The Collier
Quick and Easy Guide to

HUNTING

ROBERT SCHARFF

 COLLIER BOOKS, New York, N.Y.

A COLLIER BOOKS ORIGINAL

First Edition 1963

Collier Books is a division of The Crowell-Collier Publishing Company
Published simultaneously by Collier-Macmillan Limited, London

Library of Congress Catalog Card Number: 62-21362
Copyright © 1963 by The Crowell-Collier Publishing Company
All Rights Reserved
Hecho en los E.E.U.U.
Printed in the United States of America

The Collier
Quick and Easy Guide to

HUNTING

ACKNOWLEDGMENTS

FOR THEIR HELP in furnishing illustrations, I wish to thank the following people and manufacturers: William H. Browning of the Montana Chamber of Commerce; Willard T. Johns, Jr., of the Pennsylvania Game Commission; Robert A. Dahne of the Florida Game and Fresh Water Fish Commission; Charles Parker of the North Carolina Department of Conservation and Development; Kenneth B. Hard of the Suffolk Lodge Game Preserve; Dr. Frederick Dale and Bernard L. Flanagan of the United States Department of the Interior, Fish and Wildlife Service; N. Hallendy of the Canadian National Film Board; Clayton Seagears of the New York State Conservation Department; Lawrence Durkin of Ducks Unlimited, Inc.; James Dee of Sporting Arms and Ammunition Manufacturers' Institute; Vernon Helmke of the Wisconsin Conservation Department; Marlin Firearms Company; Bausch & Lomb Optical Company; Browning Arms Company; Winchester-Western Company; and Remington Arms Company.

ROBERT SCHARFF

Stony Brook, New York

CONTENTS

The Collier
Quick and Easy Guide to

HUNTING

Chapter One

LEARNING ABOUT SHOTGUNS

THERE IS NO more healthful sport than hunting and no sport more closely linked to the traditions of American heritage. Whether you follow your dog through the fields in search of upland game, hunt the lowland for waterfowl, or prowl the woods for deer, you take something from the experience that can't be defined in words, and seldom even in thoughts. The game bag itself is merely a by-product to the majority of sportsmen—a rather surprising but welcome addition to the larder.

The main equipment of the hunter is his weapon, and the proper ammunition to go with it. This can be a shotgun or a rifle depending upon the game sought, and upon the state laws where the weapon is to be used. In this chapter, we'll concern ourselves with shotguns and how to use them.

Today nearly twenty million Americans regard hunting with a shotgun as the ultimate in shooting sport. The fowling piece became an American institution with the landing of the first white men upon our shores. All the traditions of the ensuing centuries are embodied in the love of the American sportsman for his shotgun, and the healthful, zestful things his shotgun represents.

Styles of Shotguns

There are six popular styles of shotguns, or, as they are often called, scatterguns. These are the single-barrel single shot, the pump or slide action, the double-barrel, the bolt-action repeater, the over-under or superimposed double and the autoloader. The gun style you choose is a matter of personal preference. Any of them is good in the right hands, poor in the wrong ones. There is absolutely no difference among them in range or killing power. Many good shots use each kind.

Before launching into a discussion of the relative merits of different styles and sizes, let's consider what we mean by "gauge" for the beginner in gunnery. The gauge of a shotgun refers to the cylindrical diameter of the bore between the chamber and the choke, and was originally based upon the number of balls of pure lead precisely fitting the bore that would make a pound. Thus, a 12-gauge bore will accept a lead ball weighing one-twelfth pound avoirdupois; a 20-gauge, a ball weighing one-twentieth of a pound; a 16-gauge, a ball weighing an ounce, and so on. The modern exception is the .410-gauge, which is not based on the above system, but actually measures .410 inches, with possible slight variations by different makers. Present-day manufacturing practice differs slightly, but the following are average bore diameters of leading factories:

10-gauge = .775 inch	20-gauge = .613 inch
12-gauge = .729 inch	28-gauge = .550 inch
16-gauge = .666 inch	.410-gauge = .410 inch

As a rule, the larger gauges will kill farther than the smaller ones because they throw more shot and thus have fewer gaps in their shot patterns at long ranges. But the smaller gauges are lighter and faster, have less recoil and muzzle blast and enable the shooter to get on target quicker. Guns larger than 10-gauge are prohibited for use on migratory fowl by federal law, and some states forbid any gauge over 12.

Autoloaders (commonly known as automatics) and pumps are preferred by many to double-barrels because the double offers but two quick shots, while the automatic and pump offer up to seven. In duck hunting, however, federal regulations make it illegal to use for waterfowl hunting a gun capable of firing more than three shots without reloading. This means that the magazine of a five-shot pump gun, for example, must be plugged, so that guns of this type will hold but two shells in addition to the one in the chamber. However, that extra third shot is often very important. A duck merely winged with the first shot hits the water and begins to swim rapidly away, mak-

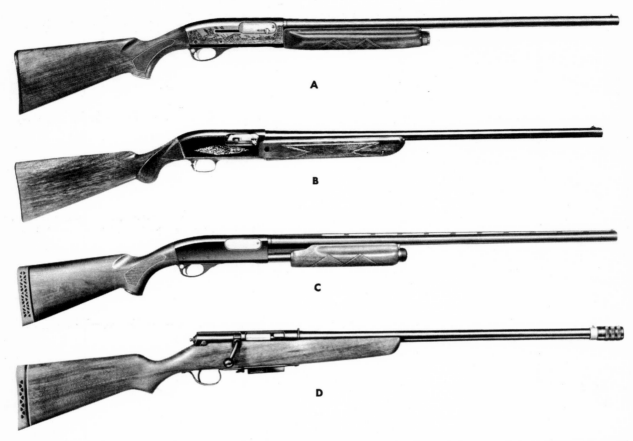

Fig. 1.1 Types of shotguns: A. Three-shot autoloading. B. Five-shot autoloading. C. Pump action. D. Bolt action with variable choke.

ing for marsh cover if possible. Killing a duck on the water is sometimes more difficult than killing one in the air. The third shot may mean the difference between a duck only wounded and one irretrievably lost, especially when you don't have a retrieving dog at hand. Several states also have laws forbidding the use of shotguns of more than three-shot magazine capacity for certain game. If you wish, most sporting goods dealers will plug your autoloader or pump gun when you purchase it.

Bolt-action shotguns are not so expensive to manufacture as the double, automatic, or pump. They work well, but they aren't so popular as the other repeaters. Most shooters can operate a pump action faster than the bolt-action type. The action must be long, and this increases the over-all length. To operate the bolt, it's necessary to reach far forward and this is hard to do without disturbing the shooting position.

There are basically two types of doubles: the side-by-side double-barrels and the over-under double-barrels. While the former is the more common, the

over-under double gun has gained in popularity in the last few years. It offers the advantages present in the side-by-side double, but it has the added advantage of giving you only one barrel to look over while you're shooting. Most beginners seem to prefer looking over one barrel. The over-under barrels are located on the vertical plane through the gun so that the recoil comes straight back. Some gunners prefer this to the side-by-side double, with the right barrel forcing the stock against the face (of a right-handed person) and the left barrel forcing the stock away from the face. The type of trigger arrangement for double scatterguns also is a matter of preference. Some claim that doubles are useful because they give instant selectivity for each barrel. The single-trigger gun is available in the selective and non-selective style. While the latter is cheaper, most shooters prefer the selective single- or double-trigger arrangements for reasons discussed later in this chapter.

A major argument in favor of the double, regardless of type, is that it is available with two barrels of different choke—one for close, the other for long

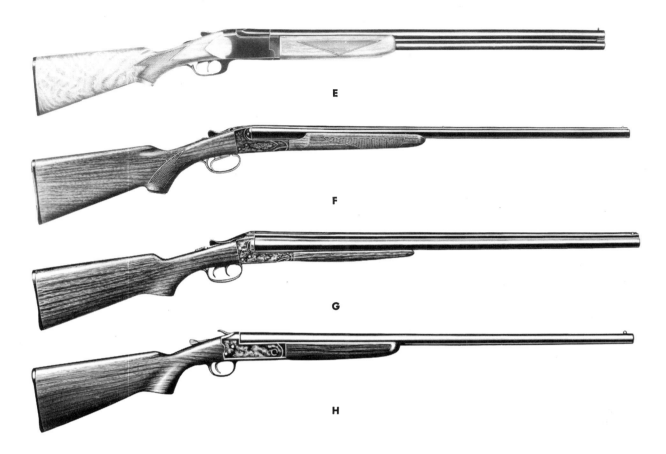

Fig. 1.1 (Continued) E. Double-barrel—over-under. F. Single-trigger, side-by-side double-barrel. G. Double-trigger, side-by-side double-barrel. H. Single-barrel.

shots, both instantly available. A word about the choke: the interior of a shotgun barrel is a smooth, round cylinder, except for a slight constriction near the muzzle. This reduction in the size of the bore is called "choke." The purpose of this constriction is to pack or concentrate the shot string, thus obtaining a closer pattern. If the bore were absolutely uniform clear to the end, the shot would scatter widely and the effective range would be very short. The degree of choke is measured by the percentage of pellets in the charge that strikes within a thirty-inch circle at forty yards. This is the "pattern." The various chokes commonly furnished and the per cent patterns they should be expected to shoot are: full choke, 65 to 75 (occasionally more); improved modified (three-quarter choke), 55 to 65; modified (one-half choke), 45 to 55; improved cylinder (one-quarter choke), 35 to 45; cylinder (no choke), 25 to 35. If you can't get a new dime into the muzzle of your 12-gauge gun, it is full choke. If you can, it is a modified choke or larger than that. Naturally, the less the choke in a shotgun barrel the bigger the pattern it will shoot

at any given range. An open-bored gun with its larger pattern is an aid to hitting at short range. A full-choke gun that holds its shots together more tightly will kill at greater range.

By means of a variable device that is easily adapted to single-barrel guns—including autoloaders and pumps—different degrees of choke may be established in your gun. With the choke closed, you get the full range of your shot. In windy weather, for example, when the ducks set their wings firmly against the gale to drop in, you'll get many opportunities at close range. This is the time to open up that choke tube so you won't blast your future wild duck dinner beyond recognition. The adjustable choke also may have considerable utility if you use your gun for upland shooting and skeet as well as for duck hunting. A variable choke is usually quite difficult to change after the bird is in the air, however. An experienced user of a double-barrel gun, on the other hand, can pull either trigger, thus shooting either his fully choked long-range barrel or the modified barrel that is better for close shots. This is

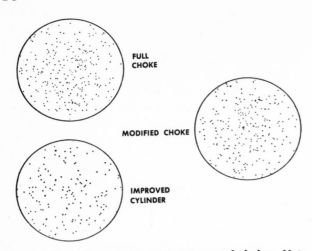

Fig. 1.2 The effect of the various types of chokes. Note that the full choke gives the greatest concentration of shot while the improved cylinder gives the least.

a definite advantage of double-barrel scatterguns, especially if the gun has a selective trigger arrangement.

In general, the single-barrel shotgun is not adequate for the beginning hunter. Too many crippled birds will get out of range before the gun can be reloaded.

Standard American chamber length is 2¾ inches, and it's used in the 12, 16, 20, and 28 gauges. Most .410 shotguns are chambered for 3-inch shells, however, and so are Magnum 12- and 20-gauge guns. The 10-gauge Magnums formerly made here, but now made only in Europe, have 3½-inch chambers.

Selecting the Shotgun

The commonest mistake shotgun buyers make is in trying to get an "all-round" gun. There is no such shotgun manufactured, and there probably never will be. It's a proven fact that a long-barreled, straight-pitched waterfowl or trap gun is next to useless on fast-flushing upland game or on the skeet ranges. The field-grade guns, barrels cut to 26–28 inches, and with a variable choke device installed, come as close as possible to being the mythical "all-round" guns, but they lack a great deal in being satisfactory for all types of shooting.

The best known method for you to use is to sit down and figure out just what kind of game you are going to hunt most. (Recommendations of various game hunted with scatterguns are given in Chapters 3 to 7.) If you're going to hunt quail more than any other game, for example, then you should by all means concentrate on getting a perfect quail gun. You'll just have to struggle along the best you can when shooting waterfowl, but the main point is that

you have the right gun for a specific purpose. With that you can do excellent shooting in that area.

A recent development by one shotgun manufacturer—it's bound to spread to others—that may change all this is use of interchangeable barrels. With this arrangement, you can use the shotgun one day for hunting quail, and switch barrels for another day's duck hunting jaunt. No tools are needed to make the switch for each different hunting trip.

Another *very* important factor in selecting a gun is to get it to "fit" you properly. By this is meant the way that it comes to your shoulder. It should come up easily and naturally, and when you press your cheek against the stock your eye should be perfectly aligned to look down the rib or over the receiver (the part that houses the action) and past the front sight at the target. We might say that, ideally, a shotgun should fit a man as well as his suit of clothes.

Generally, the four most important dimensions to be considered when fitting a gun stock to your needs are: drop at the comb, length of "pull" (length of stock), drop at the heel and the pitch. If you can afford a custom-made gun, you can order any freakish stock measurements you wish. If you do, however, the odds are that you'll soon trade it in (at a great loss of cash) and get another, whether custom-made or not, which will have a stock approximately the same as the standard gun that you can purchase over the counter. Manufacturers, when designing their shotguns, work out average stock dimensions that will be suitable for most gunners of average stature. There isn't too much difference among the stocks of the more popular shotguns, but there is enough so that you will usually find one that suits you best. Then there is the type or structure of the

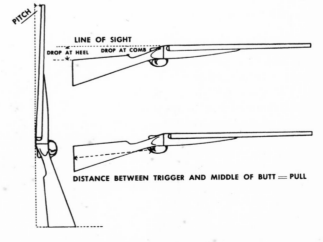

Fig. 1.3 Major dimensions of a shotgun.

gun itself to consider. For instance, you might find a double-barrel gun unsuited to you individually, while an autoloading or a pump gun with essentially the same stock dimensions might fit you perfectly. This would likely be due to the variation in the type of gun rather than that in the stock alone.

The first requirement, above all else, is that proper gun fit include the shaping of the stock so that it won't hurt you when the gun is discharged. Such proper shaping depends upon the contour of your face, particularly the location and prominence of your jaw and cheekbones. If your face is a perfect "long oval" and your cheekbones not too prominent, perhaps a high comb—the portion of the stock coming into contact with the cheek—will serve you well. High, thin combs are of the English persuasion—but they bang the cheekbones of many men. Low, rounded combs that fit under the cheekbone and line up against the fatty portion of the cheek will serve you well to line up the eye and front sight. Finally, a Monte Carlo comb may be needed to provide a fuller,

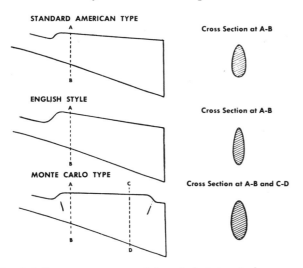

Fig. 1.4 Common types or styles of shotgun stocks.

rounder comb than either of the other types—with the added advantage of holding the eye at an exact level, whether the gun is swung right or left.

The stock design is a matter of preference. For most double-barrel guns with two triggers, the majority of hunters like the English style of straight-grip. For a single-trigger gun, or an autoloader or a pump, the pistol or half-pistol grip is acceptable, but it should be sharply curved to fill the hand, and with its lower forward edge located from three and one-quarter to four inches from the center of the trigger, according to the size of your hand.

A beavertail fore-end on a double, the big full fore-end of the automatics, or the trap-type slide

handles of pumps enables you to adapt yourself to a stock that may not be just right by holding the right hand back if the stock is too long, forward if it is too short. A beavertail fore-end will improve any gunner's shooting from 10 to 30 per cent. In addition, a good beavertail cuts down recoil at least 25 per cent because it enables the left hand to take up a lot of it. If the gun is being used exclusively for ducks, it may have a shorter stock than normal since you are generally bundled up in heavy clothing while shooting.

Drop and pitch are important elements in fitting too, since they have a direct bearing on the point of impact of the shot charge out where the target is winging its way. Drop merely regulates the height at which the head is held in pointing the gun at the target. Persons with long necks and sloping shoulders require more drop to put the comb up against the cheek and the butt down against the shoulder. Normally built persons should get along with as little drop as possible, since excessive drop may cause undershooting if the butt happens to slide too far up on the shoulder. Most men will be fitted best by a comb drop of from one and one-half to one and three-quarter inches from where the face hits the comb stock.

No amount of drop—too much or too little—affects the point of impact at the target as does the pitch of the butt. Pitch is the angle at which the butt plate is set in relation to the line of sight, and it is measured at the muzzle. If a gun has too little pitch, it tends to slip down under the armpit, and hasty shots are likely to be thrown high. If it has too much pitch, the butt tends to slip up, and hasty shots are thrown low. Pitch is right when you can forget about it. If the gun comes up to the shoulder and the butt sticks firmly there, then the pitch is all right.

The stock should be short enough for the gun to come smack to the shoulder without catching on clothes, and for the cheek instantly to hit the proper place on the comb. Here's a rule that works for most people: The stock should be just long enough to fit in the hollow of the arm when the finger is on the trigger. The average man is well suited with a stock from fourteen to fourteen and one-half inches long. A boy or woman often will be most comfortable with a stock of thirteen and one-half inches, or even thirteen and one-quarter inches long. (This distance between the trigger and the middle of the butt is called the pull.) It's a good idea for the beginner to get a stock that he thinks is a hair too long, because anyone can shoot with a stock that is a little too long more handily than with one that is too short.

Another quick method of determining the proper

stock length for you is to place the butt in the hollow of your elbow and if the trigger finger naturally reaches the trigger, the length isn't far wrong. Now, look at any small mark and throw up the gun, as for a snap shot, without conscious aiming. If you are sighting directly down the barrel, the stock fits you pretty well.

Those are the major factors in gun fit. Good balance should be the last adjustment, and though many people ignore this factor, it's still the difference in many cases between having a perfectly fitted gun and an almost-perfectly fitted gun. Heavy, powerful shooters should have the balance more toward the barrel. If the barrel is too light, the strong shooter will tend to put muzzle whip in his swing. Shifting the weight to the front will slow down the swing until it is steady and crisp. Shooters who are more slightly built should, by the same token, shift the weight to the stock. This will prevent them from making sluggish swings.

What about the barrel length? In order to get the greatest or the ultimate penetration, a long-barrelled gun is considered best by many old-time shooters. Actually, with the modern shells, barrel length, as far as ballistics is concerned, isn't important at all. The major consideration is how the **gun** is to be used. The short barrel makes a gun faster, livelier and better for snap-shooting. The long barrel gives a somewhat steadier swing, a longer sighting plane and less muzzle blast. This latter type is best for duck hunting, while the former is preferred by upland gunners.

The weight of your scattergun is another factor based on how you plan to employ it. In waterfowl shooting, weight isn't too important. But in upland gunning, the weight of your gun becomes a factor because you'll be carrying it all day, and you'll need a fast-handling gun to take quick shots in close quarters. Under these conditions, top weight should be about seven and a half pounds, minimum around six. You'll use light loads, so recoil is as important as it would be to the duck hunter. To clarify the matter of recoil or "kick," it depends upon the ratio between the gun weight and the velocity and weight of the shot load. The higher the velocity and the heavier the shot charge, the more any particular gun will kick (also true of rifles as anyone who has fired both a .22 and a 30-06 caliber rifle can testify). Duck guns are heavier than upland guns because they must absorb more of the recoil of the heavy loads that ordinarily are used for ducks. Light loads in these heavy guns would kick even less, but heavy loads in a light gun are uncomfortable. It's true that "apparent recoil"—the amount that is felt by the

shooter—depends to a certain extent on the gun design. A gun with good "balance" seems to kick less than one that is poorly designed. Also, some of the recoil is absorbed in operating the mechanism of an autoloading shotgun.

Most shotguns are fitted at the factory with butt plates of black plastic, which are suitable for general use. A rubber recoil pad will cushion the jolt of a gun handling powerful duck or goose loads. The rubber pad can't reduce the gun's kick, but it saves your shoulder from bruises. When the pad is new, it often tends to catch on your clothing as you bring the gun to your shoulder and this trouble can be lessened by rubbing a little talcum powder into the end of the pad.

The type of sight arrangement for your shotgun is a matter of personal preference. Most just have a small front bead, while some have an additional shallow groove or indentation on the receiver that can be used as a rear sight. Most good scattergun marksmen don't line up the rear and front sights in the manner a rifleman does. Actually, precision sighting isn't necessary with a shotgun employed for flying game. As a rule, the experienced shotgunner isn't even aware of the front bead, but rather his vision runs along the top of the barrel to focus on the airborne game. The muzzle of the gun is his front sight and he squeezes the trigger when the bird is just above it.

Some duck hunters use a concentric-ring-type sight. The general principle on which this works is that it can judge the distance of the duck by the amount of space it occupies in the sight, and by solving a simple trigonometric problem in your head as the duck flies over the decoys, you determine whether to lead him by one ring or two. Hunters who use their shotguns with rifled slugs for deer hunting often use precision sights to good advantage. If you are one of these hunters, you can mount rifle-type receiver sights or even a low-power scope (see Chapter 2 for details) on your shotgun. This, in effect, converts your scattergun into a smoothbore rifle.

When purchasing your gun, be sure to get a case for it. The leg-of-mutton cases and their less expensive cousins, the double-section canvas cases, which necessitate taking the gun apart before inserting it, are good especially for storage and traveling. They are, however, a nuisance to take out to a blind or in the duck boat. This is especially true on a cold morning, when you have to assemble and disassemble a gun with hands about as flexible as a pair of flounders just removed from the home freezer.

To overcome this disadvantage, you may purchase a full-length case. With this type, your gun is ready for use as soon as you take it out. The best case of this style is the one made of sheepskin with the wool turned in. The wool gradually absorbs oil from the gun and protects it. The thickness of the case also prevents the gun from receiving any scratches and dents. Its main faults are that this type of case is not easily carried or stored and is not waterproof.

Loads and Shots

Shotgun loads differ basically in only two ways: the amount of powder and the size of the shot. Formerly, most manufacturers marked each shell with three important bits of information—namely, the size of the shot, the weight of the load of shot in ounces, the dram equivalent in black powder. Today, however, they print only the shot size on the shell, and full information appears only on the box. In some cases this vital information doesn't even appear there.

The standard or "field" load, for example, for the 12-gauge shell is usually:

> 3 drams equivalent of powder
> 1⅛ ounces of shot.

The so-called express, super or high-velocity load for the 12-gauge shell is usually:

> 3¾ drams equivalent of powder
> 1¼ ounces of shot.

Thus the super or high-velocity load has approximately 25 per cent more powder than the standard load; but, inasmuch as the super load has to push only 11 per cent more in weight of shot than does the standard load, it throws this pro rata lighter load at a higher velocity (hence its name). This higher velocity gives a greater shocking power to the pellets that actually hit the game (about 25 per cent more at forty yards), but, more important than that, it increases the killing range. These few extra yards of killing range often make the difference between finishing off a cripple or losing it. This is especially true when hunting waterfowl. But, for most upland game birds, the standard field loads are in general ac-

ceptable, except in cases of pheasant at long ranges, doves flying very high, etc. In such instances, load won't be half so important as the accuracy of the man behind the shotgun.

Shot sizes run from No. 12, with over 2,300 to the ounce, to 00 Buck (buckshot), with 130 to the pound. Buckshot loads are employed for deer shooting, when shotguns are used for that purpose. (Some states permit only the use of shotguns for deer hunting in certain areas within their borders.) For all upland birds, waterfowl (often called lowland birds) and small game, sizes from No. 10 to No. 4 are most popular.

A look at the chart of standard shot sizes here will give you some idea of the number of pellets in shells in various gauges and at different loads. Up to perhaps forty yards or so it may be assumed that the smaller the shot (i.e., the larger the size number of the shot) the denser the pattern made by it will be, and thus the smaller the gaps between the pellets. Beyond that, the lighter shots, being more easily affected by air resistance, drop off rapidly in their velocity and thus in their killing power. At such a distance, if we compare the shocking power of a No. 7½ pellet to that of a No. 4 pellet (assuming their velocities to be the same, an assumption that increases in error with the range), we find that it would take about three No. 7½ pellets to equal the shocking power of one No. 4.

Number of Shot in 1¼ Ounces
Load for Standard 12-Gauge Shell

size of shot	7½	6	5	4	2
number of shot	437	281	212	169	112

Number of Shot in 1⅛ Ounces
Load for Standard 16-Gauge Shell

size of shot	7½	6	5	4	2
number of shot	394	253	191	152	101

Slug loads are also made for shotguns. These contain a single slug, rifled (spirally grooved) to make it spin. They're used for deer, black bear, and wolf

	SHOT									BUCK SHOT				
No.	12	9	8	7½	6	5	4	2	BB	4	3	1	0	00
Diameter in Inches	.05	.08	.09	.09½	.11	.12	.13	.15	.18	.24	.25	.30	.32	.33
Approx. Pellets in 1 oz. / Approx. Pellets in 1 lb.	2385	585	410	350	225	170	135	90	50	340	300	175	145	130

Fig. 1.5 Standard shot sizes.

hunting by many hunters who don't own rifles. They are fairly accurate and always deadly *at short ranges*.

The following chart gives suggested shot sizes for various game. Further information on the proper load and shot sizes for different species of game can be found in Chapters 3 through 7.

GAME	SHELL	SHOT SIZE	SUGGESTED CHOKES	WHAT EXPERIENCED HUNTERS SAY
DUCKS	High-velocity	4, 5, 6	FULL—For Pass Shooting MODIFIED—Over Decoys	Use No. 4 shot for long range and pass shooting. For normal range—No. 5 or No. 6 shot while some hunters use No. 7½ shot for closer range shooting over decoys.
GEESE	High-velocity	BB, 2, 4	FULL	Goose hunters need wallop to fold up their birds so they use the big loads with large shot. Many hunters prefer No. 4 shot for a denser pattern at shorter ranges over decoys.
PHEASANTS	High-velocity or Standard	5, 6	MODIFIED FULL—For Long Cornfield Shots	For cornfield shooting where long shots are usual—better use No. 5. On a normal rise over dogs and for all-round use No. 6 is the favorite. Bigger shot may be dangerous when you are hunting in large groups.
GROUSE OR PARTRIDGE	High-velocity or Standard	5, 6, 7½, 8	IMPROVED CYLINDER, or MODIFIED—For Brush Work FULL—For Open Ranges	On the smaller birds such as ruffed grouse or Hungarian partridge use the smaller shot. The big western grouse (sage, sooty, and blue) call for heavier loads and large shot.
QUAIL	Standard	7½, 8, 9	IMPROVED CYLINDER, MODIFIED	For early season shooting on bobwhites when feathers are light some hunters use No. 9 shot. Later, they switch to No. 7½ or No. 8. On the running and wild flushing type of quail, such as the Gambels, larger shot is sometimes used.
DOVES AND PIGEONS	High-velocity	6, 7½, 8	MODIFIED	You can do a good job on mourning doves at normal ranges with the lighter loads, and No. 7½ or No. 8 shot—but for longer ranges use the heavy loads and No. 6 or No. 7½. Use the same load on band-tailed pigeons and whitewings.
WOOD-COCK	Standard	7½, 8, 9	IMPROVED CYLINDER, MODIFIED	Your choice of shot size here will depend on ranges at which your game is shot. For fast shooting in the older thickets, No. 8 shot is a good choice.
RABBITS	Standard or High-velocity	4, 5, 6	IMPROVED CYLINDER or MODIFIED—For Brush FULL—For Long Open Shots	For cottontail rabbits at normal range, the lighter loads are suitable, but for larger game such as jack rabbits and snowshoe rabbits use heavy loads.
SQUIRRELS	High-velocity	5, 6	MODIFIED	Most hunters use 5s or 6s and prefer the heavy loads, particularly in the tall timber.
RAIL	Standard	7½, 8, 9	IMPROVED CYLINDER	For the little sora rail No. 8 or No. 9 does the job while many hunters use No. 7½ on the marsh hen or clapper rail.
TURKEY	High-velocity	BB, 2, 4	FULL	Choice of shot size depends on your range. If you're a good caller No. 4 shot makes a clean kill while BBs and No. 2s are best for long shots.
DEER, BLACK BEAR AND WOLF	High-velocity	Rifled Slug and Buckshot	For rifled slugs . . . any choke may be used. Full choke for buckshot loads.	For deer and black bear 12 and 16 gauge slugs are the best. 0 and 00 Buckshot are the most popular sizes for deer hunters who use buckshot.
FOX	High-velocity	BB, 2	FULL	It's a toss-up between BBs and No. 2 shot. But remember—the smaller the shot, the denser the pattern.

Fig. 1.6 How a snap shot is made. (Courtesy of Remington Arms Company)

How to Handle Your Shotgun

Skillful handling of a shotgun is a matter of speed. This doesn't mean a series of sudden, violent movements but rather a smooth, unbroken sequence of motion that gets the gun to your shoulder, your cheek on the comb and your eyes on the object to be hit—all in a split second. Roughly, the effective range of the average shotgun is 35 to 40 yards. Because of this, the experienced gunner knows that when swift-winged game flushes in the field, he must get into action instantly. In doing this his whole attention centers on the object to be hit; he isn't conscious of the movements required to bring the gun into position and fire it. You don't aim a shotgun as you do a rifle—you point it, in much the same fashion that you point your finger.

SHOTGUN SHOOTING METHODS

There are three main methods of shotgun shooting, covering all conceivable field situations. They are: the snap shot; the pointing-out lead (sometimes called half-snap shot); and the swinging-past lead (often called the swing shot).

THE SNAP SHOT. Snap-shooting is often necessary to bag fast-flying upland game birds when they make an unexpected appearance at close range (less than 25 yards). With this type of shot you simply bring up your gun quickly from a dropped position, point instantly at the spot in mid-air where you judge the bird will be—or directly at the bird if it's *very* close —and pull the trigger at the instant the gun reaches this point. The decision to pull the trigger must be made while the gun is being raised. You can't do otherwise. In such a case, should you follow the target with your pointing gun, attempting to get ahead of it with your point and fire, you would have to move the gun practically as fast as the bird moved—an impossibility.

Accurate snap-shooting is extremely difficult and any hunter who depends on it to bring in game will generally have an empty bag at the end of the day. Unless absolutely necessary, you should scrupulously avoid snap-shooting, at least until you have mastered shotgun shooting as a whole.

THE POINTING-OUT LEAD. In pointing out, you add gun swing or follow-through, deliberation and control to the snap shot. In other words, you:

1. Mount the gun to your shoulder.
2. Press the trigger to release the shot-charge.
3. Swing the gun muzzle in a horizontal arc, at exactly the same apparent speed as the movement of the target, and maintain a forward allowance in advance of the target which you have mentally calculated to be equal to the forward movement of the target during the time of flight of the shot-charge.

If this sounds a bit complicated, just remember that a single mental process controls the three physical reactions required to produce a definite result. Once having received the go-ahead signal from the brain, every member of the body concerned in the business of pointing and discharging the gun becomes automatically subservient to the eye. In effect, the brain tells the eye:

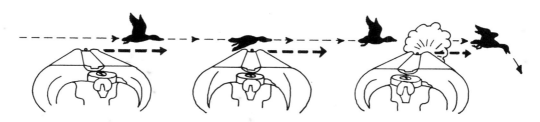

Fig. 1.7 How a pointing-out lead shot is made. (Courtesy of Remington Arms Company)

"Get that gun muzzle out ahead of the target, and keep it there until the charge lets go!"

Once having received these general instructions from the brain, the feet, legs, hips, shoulders, arms, hands and head can proceed with their respective jobs *at the same time,* all coordinated by the eye.

The ideal swing-and-mount motion will bring the gun muzzle to the line of flight of the target at exactly the proper forward allowance. At this point, the arc described by the gun muzzle levels off slightly to conform to the anticipated path of the target. Furthermore, the movement can be accomplished at one standard pace or rate of swing—the same rate of pace as the apparent speed of the target—if the gun is mounted while swinging. Otherwise, the rate of swing would have to be accelerated to catch up with the target and to pass it to the required lead. Then, the speed of the swing would have to be retarded to the exact speed of the target in order to hold the proper lead. It follows that to swing the gun in a prescribed arc at one standard rate of pace will be easier to learn—and infinitely easier to remember —than to attempt to introduce two separate and distinct speeds into the operation. Accordingly, on the basis of your own analysis, you rewrite the three rules for pointing out, as follows:

1. Begin swinging the gun muzzle to the right at exactly the same rate or pace as the apparent speed of the target. *At the same time . . .*

2. Begin mounting the gun without checking or altering the swing in any manner, with the object of bringing the line of sight to the path of the target at the proper forward allowance. *Now . . .*

3. Initiate the pressure on the trigger, which will cause the gun to be discharged while in full motion, maintaining its proper forward allowance ahead of the target.

Now that you have progressed from a snap shooter to a pointer-outer, you'll realize why the swing's the thing, and swing is nothing but timing. If you're lagging too much in releasing the trigger, your timing is off, and you're "riding out" your birds too far. All of this implies that pointing out is *not* an infalli-

ble system for producing perfect results. It is merely the next thing to it. No man ever lived who could hit them all. But day in and day out, the system of pointing out will produce a bigger bag than any other.

Don't forget that every shot in pointing out is a true swing—a physical movement on a pivot, just like golf or baseball or croquet. No matter if the target is going straight away shoulder high—there will be a definite *swing* as you bring the gun into position. If the proper lead, as in this case, is zero, then the gun steadies and stops, rather than swinging on in its arc.

The whole theory of pointing out is *perfect control* of every movement of the body, and its mechanical appliance, the gun. If the target—as a startled grouse —suddenly increases its speed or changes direction, the eye automatically follows the target and the gun automatically follows the eye.

If the target—as a duck poised to look over the decoys—suddenly stops in mid-air, then the eye stops, the gun stops to maintain the proper line of sight and the trigger is pulled just as automatically as in an orthodox swinging shot.

When estimating leads, always play safe by being on the *long* side. The charge of shot from your gun will proceed through the air in an elongated cone, into which the target probably will fly if the lead is too great. However, a lead estimated too short invariably results in a miss. The target has no mathematical chance to fly into the shot-charge because the entire charge will pass behind it.

THE SWING-PAST LEAD. The swinging-past method is at its best where the flight of the target is along a definite path. If your eyesight is normal and your physical reactions reasonably prompt, you can actually eliminate calculation of the forward allowance merely by increasing the speed of the swing to a pace faster than the rate of progress of the target. Then, as the gun muzzle swings past the target, you press the trigger, sighting on the target itself. What happens is this: the gun, moving in its own arc at a faster pace than the target, overtakes and passes it.

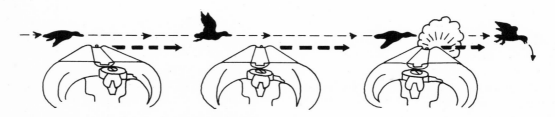

Fig. 1.8 How a swing-past lead shot is made. (Courtesy of Remington Arms Company)

The brain wills the command to pull the trigger at the exact instant the gun muzzle passes the target. In the one-fifth second required for the shooter to react to the mental command to fire, the gun continues to swing at its faster pace, and automatically builds up a forward allowance which is sufficiently exact for targets in steady flight.

The big advantage claimed for swinging past is the fact that the trigger is pulled when the line of sight is exactly upon the target—a definite object—rather than a visualized aiming point a fixed relative distance away from the target. Yet, a big disadvantage is the lack of a definite rule for regulating the speed of the gun swing. Again, sudden changes of direction of the target are difficult to detect with the faster swing required when swinging past.

As your experience increases, you'll be able to analyze your own shooting problems and definitely assign each type of shot to the proper system. Eventually the time will come—if you devote enough thought to your shooting—when you will be able to execute any shot by the most appropriate method of gun pointing and without the slightest preparation.

One of the best plans for applying the proper method is to visualize the old army method of the vertical clock. Imagine that the exact center of the clock face is the point in space immediately over your gun muzzle as you "face the shot." Then the *apparent* direction of the target can be flashed to the brain by the eye as a "two-o'clock" shot, or a "five-o'clock" shot. You'll learn later in this chapter that "facing the shot" consists actually of three movements: placing the feet in order to fire comfortably in the required direction, pivoting the body to follow the target's flight with the eyes and thrusting the gun to the "ready" position.

In game shooting, the time of appearance of the target and the direction of its flight will be beyond your control. You'll merely snap into the ready position as the target appears suddenly before you. Your clock-face zero then will be a point on or near the line of flight of the target, usually the point—as in upland game shooting—where the fleeing bird or animal is recognized as a target. Thus, the eye must register the direction of the shot from this point onward along the path of the target.

In any kind of shooting, the zero of the clock face will be that point in space on or near the path of the target which serves as a beginning point for the eye in estimating the apparent direction and apparent speed of the target.

A two-o'clock shot on the vertical clock is a target moving from left to right, and rising at an angle of about 30 degrees from the horizontal. The proper swing to produce the right forward allowance will move upward as well as from left to right. A five-o'clock shot will be descending from the horizontal at an angle of about 60 degrees as it also moves from left to right. A quail taking off on a right-quartering course is a perfect example of the two-o'clock shot, while a duck decoying from the left rear often produces a five-o'clock shot.

Always bear in mind that the *apparent* direction and *apparent* speed of the target are of vastly greater importance than its actual speed of flight. For example, the two-o'clock shot may involve a target traveling at exact right angles across your front, or it may be the right-quartering quail as in the example above. Since in either case the apparent direction at the shooter's eye is the same, then the *direction* of the gun swing from the center of the clock face toward two-o'clock will be exactly the same.

For shots at all short and medium distances with the shotgun—from 20 to 40 yards—the actual speed of the target may be ignored entirely. The *apparent* speed only need concern you, because at short and medium ranges, the velocity of the shot-charge is reasonably constant, and the relationship between the actual speed of the target and the velocity of the shot-charge remains—for all practical purposes—definite and fixed.

The eye quickly learns to estimate *apparent* speed along with *apparent* direction, and to combine both factors in its flash to the brain. After all, it's merely necessary for the eye to warn the brain that the swing of the gun must be fast, or slow, or in between, in order to overtake the target. The muscles of the body, responding to the urge of the brain, then go into action at somewhere near the proper speed to overtake and pass the target, using either the pointing-out or swing-past method. The speed of the swing is accelerated or retarded as the movement progresses, as a correction of the original estimate of the eye, with the *apparent* speed of the target as pacemaker.

In long-range shotgun shooting, actual target speed assumes vital importance. Whereas the speed of the target will remain constant, the velocity of the shot-charge will diminish rapidly with distance. The ratio between target and shot-charge speed won't be the same at 60 yards as at 40 yards. If the ratio remained the same, swinging past would be just as effective at the longer range as at the shorter, because the actual forward allowance at the target would increase in exact ratio with the range.

Prove this to your own satisfaction with pencil and

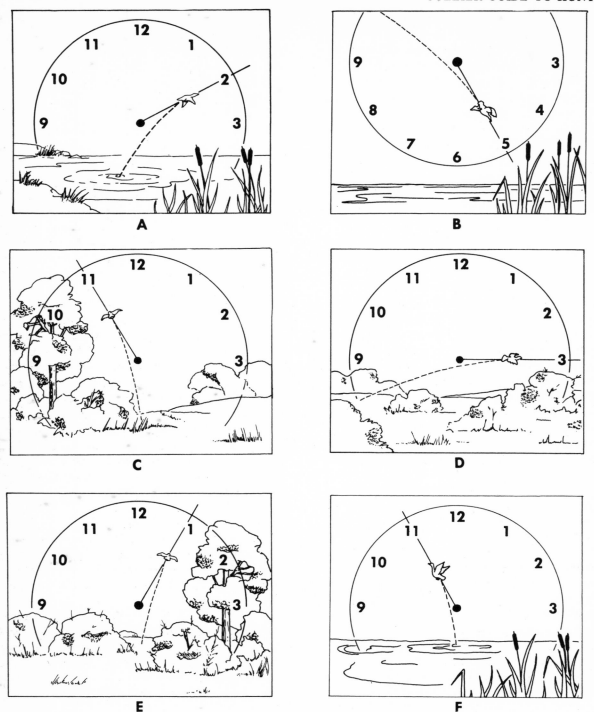

Fig. 1.9 The old army method of visualizing your gun swing to the target against an imaginary clock face is a good one for game shots. In (A) duck has jumped from shooter and is driving fast toward right front of gunner located in line with clock zero. In (B) wildfowl approaching from rear or high from front or sides passes close to clock dial zero, making a fine five-o'clock shot. In (C) flushed bird, driving up and away, makes a good eleven-o'clock shot. In (D) bird flushes from left, driving across gunner's front for a three-o'clock shot. In (E) and (F) bird has started almost straight up and veered slightly to right or left, making orientation from clock zero easy. Remember that zero or clock center is the point where gunner faces the shot. The swing from zero to a specific clock number represents rapid correction of gun alignment along the path of the fleeing target. (All photos courtesy of Sporting Arms and Ammunition Manufacturers' Institute)

paper. Merely draw the sides of an acute angle, and cut the sides with straight lines passing through points on the sides equidistant from the apex. Let one side of the angle represent the actual direction of the target in space, the other side the line of the shot-charge. Thus, while the angular lead or forward allowance at the gun remains the same, the actual lead in advance of the target increases in direct proportion to the range.

Much of the efficiency of high-speed shotgun loads is derived from their higher remaining velocity at long ranges, thus making possible shorter leads than would be necessary with loads of standard velocity. For many shooters, high-speed or long-range loads produce excellent results with the swinging-past system, even at the extreme ranges of modern wildfowl shooting.

For the average shooter, however, pointing out is far more satisfactory at long and extreme ranges. Pointing out, being essentially slower in pace than swinging past, permits more exact correction of swing-direction and swing-speed, based upon the visible relationship between line-to-target and line-of-flight of the shot-charge. The eye actually estimates this distance in pointing out. In swinging past, there is no such estimation, the lead being entirely dependent upon speed of swing.

A good rule is to observe the distance at which you take your shots, in comparison with your shooting companions. If you are slower in "getting on" your targets, no doubt pointing out will be best for you until you learn to speed up your timing to deliver the shot in reasonably fast time. Then, and then only, will swinging past produce the best results.

THE GUN AND THE TARGET

Shooting is a sport of controlled relaxation. The obvious purpose of relaxation is to assist coordination. A blocked brain, fixed eyes and frozen muscles defeat coordination by preventing relaxation. From the instant you take your stance, and until the shot is delivered, smoothness must characterize your every mental process and physical reaction. Thus the proper way to approach your shooting is to resolve, first of all, not to do anything that will interfere with smoothness of swing.

One way to acquire smoothness of swing is to practice a little "dry shooting" with a walking stick or some similar tubular object three or four feet long. If you or your neighbor owns a playful dog, draw him into the game. Try sighting the stick at the dog as he plays around you, being careful to keep the end of the stick pointed exactly at your unwitting assistant. Notice how easy it is actually to

see the tip of the stick and the dog at the same time —how easily the tip of the stick follows every movement of the "target." If no dog is available, simply sight the stick quickly at objects on the wall, shifting from one to the other as rapidly as your brain can will the movement and your eyes and hands can obey the command of the brain.

If, later on, you experience difficulty in lining up your shotgun on a moving target, remember your experience with the stick. *Then* there was no difficulty whatever in keeping both the target and the point of the stick in perfect alignment. You knew the end of the stick was right there where you wanted it. You were not worrying about releasing a trigger at the proper moment. No thought of pointing out or swinging past intruded upon your mental or physical processes. All you had to do was follow the target with the end of the stick, no matter how the target leaped or changed direction.

The smooth, easy following of a moving target with the muzzle of your shotgun is exactly the same as following the dog with the stick. However, if you don't strain mentally or physically, it's really a lot easier. Your shotgun has a crook in it to make it line up easily with your eye. It has a straight edge in the form of a rib down the top of the barrel (or between the barrels if it is a double gun) that automatically guides your eye to the front sight. If you never learn anything else about wing shooting beyond following the target with the front sight, you'll bag a lot of game.

THE BRAIN AND THE EYES

The brain has only one function in advance of that all-important flash from the eyes—"There's the target!" That function is to create the proper state of mind to permit the body to perform its functions easily and smoothly.

All good shooting is a result of proper direction of the conscious mind. All poor shooting results from combined errors of the mind and the body, which may be induced either by conscious or subconscious interference with a normal relationship between the mind and its servants—the eyes, the hands, and all the rest of us.

The most common fault of the conscious mind is an improper approach to the shot. If the mind prepares itself for the shot with a "Get this bird! Get this bird!" fixation, the same fixation is transmitted to the muscles of the body. Bound muscles destroy smoothness of swing. A bodily as well as a mental fixation exists. Even the eyes become fixed with a glassy stare, and are physically incapable of performing the work assigned to them.

The proper mental preparation, as you get ready to fire each shot, is a "Watch for the target!" attitude. This induces an alert, watchful consciousness of the work to be done by both mind and body. The eyes, in their primary function as agents of the brain, don't become fixed. Rather, they're held at universal focus, ready to change direction instantly upon the appearance of the target. This thing called determination is all right in its place, and it even has a place in shooting, if properly applied. If determination—to you—means a set jaw and a fixed stare, dispense with it at once. You'll bag more game if you take your shooting less seriously.

The most common fault of the subconscious mind is flinching. Anticipation of recoil, muzzle blast, a bump on the jaw, or some other physical discomfort blocks the normal mental process so necessary to proper functioning of the body. Again, intrusion of some extraneous thought as the mind concentrates on the job of the moment may interpose a mental block just as disastrous to good shooting as a physical manifestation. Inability to keep the mind on the job of the moment is a common fault, even with good shooters. The remedy for this state of affairs is to keep your mind on your business.

Physical manifestations of flinching may be classified as downright gun-shyness. The conscious mind isn't afraid of the discharge of the gun. The subconscious mind, however, resents something about the procedure. If ever there was an excuse for the ancient platitude, "an ounce of prevention is worth a pound of cure," that excuse applies to the fault of flinching. Continued use of an ill-fitting gun, heavy loads in a light gun, a gun with too short barrels, or any one of a hundred ill-advised errors of judgment may cause flinching. Plain, everyday horse sense would have prevented 99 per cent of all cases of flinching since the beginning of the sport.

Since the primary function of the eyes is to act as agents of the brain, they may be expected to conform to mental processes more nearly than any other members of the body. In the section on "Pointing Out," it was shown by diagram that the eyes can and must combine two definite assignments in delivering the shot, these being:

1. To serve as agents of the brain in setting off the mental processes necessary to the delivery of the shot.

2. To operate as a range-finder to determine the location of the target, and its *apparent* direction and *apparent* speed.

The third important function of the eyes—that of aiming or pointing the gun—comes into play *after*

the brain has been set to functioning, and *after* the target has been located and its apparent direction and apparent speed reported to the brain. As explained in "The Gun and the Target," this third function of the eyes should become as nearly mechanical as possible. Shooting skill will improve in direct proportion to the achievement of this ideal.

Mankind has never been able to improve upon the number and arrangement of the eyes in performing any task involving the apparent direction and apparent speed of an object. Mechanical range-finders, binoculars and ordinary field glasses all employ two lenses set some distance from each other. The old-fashioned parlor stereopticon is perhaps the best example of them all. At the same time, monocular instruments are used universally in the process of lining up one object on another, or placing an object in a definite position with respect to another. The telescope, the surveyor's transit and the mariner's sextant are examples of devices of this type.

From the foregoing, you will deduce that binocular action of the eyes best performs the functions of setting off the mental process and acting as range and direction finder. Monocular action is best for alignment of the gun upon or in front of the target. Therefore, shoot with both eyes open! After the eyes have performed their two binocular functions, that something which oculists call "accommodation" will cause the action of the eyes to become monocular in shooting parlance, your "master eye" will take command, and the gun will be aligned upon the target by the master eye, assuming that the gun must invariably be fired from the shoulder on the same side as the master eye.

The accepted test for determining the master eye is known to all experienced shooters. You simply hold both eyes open, and align your finger upon some object. If you suspect your right eye of being your master eye, now close the left eye. If the finger remains aligned upon the object, your suspicion was correct, and your right eye is the master eye. If the finger moves out of alignment with the object, then you guessed wrong—your left eye is the master eye.

Having determined that one eye or the other is the master eye, then continue the test to determine your accommodation. Close the master eye, and align the finger upon the object with the weaker eye. Now open the master eye, returning to both eyes open. The finger should jump immediately out of alignment with the object. If it doesn't jump immediately and positively, then consult a good oculist at once.

Fig. 1.10 Footwork is very important in good shotgun shooting. The proper footwork for various shots is shown.

PASSING SHOT LEFT TO RIGHT   OVERHEAD IN-COMING SHOT   INCOMING SHOT PASSING TO LEFT   INCOMING SHOT PASSING TO RIGHT   SWINGING ON TARGET WHICH HAS PASSED

GROOVING THE SWING

Since the brain is the master engineer of your shooting, and the eyes are the chief assistants of the brain, all other muscular action may be combined into one physical function—grooving the swing of the gun to keep it aligned on the target until the shot-charge is unleashed.

Practically every muscle of the body is brought into play in grooving the swing. The lower part of the body, from feet up to and including the hips, regulates lateral movement. The upper part of the body controls vertical movement. Coordination of all these muscles must be insured by a proper shooting position, which in itself must combine the factors of torsion and balance. Torsion initiates and controls lateral movement. Balance controls and regulates vertical movement, at the same time permitting final minor adjustment of the swing by the arms and shoulders. Thus we arrive at a fixed relationship between torsion and the lower part of the body, and between balance and the upper part of the body. The feet, legs and hips must be so placed as to provide proper torsion to insure lateral movement. The upper part of the body must be so balanced as to permit vertical adjustment of the arc of the gun swing. The normal placement of the weight of the body, as well as the weight of the gun, the distribution of that weight, and the method of swinging it must all be considered in assuming a proper shooting position.

First of all, the shooter must so place his feet "to face the shot"—to deliver the shot-charge at the point where he expects to hit the target. In upland game shooting, targets will be slightly above the horizontal plane of the gun muzzle but not far enough above that plane to require overhead shots. Since modern shotguns are designed to point naturally just above horizontal, when held with the butt flat to the shoulder, it follows that an upright, natural shooting position will serve best to keep the axis of the body's center of gravity perpendicular to the horizontal plane.

Just as in golf, a natural pivot, not a sway, will produce the smoothest swing. Widespread legs, hips held askew, abnormally bent knees—all these affectations merely serve to destroy torsion and balance. While it's true that the weight of the gun in front of the body will displace the center of gravity toward the front, this displacement isn't so great in a normal person as to require abnormal measures of control. At most, the weight of the gun in shooting position merely shifts the center of gravity to the left leg (in the case of a right-handed shooter) and thus the left leg becomes the pivot leg and the right leg the balance or "steering" leg. The feet are the twin platforms of the body, and so all discussion of shooting position must begin with the feet.

In "facing the shot," the gun normally crosses the left toe in a right-handed shooter. This means that the left toe will point a little to the right of the exact spot where the shot-charge is to be placed. Since the feet give a firmer foundation to the body if they are separated at an angle, the right foot will be a few inches back of the left, and with the right toe turned still farther to the right. The shooter's conformation will regulate the exact distance between the feet and the exact angle between the toes of the two feet. Generally speaking, turning the right toe too far to the right restricts ease of movement to the left. A good rule is to assume a position that is perfectly comfortable and without muscular strain through any possible arc of lateral swing. Try it a few times, and you will find that the feet find their natural position and their natural angle without any conscious attention on your part, provided you face the shot.

Most of the weight of the body will be upon the left foot, evenly distributed as between toe and heel. That part of the body's weight borne by the right foot will be principally upon the toe. The heel of the left foot thus can never leave the ground without upsetting the balance of the upper part of the body. The heel of the right foot may leave the ground in the process of "steering," if it seems more comfortable to swing in this manner. However, if the feet are held reasonably close together under the body, it will not be necessary to raise the right heel to obtain a smooth, easy swing.

Having faced the shot, pivot the lower part of the body—without moving the feet—to face the spot where the target will appear: the zero of the vertical clock. The muscles of the feet, legs and hips will then be under torsion and ready to swing back to the position at which the shot is to be delivered. This torsion, it has been explained, is best achieved by a pivot and not a sway. If the knees are bent abnormally, pivoting becomes impossible. A shift of weight to one side is inevitable, and weight does not always shift back to its original position. Thus, after the feet, the knees become the next important consideration in the swing.

Straight legs twist, or take on torsion, much easier than crooked ones. At the same time, the knees must not be locked, or pivoting is impossible. Just enough "break" or bend in the knees to permit free pivoting is the ideal position for these members. At first, this position may be assumed consciously, and tried out tentatively in your bedroom or anywhere else. It isn't necessary to stand upon a shooting ground in order to cultivate a proper shooting position.

The hips should be level, permitting their pivoting—and that of the upper part of the body—in a horizontal plane. If the hips aren't level, balance of the upper part of the body is destroyed, and the resulting swing will be upset by the displacement of the center of gravity. In other words, the swing will be low at one end, high on the other. Or, it may start in the proper arc, only to become high or low as the shifting of balance interferes with the smooth continuity of the swing. Too much stress can't be placed upon this point of the smooth, even *level* pivoting of the hips upon the foundation of the feet and legs.

One of the primary reasons for a smooth, level swing is to prevent "canting" the gun—rotating the sighting plane on its long axis, so that the front sight isn't exactly on top at the moment of firing. Canting isn't the serious fault in shotgun pointing that it is in rifle and pistol shooting, since the sighting plane will place some part of the pattern on the target, even with the gun canted, provided you sight along the rib. The big difficulty is trying to sight along the sighting plane with the gun canted. The head is displaced from its normal position, and thus the result of excessive canting will be improper pointing and a missed target.

It has already been pointed out that if the hips are level and the body upright, the upper part of the body will retain that perfect balance so necessary to produce the vertical component of the gun swing. In a natural, upright position, the torso, shoulders and arms point the gun naturally and normally at a point in the foreground just above horizontal. Thus, you can lower the gun by bending forward at the waist and continuing the movement through the arms and shoulders—which moves the balance of the body forward. Conversely, you can elevate the gun muzzle by bending upward or backward at the waist and continuing the movement through the shoulders and arms, which has the effect of shifting the balance backward.

In the movement of depressing the gun muzzle, the left foot takes more of the weight of the body, checking the transfer of weight to the left foot when the gun muzzle has been sufficiently depressed. Conversely, more weight is transferred back to the right toe by the movement of elevating the gun muzzle—the shifting of balance being checked by the right toe when sufficient weight has been transferred. All of this shifting must be accomplished without the slightest disturbance of the torsion factor and this is impossible if the body is bent too far forward, or is held rigid in a too-upright position.

The transfer of weight from one foot to the other is so slight, with a good shooting position, as to be imperceptible. It's mentioned here merely as a check-point in determining whether or not you have achieved proper balance. If you're conscious of the shifting of the weight, your feet are too far apart, your knees are bent too much, or abnormal placement of some other member of the body is serving to destroy balance and probably torsion as well. Check yourself thoroughly. Make sure you are swinging from side to side, and up and down, with the least possible shifting of weight, and with the smallest practical displacement of feet, knees and hips.

With the torso held reasonably erect—remember the center of gravity of your body is slightly forward because of the weight of the gun—your shoulders must conform to the job of the arms in holding the gun in the proper position. Since the left hand and arm must be well under the fore-end of the gun to support it properly, your left shoulder will be relatively low. Since the right hand must grasp the gun at the grip, the right shoulder will follow the right elbow. If the right elbow is held high, the right shoulder will be relatively high. If the elbow is held down, hanging relaxed in a natural position, the right shoulder will be a little higher than the left.

However, a high right elbow tends to straighten out the shoulder and thus present a flat surface against which to place the butt of the gun. Again, a high right elbow serves to elevate the wrist of the right hand, which is desirable from the standpoint of coordination of the hands. A good compromise is to shoot with the right elbow moderately high—not so high as the horizontal position of the rifle shooter, not so low as to permit the upper arm to touch the chest. Midway between the two extreme positions will be just about right. The shooter can judge for himself what is best after studying the functions of the arms and hands.

The arms simply follow the hands and thus the hands become all important in regulating the position of the entire upper body. The old school of American shotgun shooting was based upon pivoting the gun with the left hand against the right shoulder, thereby leaving nothing for the right hand to do except pull the trigger. The newer school prescribes a much more important duty for the right hand—that of cooperating with the left hand in pointing the gun as a two-handed movement, perfectly coordinated as to tensity of grip and ease of movement. This change in technique is responsible for the change of dimensions of the modern shotgun from the old; for the abandonment of the "crooked" gun in favor of the modern, straighter type.

The right hand—in the case of a right-handed shooter—also has the responsibility of releasing the trigger. The index or trigger finger must not be frozen by too tight a grip with the right hand. Likewise, it must not freeze as a manifestation of the fault of flinching. It must be flexible in order to obey the command of the eye instinctively, immediately—not so flexible as to require a general tightening of all the muscles of the hand in order to produce a firmness in the muscles controlling the trigger finger. This general tightening-up will cause the shooter to shove or jam the right hand into the trigger-pull, resulting in canting or even actual displacement of the muzzle.

Reams and volumes might be written on the subject of trigger-pull alone. Suffice it to say here that the slow process of "squeezing" the trigger, so necessary in accurate shooting with the rifle and pistol, is too slow for shotgun shooting. Again, in squeezing the trigger, the rifleman isn't supposed to know when the sear, the catch, will be released and the gun discharged. The shotgun shooter *must* know when the trigger will release in order to estimate his forward allowance properly. Therefore, he will pull or slap the trigger sharply, but not so sharply as to communicate the motion to the gun itself. "Pulling" a trigger may be described as a contraction of the muscles controlling the index finger, with the index finger already curled around the trigger, and in close con-

tact with it. "Slapping" the trigger consists of bending the index finger from a straight position along the trigger guard, *not* in actual contact with the trigger when the movement is begun. It follows that one method or the other will be better for *you*. The better method will be the one which communicates the least possible movement to the gun, the least possible disturbance of alignment.

The whole business of gun pointing may be summed up in this thought: the ideal is to preserve the illusion of pointing a stick, which is obviously a two-handed movement, founded on natural instinct, and assisted tremendously by modern changes in gun design. The new, so-called beaver-tail fore-end is intended to keep the hands at the same level in pointing the gun, just as they would be in pointing a stick. Naturally, the major part of the job of starting and stopping the gun, in swinging, is assigned to the left hand, because its arc represents an outer circle of the swing, while the arc of the right hand represents an inner circle. In the main, however, the two hands work in unison after the left hand has started the swing from its normal position of support under the fore-end. It follows that your gun will be pointed more accurately the farther you extend your left hand out toward the muzzle. You extend the pointing base, which is the distance between the hands, and thereby obtain more uniform control of the swing. At the same time, you sacrifice speed at the gun muzzle in favor of steadiness. Everything about this shooting business is a compromise somewhere along the line. If you hold your left hand back toward you on the fore-end, it can swing through a shorter arc, thus increasing its speed of travel, and relatively increasing the speed of swing of the gun muzzle.

There remains to be discussed the position of the head in relation to the gun, and to the other members of the body. This already has been touched upon in the discussion of gun fit. Suffice it to say that the right cheek is the means of locking the eye to its position slightly above and behind the back end of the rib or barrel. The cheek should be able to find this position merely by a forward inclination of the head—the less dipping and ducking the better. At the same time, the pressure of the cheek should not be so heavy as to place a drag upon the hands, the arms and the rest of the body in aligning the gun.

The cheek must ride the comb of the gun stock, invariably, without the slightest variation in position or pressure. It is easy to show by mathematics just why this rule is axiomatic and the most important in shooting technique. A far easier method of proof, however, is to visualize what happens in the case of a right-handed shooter swinging to the right. The entire movement of the gun is away from the cheek. If pressure is relaxed, the head lags behind the swing, and when the shot is delivered, the eye is *not* in its proper position to point the gun. This would not occur in pointing a stick which can be held by the hands in front of the master eye. But a gun has a stock for the purpose of absorbing recoil against the shoulder, and the master eye must adapt itself to the position defined by the very construction of the gun.

It may be stressed here that the tendency of the head to lag behind the swing in shots crossing from left to right is responsible for making this type of shot the hardest in game shooting. It isn't that a right-handed shooter swings more naturally to the left. If his shooting position is correct, he can swing either way with equal facility. It is merely that a swing from right to left carries the cheek—and the master eye—along with it, and thus insures perfect alignment of the gun muzzle upon the target.

On the same principle, the nearer the comb line of the gun stock approaches parallel with the horizontal, the more accurate the placement of the eye through all parts of the gun swing, either from left to right, or right to left. A swing to the right serves to pull the cheek back along the stock. A swing to the left moves it forward. If there is a big difference between drop at comb and drop at heel, the height of the eye above the sighting plane increases or decreases with movement to the side.

OFF-SEASON PRACTICE

All too many scattergun hunters take their guns out of moth balls the night before the season opens, and the results are quite inevitable—their shooting is rusty. Skeet shooting is a great teacher of quick, sure gun handling. Trapshooting from a platform is not nearly so good, since you will get nothing but going-away shots. In any case, both of these shooting games require a fixed field setup, something not available to most shooters unless they are members of a gunning club. Therefore, for shotgun practice, your best bet is a hand trap—the kind with a spring and cocking mechanism, rather than the whip type —which you can use wherever you can find a safe shooting area—a minimum of 250 yards.

Then pair off with your hunting partner, one throwing, the other shooting. Start with the easy straightaway or crossing shots to get the feel of your gun. Then switch to quartering angles from both the right and left sides. If you find that you're missing consistently on any quarter, keep shooting at this same angle until you find the right swing and lead. That's the advantage of hand-trapping over skeet.

You can work out your shooting difficulties at once without having to shoot a great many full rounds in order to solve your swing on any particular shot. Even if it is a warm, preseason day, wear the type of jacket you would wear were you actually in the field. If you can score consistently in this hand-trap contest, you're ready for the opening of the hunting season.

Care of Your Shotgun

Back in the days of black powder and corrosive (chlorate) primers there was no question about gun cleaning. Either it was done (and a messy job it was) promptly after the day's shooting, or the gun owner could be quite certain that the morrow would reveal the first streaks of rust. With modern non-corrosive and non-fouling shot shells, however, the situation is quite different. Neither the powder nor primers in present-day ammunition are of themselves rust promoting. Does this then mean that cleaning is unnecessary? Definitely not. With the possible exception of a few really dry-air locations, gun cleaning is the best insurance against the ravages of rust that is born of temperature changes and contact with moisture-bearing bodies.

Common experience has shown that moisture has a way of getting into everything, and those surfaces suffer most that are difficult to inspect closely for first traces. The interior of a shotgun barrel is a prime example of this situation. The blued outside metal surfaces require cleaning and oiling too, for they are ever vulnerable to rust-producing perspiration, rain, snow and condensation. Fall hunting conditions, of course, cause the major enemy to a sportman's gun—rust. Once the reddish-brown streaks appear on steel, it is proof positive that damage has been done. Rust is visible evidence of metal that has been eaten away, and this metal can't be replaced.

First need is a good cleaning rod. For shotguns, it is usually made of aluminum or wood and may be one solid piece or jointed. The solid rod seems less inclined toward breakage under severe usage, while the jointed rod is by far easier to pack along on the hunting trip. (Many shooters have one of each—the solid for home use and the jointed for field use.) Whatever the style or material, the rod should be of the type that has a handle at one end and is threaded at the other to accommodate tips for various uses. Shotgun rod kits usually include a slotted tip, a wire brush and a felt or wool swab. Patches can be purchased cut to size for the gauge of gun to be cleaned, or they can be cut to size from

Fig. 1.11 You can practice your shotgun shooting off-season with a hand skeet device such as shown below.

pieces of Canton flannel. Actually there is little, if any, saving of money realized from buying Canton flannel and cutting one's own patches. To do a thorough job, patches must be of the right size. If too big, the risk of getting patch and rod stuck in the barrel is great. Powder solvent, a can of light oil, a tube or small can of gun grease and a supply of clean rags complete the required basic equipment list.

It won't take you five minutes to swab out your barrels at the end of a day's sport, nor half a minute to rub a little grease over the outside of barrels and lock work. Do this, and year after year, your gun will be new and perfect, inside and out. Never plug up your barrels with anything, for moisture will condense inside and cause rust to form. Use a light oil for lubricating action parts—3-in-1 Oil is good for this purpose. But don't depend on it as a barrel cleaner because it just isn't one, and moreover, it will evaporate and allow rust to form. Use a good gunpowder solvent especially made for this purpose and apply it as directed by the manufacturer. Also rub a few drops of boiled linseed oil into the stock and fore-end every time you think of it, and scrub the oil out of the checked portions with a stiff-bristled hand brush. If linseed is not available, then automobile cake wax will aid in keeping the stock water-repellent.

If you have just shot in the rain or snow, you should disassemble your gun as soon as possible after getting under cover. Wipe the entire outside surface with a dry rag with no oil on it, for the oil and water drops will form an emulsion that may subsequently form rust on the gun. Then go over the entire outer surface of the barrel and metal parts with a well-oiled rag. Give the same treatment to the inside of the barrel or barrels, in which some raindrops may be lurking, too.

Before putting your gun away for any length of time, or if you have been shooting for several days

in succession, it is advisable to run a swab soaked in powder solvent through the barrel to be sure that you aren't getting any lead fouling in it. Soft shot, like corrosive primers, isn't employed any more in the manufacture of commercial shells. All modern loads use chilled shot, which is a great deal harder and a lot less likely to stick to and mark up the barrel. However, in spite of the chilled shot, this problem does arise. The best cure is a liberal application of powder solvent, followed by the judicious use of a wire brush soaked in the same preparation. If this doesn't remove the lead foulings, take the gun to a gunsmith to do the job. Don't try to scrape it out with a metal object, since this will only scratch your barrel, and it will lead up again more quickly than ever.

At the end of the season—or rather, immediately after your last trip for the season—clean the gun very carefully and coat it with a good grade of high-viscosity oil or good gun grease. Apply it liberally, put your gun in its case and store it in a dry place —not the basement. If you have noted any difficulties with your gun, have it checked by a gunsmith before you store it. When, after several years' service, the bluing becomes worn, it's good business to have the whole gun refinished. Modern gunsmiths can do a job equal to factory work at moderate cost, and it keeps your gun like new, with maximum trade or sales value.

Before any gun is fired the first time after cleaning or storage, enough patches should be run through the barrel to remove any oil or grease that is present. In the case of a new gun where the grease is thick, carbon tetrachloride or a petroleum solvent can be used to advantage on patches and a wiping cloth. Oil or grease in a barrel can be the cause of flyers on the first few shots, and if present to any appreciable degree when the gun is fired, it may well result in damage to the gun.

Chapter Two

LEARNING ABOUT RIFLES

FROM THE OLD smooth-bore musket of colonial times, through the development of the frontiermen's famous Kentucky rifle, down to today's precision firearms, the rifle has played an important part in our nation's progress and expansion. Today's rifle-man-hunter has a wide choice of rifles from which to choose—from the little single-shot .22 rimfire to ultra-modern .300 Magnums which can deliver a killing blow to the biggest game animals at extremely long ranges.

How to Choose a Rifle

The rifle is a gun employed to shoot a cartridge or shell loaded with one large shot and is designed to deliver it at long ranges. This is where it differs from the shotgun which, as discussed in Chapter 1, was designed to deliver many small pellets over a short distance. In order for a rifle to deliver its single shot or bullet for a long distance and still have sufficient killing power, it's necessary for the shot to leave the barrel at a high velocity. To accomplish this, a rather large charge of fairly fast-burning powder must be employed to give the bullet a tremendous shove. This, in turn, necessitates the use of a metal case to house the charge and hold the base of the bullet. It also means that rifles are usually quite heavy so that they won't blow apart by the discharge. In addition, the recoil shock of the explosion and of a bullet given such a hard push would cause a too-light gun to jump so that the extreme accuracy —so important to rifle shooting—would be impossible.

So that a bullet can keep on an accurate course, it is necessary for it not only to travel straight ahead, but it must rotate as it goes toward its target. To accomplish this, spiral grooves or rifling are cut inside the barrel throughout its entire length. The discharged bullet expands against these grooves or rifling, thus follows their exact spiral, and its spin-

ning motion is begun. Upon the number of spirals depends the rotation speed of the bullet. Too fast a spin of a high-velocity bullet may impair rather than help its accuracy. Therefore, it's important to follow the manufacturer's recommendations as to the proper cartridges to use since the manufacturer has rifled the barrel to give the best average results in accordance with the ammunition intended in that rifle.

The caliber of a rifle is, in the simplest of terms, the diameter measurement of the hole or bore in its barrel, stated in decimal fractions of an inch. This bore diameter is measured across the actual barrel and does not take the rifling or grooves into consideration. For example, the bore diameter for a .30-caliber rifle measures .3000 inch. (In the United States, we generally drop the extra ciphers.) Unfortunately there is no standard calibration system employed by gun manufacturers in the same manner as standard gauges of shotguns. For example, in the caliber .25/20, the "20" means the powder charge in weight; .250/3000, the "3000" indicates the muzzle velocity of the bullet; .30/06, the "06" designates the year the cartridge became standard; and, in the case of the .30/30, no one is absolutely certain what the last "30" stands for. In a few cases, the decimals don't even stand for the true caliber—the .303 Savage is actually .300, while the .220 Swift and .218 Bee have a bore diameter of .219 and .217 inches respectively. There are many other examples where confusion exists.

In selecting a rifle, the choice of caliber will depend on the following important factors:

1. Consider the type of game you plan to hunt. You can't, obviously, hunt varmint with the same caliber rifle as you would big game such as bear, elk, moose, etc. Specific recommendations for the various species of wild game hunted by rifle are made in Chapters 5 through 7.

2. The type of country and section of the United States where you plan to do your hunting

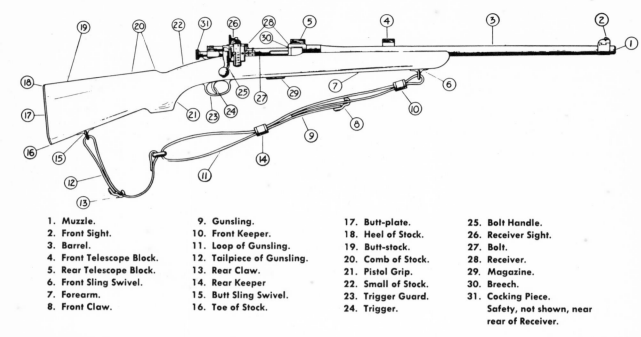

1. Muzzle.	9. Gunsling.	17. Butt-plate.	25. Bolt Handle.
2. Front Sight.	10. Front Keeper.	18. Heel of Stock.	26. Receiver Sight.
3. Barrel.	11. Loop of Gunsling.	19. Butt-stock.	27. Bolt.
4. Front Telescope Block.	12. Tailpiece of Gunsling.	20. Comb of Stock.	28. Receiver.
5. Rear Telescope Block.	13. Rear Claw.	21. Pistol Grip.	29. Magazine.
6. Front Sling Swivel.	14. Rear Keeper	22. Small of Stock.	30. Breech.
7. Forearm.	15. Butt Sling Swivel.	23. Trigger Guard.	31. Cocking Piece.
8. Front Claw.	16. Toe of Stock.	24. Trigger.	Safety, not shown, near rear of Receiver.

Fig. 2.1 Nomenclature of a small bore rifle. (Courtesy of Sporting Arms and Ammunition Manufacturers' Institute)

must be taken into consideration. For instance, in the eastern portion of the country, where a good part of the rifle-hunting area has dense cover so that game is seldom at ranges of more than 100 yards, a heavy, long-barreled rifle isn't required. The western hunter, on the other hand, who does much of his big-game hunting in the wide open spaces wants a rifle that will deliver its bullet in a flat trajectory and a high velocity, for many of his shots will be taken at ranges varying from 100 to 300 yards.

3. Some states have outlawed certain calibers in given sections of their state (a few have outlawed rifles altogether in certain areas), while some have laws stating that certain species of game must be hunted with rifles no lighter than a specified caliber.

4. The cost of a rifle varies to some extent, depending on the caliber. Decide how much money you would like to spend.

TYPES OF ACTION

The action of a rifle means the type of device it has for reloading. For hunting purposes, a single-shot gun is next to worthless, since the one or more extra shots that may be needed to bring an animal down has to be done more quickly than can be reloaded by hand. Repeating rifles, with magazines holding extra shells, are therefore most useful and popular. There are four types in common use today: the lever action, the slide action, the bolt action and autoloading.

THE LEVER ACTION. This type of action employs the back of the trigger guard as a lever in which the three last fingers of the right hand fit. Once the shot is made, these fingers push the lever down and ahead, then back and up, ejecting the used cartridge case and throwing another shell from the magazine into the barrel. It is a simple, foolproof and safe action. For these reasons, it's an ideal gun for the beginning rifleman. But, the very structure of the lever action rules it out when it comes to handling the big bore, high-velocity loads necessary for long range shooting. But for the hunter who does almost all of his shooting at ranges under 150 yards, and wants a light, handy rifle for climbing the ridges and pushing through the thickets of the eastern covers, the lever action rifle is a good choice.

THE SLIDE ACTION. This action, often called the pump action, uses the fore-end or handgrip below the barrel to accomplish its task. When the rifle is fired, this handgrip, which rests in the left hand, is pulled back and pushed forward to eject the spent cartridge and to replace it with a new one. This permits the hunter, if he doesn't get a clean hit on his first shot, to keep his rifle sights on the running animal while ejecting the empty and chambering a fresh shell with a flick of his forearm. This action, while simple to operate and considered a "fast hander," has never gained too great a popularity among hunters. Most rifles containing slide action are usually of moderate weight and have good accuracy up to about 150 yards.

THE BOLT ACTION. To accomplish this action, a knob, placed at the right side of the gun near the trigger, is grasped, shoved upward to unlock the gun breech, pulled backward, ejecting the used cartridge, thrust forward carrying the new shell from the magazine and then pulled down to lock the breech again. For long-range shooting, or for game that is brought down more readily with a fast, heavy bullet, the bolt action rifle has no peer. While not so fast to operate as the other three actions, it is undoubtedly the all-round best and most popular with experienced hunters.

THE AUTOLOADING ACTION. This action is as nearly automatic a one as possible. With it, the recoil power of the shot is employed to eject the spent cartridge and throw another into the barrel. The trigger may then be pulled again and the next shot fired without any manual action on the part of the hunter. Its ease of operation gives more shots in a shorter time, thus increasing the firepower of the weapon. It is good for short and medium range hunting (up to 150 yards), but is heavier than most other guns of the

Fig. 2.2 Types of rifles: A. Lever action, with gunsling and telescopic sight. B. Slide action. C. Bolt action, with gunsling. D. Autoloading action.

same caliber. Due to its almost automatic feature, a few states have made it illegal to use for certain game species.

Before deciding on the action you wish, however, you should first make up your mind as to the caliber rifle you wish. Manufacturers usually only make certain actions in certain calibers.

FITTING A RIFLE TO YOU

While the fit of a rifle isn't quite so important as when selecting a shotgun because you generally have more time to shoot—hence you can do a better job of making your anatomy conform—one that fits nicely is a joy to shoot.

Anyone does better shooting with a well-designed stock that fits him than he does with one that doesn't. So that the rifle can be held firmly and steadily, there are four points of contact with parts of your body—the cheek against the comb, the shoulder against the butt, the left hand on the fore-end and the right hand at the grip. The comb should be thick enough and high enough so that the pressure of the cheek against it steadies your aim and completes the essential pressure triangle of butt, grip and comb for steady holding. The cheekpiece should be so shaped as to give added support to the face and steadiness to the rifle. The drop at the comb (in combination with the thickness) should put the eye in line with the sights, but not be so high or thick as to injure the cheek from recoil. The drop at heel should put the butt comfortably at the shoulder and yet be at a minimum so that recoil effect is lessened. The pitch of the butt should be at an angle which prevents it from sliding up or down. The fore-end should be of such a size and shape that it will keep the hand away from the hot barrel and will assist you to control your rifle in the case of a fast swing. The pistol grip should be so shaped as to let you hold the butt against your shoulder for steadiness, and at the same time leave your trigger finger free to squeeze the shot off at the proper moment.

While all items are major considerations, the most important one is probably the comb. It should be just high enough so that the cheek presses firmly against it to steady the rifle. With the cheek so pressed, the aiming eye should be right in line with the sights. If the comb is too low, the cheek doesn't touch it, thus butt-grip-comb triangle is broken. If the cheek fails to make proper contact with the comb, you usually try to make your left hand do the work your cheek should do. Should you hold too far out on the fore-end and try to complete the triangle by pulling the butt back against the shoulder with

your left hand, you are doing a task which should be performed by your hand at grip.

The rifle stock generally has more down pitch than the shotgun, simply due to the fact that it is aimed in a different manner. While the down pitch in a shotgun may vary anywhere from ¼ to 2 inches, the rifle's may be from 3 to 4½ inches, and sometimes more. The reason for this big difference is that with a scattergun the hand holds the butt firmly but rather lightly against the shoulder, whereas the rifle butt is held very hard. The drop at the heel is usually between 1 and 1⅜ inches. Thus when expressed in terms of drop from the line of iron sights, it would mean a drop at the comb of approximately 1⅝ inches, and a drop at heel of about 2⅝ inches.

The length of the pull is generally from ½ to 1 inch less than that on the shotgun. It should be such that the rifle comes up quickly with no tendency to catch in your clothes. But, it should be long enough so that upon recoil it won't hit your thumb into your nose when the thumb is correctly around the grip instead of along the grip.

While on the subject of the grip, remember that a good pistol grip can help your shooting because of the task the right hand must do in keeping the butt firm against your shoulder. The pistol grip shouldn't be extremely "full" (sharply curved). If too sharply curved, the hand is cramped. If there is no curve, or if the curve is the arc of a circle, the hand isn't properly supported. The best-feeling grips usually have a slight parabolic curve toward the grip cap. The circumference of the grip should be between 4½ and 5 inches and its forward edge about 3⅜ to 4 inches (depending on the size of the hand) from the center of the trigger and about 1½ to 2 inches below the center of the trigger.

The fore-end should generally be about 10 inches long from the forward edge of the receiver ring to the end of the fore-end tip. This is a good proportional length for a 20- or 22-inch barrel, but could be slightly longer for a 24-inch barrel. Many excellent fore-ends are just about circular in cross section, but a slight pear-shape or semi-beavertail probably is more comfortable and may give better control.

As a rule, the straighter the stock the better. With a straight stock, the rifle recoils in a straight line and, if the buttplate is large enough to distribute the recoil over a wide area, no one is going to get hurt. The small buttplate that concentrates recoil is poison. So is the crooked stock with or without a Monte Carlo, as the comb rises from recoil to hit the shooter on the sensitive cheekbone.

Remember that when selecting a rifle to fit you the important considerations are how firmly the comb and the cheekpiece support your face, how well the pistol grip fits your hand, how fast you can get it into shooting position and how steadily you can hold it when you squeeze the trigger. All else—style, stock shapes, wood, decorations, etc.—is a matter of personal preference.

RIFLE SIGHTS

It is very important that your rifle has the proper sights. While there are several different iron sights available, there are only two basic types—open sights and peep sights.

In the open type sight arrangement, the front sight is usually some sort of "bead," often enclosed in a metal ring or cylinder. The rear sight is simply a V- or U-shaped piece of metal into the bottom of which the front sight is aligned. With the front and rear sights blackened, and in shooting at a black-and-white target, it's possible to obtain good accuracy with open sights. But with most open sights, accuracy falls off quickly when conditions are less ideal. Even the best open sights, the shallow U's and V's, cut off half the view of the game. The worst, like the full buckhorn, cut off at least three-fourths of the view. The hunter wants to see what he's shooting at, hence tends to boost his front sight up high above the notch so he can see. With the narrow V's, there is an increasing tendency to shoot high in poor light, or even in fair light. The closer you get to the bottom of the V, the dimmer the light grows. Hence, the front sight is hard to see.

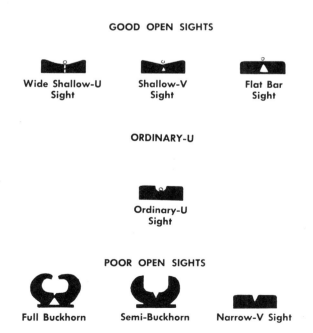

GOOD OPEN SIGHTS

Wide Shallow-U Sight Shallow-V Sight Flat Bar Sight

ORDINARY-U

Ordinary-U Sight

POOR OPEN SIGHTS

Full Buckhorn Semi-Buckhorn Narrow-V Sight

Fig. 2.3 Examples of good and poor open type sights.

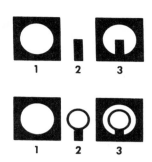

Fig. 2.4 Peep sights and sight pictures: 1. Rear sight. 2. Front sight. 3. Combined sight picture.

The peep type sight is a far more scientific device than the open sight, as it is based on the sound optical principle that the eye naturally centers objects seen through a hole. Roughly, the peep sight is a disk with a small hole in the center, through which you look, aligning the front bead in the center of the hole. When employing an open sight, your eye must try to focus on 1) the rear sight, 2) the front sight and 3) the target. Sometimes this can be rather difficult, especially if you're a middle-aged man whose eyes aren't so elastic. But, with the peep type you don't look at your rear sight but through it. All you do is put the bead on your target and squeeze the trigger. For this reason the peep sight is preferred by most hunters, except where fast, quick shots are generally employed. In such cases the good open sight is best.

TELESCOPIC SIGHTS

The telescopic sight is, fundamentally, a rear sight made in the form of a telescope. The advantages of telescopic sights—a greatly clearer target picture, focal-plane sighting and precision aiming—have long been known to target and bench-rest shooters. Only in recent years, however, has there been a pronounced swing to scope sights for game hunting. Today, some hunters still feel a question about the dependability of such "delicate" equipment in hard field use, or under adverse weather conditions. Some think iron sights are faster or safer. But anyone who has seen the increase every year in the number of scope sights in the field knows that the scope is "here to stay." There are sound reasons.

For deer hunting in thickly wooded country, for example, a 2½ power scope sight, mounted low, close to the receiver, giving the shooter three to five inches of eye relief and a field of view of 30 feet or more at 100 yards, is ideal. The long eye relief permits safe use on rifles of heavy recoil, and a wide field of view enables the hunter to keep running game in his sight picture, permitting easy swing-ahead

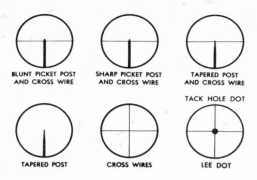

Fig. 2.5 Some popular styles of scope sight aiming reticules. (Courtesy of Florida Game & Fresh Water Fish Commission)

or lead. Mounted in sturdy, rigid mounts, these low-power scopes have wide-latitude, or universal, focus. Once set, unlimited clear vision should be achieved, beginning at about 25 yards.

Contrary to belief, when properly mounted, the hunting scope is the fastest of all sights for quick shots at running game in thickly wooded areas, for you have but one sight to align on your target—the reticule. The arguments advanced against the superiority of scope sights for brush shooting usually come from hunters who have made costly mistakes in scope selection, mounting and adjustment.

A scope sight is a great boon for shooters who have defective vision that is not fully corrected by the wearing of spectacles. Within the range of focusing latitude of the better quality scope sights, an adjustment for perfect vision can frequently be found. Shooters who wear bifocals should use the distance prescription segment of their eyeglasses when taking aim through a scope.

Whether you enjoy normal vision or wear glasses, focus the scope for clearness and "blackness" of the reticule alone. Begin by loosening the eyepiece clamping ring, which is usually the second knurled ring rearward of the rear mount, and then point the scope towards clear sky. Slowly turn the eyepiece out (counter-clockwise) until the image of the reticule is fuzzy and plainly out of focus; then turn it in (clockwise) until the image is sharp and clear. *Then stop!* If you adjust beyond this point, there will be a strain on the aiming eye and the eye will automatically try to accommodate an incorrect focus, something you don't want to happen. And don't strain your aiming eye by prolonged examination of the reticule; instead, take quick peeks to see if the reticule looks distinct the second you take aim. Satisfied on that score, screw up the clamping ring to

lock the eyepiece in correct, permanent position. Once determined, this setting will not have to be changed until major changes take place in your eyesight.

Although the hunter sees the details of his target more distinctly and is able to aim more accurately with a scope sight, the optical sighting aid does nothing magical. A scope sight improves upon conditions already present. It can't introduce desirable extra illumination. The light must be there already; the scope's optics merely utilize existing light and other sighting factors to maximum advantage.

If you plan to hunt mountain sheep, antelope, mountain goat, or game that is in the open and unsuspecting, a 6-power scope may be the answer, provided you can shoot from the prone or sitting position. From such positions it's possible to "hold" with enough steadiness to eliminate the movement of the cross hairs all over the target. But, if you don't have any expectation of getting a shot at ranges greater than 150 yards, you'll find the 2½-power scope will meet your needs. Also this provides you with a field of view of between 40 and 50 feet, more than twice that of a good 6-power scope. For those who want 2½-power for some shooting, and 5-power in the event of need, some manufacturers have now turned out scopes in which the magnification can be doubled by the mere twist of a knob.

To guide those who want to know the field of view of the average scope sight in various powers, here it is. The field of view is given in feet at a range of 100 yards.

> 2-power — 45 feet
> 2½-power — 40 feet
> 4-power — 30 feet
> 5-power — 25 feet
> 6-power — 20 feet
> 8-power — 15 feet

It may surprise you that you don't actually see the target with a scope. Instead, you see an image of the target, and in a properly adjusted scope the image seen and the imposed reticule appear at the same distance and in the same plane. This picture must be bright and clear right out to the edges of the lens, without distortion or color fringe. When you look into a scope sight's big eyepiece or eye-lens you should see your target and immediate surroundings and the aiming reticule all accurately focused, distinct, well lighted and greatly magnified.

Conventional cross hair reticules obscure less of one's target than the post or post-horizontal styles of reticules, enabling the shooter to "quarter" his target on clear shots, but against widely varying backgrounds or in thick but delicate growth, the post style will win hands down in definition and speed of alignment. If your preference is the post-type reticule, it should appear perpendicular to your vision as the firearm is placed to the shoulder and aimed. Where the reticule is one of the popular cross hair types, both hairs should be accurately positioned—that is, the horizontal one should be perfectly level and the perpendicular one should be precisely erect.

In mounting a scope sight on a rifle, it is highly important that the scope tube be positioned so that instantaneous eye alignment and full view of reticule and target images occur each time the rifle is shouldered. It shouldn't be necessary to first move the aiming eye forward or backward to find the scope's area of maximum clarity and eye relief. The hunting scope is correctly positioned when you can throw the rifle to your shoulder with eyes closed, then open your eyes to find everything in instant, full focus—full field of view, aiming reticule and target.

If, as frequently happens when a scope sight is mounted on a rifle with a factory stock having a comb height originally shaped for metallic sights, you have to lift your face from the stock's supporting comb to get best vision alignment, then you need to raise the height of the comb of the stock. This can be done either by adding a walnut rib, screwed or glued in place, or by installing a lace-on leather and rubber comb pad, available in various comb heights. In using a scope, or any of the metallic sight combinations, the shooter's face should receive support from the firearm's stock comb—a most steadying influence to the aiming eye and to natural sight alignment.

To be a fully effective sighting instrument, the scope sight must be free of parallax—the apparent movement of the scope's reticule as the aiming eye is moved around the field of view. Technically, parallax means that the reticule isn't in the plane of focus of the scope's object lens, and that your aim won't be correct until the condition is remedied. To remove parallax from a hunting scope, place the rifle and mounted scope upright on a bench rest or similar support, rifle steady and unmoving. Loosen the small screws holding the adjustment turrets just a wee bit and then use a screwdriver handle to gently tap the turrets forward or backward, as required, until no parallax is present. This condition is achieved when there is no longer any apparent movement of the reticule as the aiming eye is shifted. Removal of existing parallax can be a time-consuming job in some

Fig. 2.6 For ordinary scanning, big game hunters commonly carry binoculars, which afford a wider field of vision than the more powerful scope. Some even use a spotting scope (far left) for this task. (Courtesy of Bill Browning, Montana Chamber of Commerce)

instances, but it must be done. Carefully following the instructions furnished by the scope's maker will make the job easier.

On the average, a mounted scope sight will add only about three-quarters of a pound to the weight of a rifle.

Rifle Ammunition

Like the caliber of a rifle, ammunition employed with it is without a fully standard system of nomenclature. In other words, there are some cartridges whose names don't match the true caliber either of their bullets or of the guns which will fire them. This lack of uniform designation of rifle ammunition is due to the fact that manufacturers are constantly developing new and better loads for the hunting public. But for the beginning hunter, it is very important that he teaches himself the basic difference in types of ammunition and how each should be used. Before going into this, let's examine the cartridge itself.

The cartridge case has two important functions: one being to hold all the parts together in a package convenient for handling and the second being to keep the powder gas in the gun, where it belongs when the cartridge is fired. Since the gun itself isn't gas-tight and since the pressure inside the rifle quickly builds up to over twenty thousand pounds per square inch when the trigger is squeezed, the task of the case in keeping the gas under control is very vital. In appearance, the case is a cylinder of a copper alloy such as brass, open on one end, with a flat-bottomed bulge on the other end.

The priming mixture, to some extent, could be considered the match that ignites the powder. You normally won't see the priming mix, since it's located in the flat-bottomed bulge on the end of the cartridge case. The modern smokeless powder used in rifle ammunition is relatively hard to set on fire and without the primer we would have trouble getting it to ignite. It is the burning of the powder in the rifle that is the source of concentrated energy. When all of these components are assembled, the priming mix is held firmly in the base of the case, the powder is loose in the case and the open end of the case is crimped around the tail of the bullet.

Actually the bullet could be considered the most important component of the cartridge. Yet, to all too many hunters, it's the least understood and most ignored of all the elements that affect practical shooting. For instance, the bullet's ability to overcome air resistance and fly a great distance depends on its shape and sectional density (weight compared to diameter). Accuracy of flight depends upon perfection of form and upon proper relationship of bullet length, weight, caliber, velocity and twist of rifling. And killing power depends on the bullet's actual construction, weight and velocity.

The ammunition manufacturers spend a great deal of time and money developing and producing bullets of various types which will give best results under certain specific conditions. Yet, many times, a hunter will just ask for a certain caliber cartridge, completely ignoring bullet type and weight. For a particular example, let's say a deer hunter with a .30/06 caliber rifle is sold a box of .30/06 ammo loaded with 110-grain bullets. This cartridge is loaded especially for varmint shooting, where the bullet must mushroom or open up very quickly. When well placed on a deer or larger animal, such a bullet may inflict only a superficial wound. This results in no meat for the table, a shot game animal which may die a painful and lingering death and a very unhappy hunter. A clean kill would have resulted had the proper 150- or 180-grain weight bullet been used.

At this point, it may be wise to explain the two ways game is killed quickly. The first is by disruption of a vital center. A shot in the brain and a shot which smashes the neck vertebrae will always kill instantly. All other hits depend for instantaneous kills on the distribution of shock over a wide area by tissue destruction—in other words, by spoiling meat. However, if the bullet is properly placed the tissue destroyed is not that which is ordinarily eaten. A high-speed bullet through the lung area will tear up and wreck several pounds of lungs but not much else. One in the abdomen will tear up entrails. Moreover, to get instantaneous kills, the bullet has to expand violently. The bullet which is so strongly

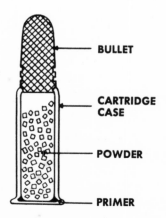

Fig. 2.7 Section through a .22 Long rifle cartridge. (Courtesy of Sporting Arms and Ammunition Manufacturers' Institute)

constructed, or has lost so much velocity, that it doesn't expand violently won't give an instantaneous kill unless the neck vertebrae or the brain is struck.

There are innumerable bullet designs: hollow point, soft point, bronze point, sharp pointed, boat-tailed, power-point, etc. While each has its special purposes related to range, weight, etc., they can all be grouped into the following five different classes of game bullets, depending on what they're to be used on:

1. The light constructed, high-speed bullets for varmint hunting of woodchucks to coyotes; bullets that will quickly expand for the kill in small, soft bodies, yet will completely disintegrate on contact with the ground to eliminate any chance of ricochets.

2. Bullets that will quickly expand for shocking power, yet will hold together for penetration of medium-size game such as deer, antelope, mountain goats and sheep.

3. The so-called all-round bullets that are heavy and tough enough to kill the heavier non-dangerous game such as moose, caribou and elk, but will still expand readily enough to be employed on medium-size animals.

4. Bullets for those animals in the dangerous category that are soft-skinned such as large grizzlies, lions, tigers, Alaskan brown bears, etc. These bullets must be heavy, but they should mushroom and hang together for sure killing penetration.

5. Heavy, non-expanded bullets designed to kill heavy, dangerous, tough-skinned animals such as the elephant, water buffalo and rhinoceros.

The type of hunting conditions and the type of terrain also affect the choice of bullet. For example, when hunting in brush or woods, you'll want a bullet of good shocking power that won't be deflected or greatly deformed on contact with twigs or small branches, yet one that will open up and make a killing wound within the animal. Such a bullet should not be too sharp of point, for a sharp-pointed bullet is more easily thrown off its line of flight. It should be fairly heavy for its caliber and constructed so that it will expand for shocking power, but hold together for penetration. On the other hand, when hunting on the open terrain of the West, the sharp-pointed bullets are ideal. Specific recommendation for the proper cartridges for specific game is given in Chapters 5 through 7.

When selecting ammunition for your rifle, you must also consider the cartridge's muzzle velocity and the bullet's trajectory. The latter is the arc described by a bullet between the rifle's muzzle and the target at a given distance. When a bullet is first propelled from the muzzle it rises slightly; then, as it loses some of its original velocity, gravity pulls it downward. The faster the bullet travels over its range, the less it will drop and the flatter its trajectory will be.

The muzzle velocity or the speed at which a bullet leaves the rifle varies with the type of cartridge and is classed into two broad categories: high-velocity and low-velocity. The high-velocity load generally has a flat trajectory which means that the point of actual aim can be nearer to exactly "on" the target at long ranges than with a relatively low-velocity bullet. This is obviously advantageous, especially for shooting mountain sheep, antelope, or bear at long ranges on the clear western plains and mountain regions, or for distant varmint shooting. But, since high-velocity bullets are generally more easily deflected off course, by hitting even a small twig, than low-velocity ones, the latter are best at short ranges in brushy or wooded country.

Cartridges are fired in two ways and are designated as either center-fire cartridges or rim-fire cartridges. In the first, the firing pin of the rifle strikes the center of the cartridge case bottom. In the latter, the firing pin strikes the rim. Almost all rifle ammunition manufactured today is of center-fire type, except for a few low-powered .22 cartridges. Remember that cartridges of one type of firing are not interchangeable in guns built for the other. Actually, in the interest of safety, *never* experiment with any ammunition other than that specifically intended to be shot in your rifle. Certain other loads may fit it, but they may also ruin your rifle, or even blow out the breech and injure you seriously. Also be sure that you know the distance at which the particular load you are using is dangerous. Some heavy loads are dangerous over a mile away.

How to Handle a Rifle

There are three primary essentials, regardless of type, in rifle shooting which must be thoroughly learned before one can even start on the road toward hunting success. These are *aiming, holding,* and *trigger squeeze,* and the most important of these is the *trigger squeeze.* These three essentials must be learned together as their coordination plays an important part. If you aim your rifle accurately, if you hold it steadily, then if you squeeze the trigger so as not to spoil the aim and hold, you'll always strike the target—provided your rifle and ammunition are accurate and your sights are correctly adjusted. Here is where coordination comes in, that is, the teamwork between eye, brain and muscle to hold the rifle and send the bullet on its way.

Even if a man is a real good shotgunner, there's no proof that he'll do a fine job with a rifled weapon. The two methods of shooting are almost diametrically opposite. When employing a scattergun you must combine swift gun-handling with quick judgment to get off a well-placed charge in the shortest possible time. There's no premium on careful holding and gentle, smooth trigger squeeze. In other words, an expert shotgunner is a trigger-jerker—when his swing is right—but a good rifleman, on the other hand, *cannot* jerk the trigger if he expects to put the bullet where he wishes.

SHOOTING POSITIONS

There are four generally accepted body positions—prone, sitting, kneeling and standing. Hunters make use of all of them on occasion. The standing or off-hand position is used only for quick shots at moving game in the field. The kneeling and sitting positions are much steadier for long shots in the field, and where game is unaware of the hunter's presence, the prone position is often taken and the sling made use of to steady the shot over extremely long ranges. Actually, you should always take the steadiest position you can since you want to place your bullet just right and kill cleanly and humanely. If you can find a quick rest over a limb or a stone, you should do so. If conditions are such that you can shoot from a prone position, do so. If you can't use a rest or lie down, you'll have to settle for sitting, or if you can't sit, then it's best to kneel. Only as a last resort should you shoot in a standing or offhand position.

The gunsling is of tremendous assistance to steady holding in the prone, sitting and kneeling positions. We don't mean to say that you can't shoot in these positions without the gunsling, but we do say that it will take you weeks and months to hold and shoot fairly well without it, and with it you can learn to hold steadily and shoot very well in just a few days. Every expert rifleman uses the gunsling in these positions.

The upper or forward half of the sling is called the "loop." When you stretch the sling along the bottom of the stock the loop should be adjusted to such a length that it will come to within about 2 inches of the butt-swivel. Exact length will differ with different lengths of arms, and can only be told from experience. If the loop is too short you can't get the rifle to your shoulder; if too loose the sling won't be tight on the arm. The rear portion of the sling is called the "tail," and it should always be so loose that it will never be stretched tight when you're in the firing position.

To place the sling on your arm, move the hand between the entire sling and the stock just in front of the trigger guard, and then bring the hand and arm back through the loop. That is, your arm should pass through the loop from its right to its left. This twists the upper portion of the sling so that its flat rests against your wrist. The left hand is then carried in a circular motion, high and left, over the forward part of the sling and grasps the forearm just in rear of the front sling swivel. With the right hand then pull the loop as high up on the left upper arm as it will go, and slip down the keeper to hold it there.

THE PRONE POSITION. To assume the prone position, having adjusted the sling on the arm as described above, you should first half face to the right of the target, then lie down on your stomach, elbows on the ground, taking particular care that you lie at an angle of 45 degrees to the right of the target, never head-on to the target. Place the butt of the rifle to your shoulder and aim at your target. If you can't get the butt of the rifle to your shoulder the sling is too tight. When the sling is just the right length it takes a little effort, but not much, to place the butt to the shoulder. The left elbow must be on the ground at a point almost under, and never more than an inch or two to the left of, the rifle. The right elbow should be sloped outward more. The elbows shouldn't be too far apart nor too close together. Regard the upper arms and the chest as the legs of a tripod; if the legs are set too far apart or are too close together the tripod will be unsteady. The forearm should now rest well down in the palm of the hand, fingers curling up over the forearm and fingers and thumb almost but not quite meeting over the top of the barrel. Don't grasp the forearm with the fingers and hold the palm away from the bottom of the forearm, but let that forearm press down hard into the palm of the hand. The sling loop should now be quite tight, binding the forearm down hard in the palm of the hand, and binding the butt quite tight against the shoulder. The sling loop should feel as though it had about 10 to 15 pounds' tension on it. The legs should be spread wide apart and should hug the ground closely, feet turned outward, and the inside of the shoes resting on the ground, or as nearly so as possible without strain; the right hand should grasp the small of the stock; the left hand should be placed near the lower band swivel so that the rifle will rest on the palm of your hand; and the cheek should be pressed firmly against the stock with your eye as near the cocking piece as it can be placed without straining.

The principal faults of the beginner are: lying

head-on to the target instead of facing 45 degrees to the right; left elbow too far to the left of a point directly under the rifle; forearm of rifle not well down in the palm of the hand; sling loop too loose or too tight; and loop around arm down near the elbow instead of high up near the armpit.

THE SITTING POSITION. Unfortunately, the prone can't be used all the time while hunting. In a flat, plains country, grass and low bushes are likely to get in the way. On a hillside, the prone position is impossibly awkward; no one can shoot with his legs higher than his head. But sitting puts the line of sight high enough so that it can be used when shooting in high grass and low bushes. It can also be used on hillsides. It's much more flexible than the prone position and can be used for running shots; a prone position generally can't. If used in connection with a sling, it is a very steady position.

Adjust the gunsling as before. (Good shooting can be done in this position without a sling, but with the added support of a sling it's very steady.) The sling, arms, hands and rifle are in the same relative position as when shooting prone. Half face to the right of the target and sit down. Rest the elbows on the knees, or just a little bit below the knees, the

Fig. 2.8 The three best rifle shooting positions: (left bottom to right top) prone, kneeling, and sitting. (All photos courtesy of Bill Browning, Montana Chamber of Commerce)

left elbow and left knee almost under the rifle. If possible stamp small holes in the ground for the heels to rest in to keep them from slipping. It is also permissible to cross the legs below the knees if you desire and if it gives added steadiness. Gradually you will find that there is just one spot on the kneecaps, or slightly below them, where the elbows will tend to rest firmly. The body should be well forward and the cheek shoud be pressed firmly against the stock and placed as far forward as possible without straining. Your left hand should be near the upper sling swivel so that the rifle will rest on the palm of the hand. But no attempt should be made to completely hold the forearm tight with the left hand. Usually the sling tension pushing the upper arms back against the shin is sufficient. But remember, as in any shooting position, that the more relaxed you are the better you'll shoot. Tension makes for tremor and tremor makes for missing.

THE KNEELING POSITION. Adjust the gunsling on the left arm as before. Half face to the right of the target. Sit on the right heel, resting the weight of the body on it. If your ankle is limber enough you may sit on the side of the foot instead of on the heel. The left knee should point toward the target, with the left elbow resting on or a trifle in front of the kneecap. The sling, hands, arms and the rifle are in the same relative position as when shooting prone, except the right elbow isn't rested. The left elbow should be a little more under the rifle than in the preceding positions. Lean a little forward to get a good balance, then train yourself to control the slight tendency to sway from side to side.

The kneeling position is nowhere nearly as steady as the sitting one, but it has the virtues of being a bit faster to get into and of giving a higher line of sight. But you should avoid placing a wobbly elbow on a wobbly kneecap, and should instead hook your upper arm over your knee and let your back muscles and sling do most of the work.

THE STANDING POSITION. The shot taken from the standing or offhand position is the hardest of all to make, but under certain conditions it must be employed, and anyone who plans to hunt with a rifle should practice it. It is the position for brush and heavy woods where game is come upon suddenly, mostly at close range, and often on the move.

Face almost directly to the right of the target. The left side should be toward the target and the feet from 12 to 18 inches apart, as seems steadiest. The left elbow should be well under the rifle. With long-armed shooters the left hand should grasp the fore-

arm well out toward its tip. Short-armed shooters will have to grasp slightly closer to the trigger guard. The right elbow may be held high or low as seems steadiest. Hold the rifle medium hard to the shoulder with the right hand, using the left hand mostly to direct and steady the rifle. The right cheek should be pressed hard against the left side of the buttstock. Let the forearm rest well down in the palm of the hand. Slight variations in this position are permissible, and after considerable experience you may find that you can vary the position with advantage.

For fast-moving game, the left hand should be pretty well out on the forearm to give leverage for a fast swing, but for a precise offhand shot the left hand should be farther back toward the receiver and the weight should rest on the heel of the palm with the elbow directly underneath the barrel. In this position the left hand merely serves as a support. The right hand pulls the rifle back against the shoulder, and, when the sights look right, you take up your final ounce of pull and the bullet speeds to the mark.

It is important that you get a good balance on both feet and the hips. If your body is out of balance you will sway and tremble. Assume an erect, well-balanced standing position without the rifle in the hands. Now when you take up the rifle and aim with it, the weight of the rifle stretched out in front will tend to pull you forward. You should now lean back just a trifle, perhaps an inch or two, just enough to counteract the tendency of the rifle to pull you forward, thus getting in perfect balance. Don't lean forward *at all* as the beginner and the poor shot usually do. The gunsling is of little or no advantage in standing positions, but often the resting of the left upper arm against the body, or wedging the left elbow into the hip, does give a slightly steadier position.

THE SECRET OF STEADY HOLDING. In all shooting positions, holding must never be a physical exercise. Don't try to hold by brute strength. Contract your muscles only enough to place your bones in such position that the bones will hold the rifle up. Then relax every other muscle. Particularly have the comb of the stock high enough so that you can lay or rest (not press) your cheek down on it so as to relax the large muscle at the back of the neck and between the shoulder blades (trapezius). Relax all the other muscles also that are not needed to hold the bones in the position. Try to make the bones hold the rifle. Relax, be lazy, be quiet, be slow, be uniform, and thus you will gradually learn to hold steady. The rifleman who fusses, frets, screws himself into an uncomfortable position, changes his position, tries to hold by brute strength never learns to hold steady.

AIMING THE RIFLE

The greatest pains and precision must be taken about the aim, because any inaccuracy in aiming results in the bullets hitting wide of the mark. You aim a rifle by first getting the front and rear sights into correct alignment, and then holding them thus aligned, moving or directing the rifle so that this line of aim is brought into line with the game to be struck.

You should use the right eye only to aim with, partially closing the left eye. If the right eye is the master eye you may be able to keep both eyes open when aiming, and this may be a slight advantage in giving you clearer vision. Always focus your eye so as to get the best combination vision of the front sight and target. Don't focus on or look at the rear peep sight, but look through it, letting it blur. Center the top of the front sight in this round blur. This may be difficult at first, but will become second nature with practice, leaving you with two objects to concentrate upon—the front sight and the target.

When you aim you must hold your breath. Take a deep breath, then let it out until the lungs become normal, and then start to aim. Hold the breath while aiming, and then attempt to squeeze the trigger exactly as described in this chapter. If it becomes difficult, or you become shaky, bring the rifle down, rest a minute, then try again.

Don't aim too long. The longer you hold your rifle in the aiming position, the more unsteady you'll become. Since it's necessary to hold your breath while aiming, the palpitation of the heart will increase if the period is too long, and this palpitation will be transmitted to the rifle. This doesn't mean, however, that you should fire at the moment the rifle is raised to your shoulder. Instead, it means that your first split second of aiming will be usually your most productive, for the longer you peer at the target the more obscure it becomes. Windage and distance must, of course, be taken into consideration. Your rear sight of the peep-type sights usually has a mechanism calibrated in "minutes of angle" that enables you to move it up or down to adjust for various distances or ranges. To compensate for a crosswind coming from the right, say, you must either aim to the right or adjust your wind gauge on the rear sight to the right—according to the strength of the wind.

With high-velocity loads to be shot at long ranges, the rifle is usually sighted in to hit the point of aim exactly at 200 yards. For low-velocity loads sighting in is usually done for 100 yards, or under, especially if most actual shots will be at about those distances.

It is important, therefore, for you to know the exact trajectory of the ammunition you're shooting. To provide this information, tables of ballistics, available from manufacturers, give complete data on the trajectory curves of rifle cartridges they supply. When reading these tables, as a rule, one "minute of angle" on the rear sight calibration will equal about ⅜ inch at 50 yards, 1 inch at 100 yards, 2½ inches at 200 yards, etc. If the trajectory of a specific load is a drop of 6 inches at 100 yards, for example, the sight is moved in the direction you wish the bullet to go—in this case up—6 minutes of the angle. Thus, your point of aim will be exactly on the target 100 yards away, and you'll hit it. Actually, you'll be aiming 6 inches high, movement of the rear sight having made the "invisible" compensation of the angle. If you change to another cartridge of the same caliber but of different ballistics, you must, of course, reset the sights to get the same result over a given range.

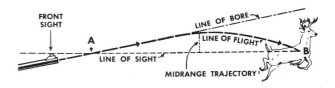

Fig. 2.9 Trajectory of a rifle bullet. Bullet starts out below line of sight, crosses it at A (15 to 50 yards from the muzzle, depending on the range from which the rifle was sighted in), rises above line of sight to midrange, then plunges downward to target B. (Courtesy Sporting Arms and Ammunition Manufacturers' Institute)

When making any adjustment of the peep sights, you must fire a trial series of shots at a known range. Then, once the sights are adjusted correctly to hit dead center at that range, if you estimate the range accurately in the field and shoot straight, you'll hit your point of aim at the sighted-in distance or, assuming that you are thoroughly familiar with the trajectory path of your bullet, you'll hold your point of aim a little lower or higher, as the case may be, for less or greater distance. Now, you can see why flat trajectory—described earlier in this chapter—is extremely advantageous. Suppose that the load you're using pushes its bullet along so that it drops about 2½ inches at 200 yards and 5 inches at 300 yards, then you can be a rather poor judge of range, but still bring down your game. By aiming slightly higher at, say, the shoulder of a deer which you judge to be 200 yards away, but which was actually 250 yards distant, you will still get a good hit.

With a telescopic sight, you have only to sight your game in the field of the telescope (once the angle of compensation for the trajectory has been made), and there, in the same focus, appearing at the same distance, is the reticule, sharp and clear, indicating the exact point at which the bullet will hit. Furthermore, by correct adjustment of the eyepiece, you can correct for what are technically known as "spherical defects" of vision—nearsightedness or far-sightedness. With this advantage, the image seen through the scope will be clearer and sharper than any image observed with the unaided eye. As one gun expert puts it, "A suitable scope sight, correctly adjusted to the eye, makes a middle-aged man see like a boy again." With rifles equipped with good scopes every shooter, young or old, starts out with an equal chance, as far as sighting is concerned.

SQUEEZING THE TRIGGER

After you have taught yourself to aim your rifle uniformly, and to hold the rifle steadily in the proper position, the next essential you must master is the trigger squeeze so you can discharge the rifle without disturbing the accurate aim and steady hold. This is one of the most important things in rifle shooting because the natural tendency is to jerk the trigger when the aim is right, and to set the muscles and flinch against the recoil and report which you know is coming, and you'll have to train yourself to overcome these natural tendencies. The difference between the poor and good shots, and between the good and excellent shots, all lies in the relative excellence of their control of the trigger.

Long years of experience in the training of hundreds of thousands of men to shoot the rifle have shown that there is one best way for a beginner to train himself to squeeze the trigger so he will not jerk or flinch. You should squeeze or press it so gradually that you won't know when the rifle is going to fire. Not knowing exactly when the rifle will be discharged, you won't know when to set your muscles against the kick; that is, you won't flinch. Therefore, during the beginning of your practice you should invariably squeeze the trigger in the following manner until it becomes a fixed habit, so you'll do it naturally in this way even when you don't think particularly about it.

Once you have aimed at your target, apply a slight pressure on the trigger with your forefinger, enough to take up the slack on the trigger if your trigger has a slack or preliminary pull, but not nearly enough pressure to discharge the rifle. It's best to press or squeeze the trigger with the first joint of the forefinger because this is the most sensitive and delicately trained portion of the human body. Some marksmen prefer to use the second joint. It really doesn't make much difference which you use. As soon as you become well set in the position, take a deep breath, let the lungs become normal, and then start your effort to hold steadily and aim accurately. Keep the sights on target, increase the pressure of your forefinger on the trigger ounce by ounce. During one of the moments when the squeeze or pressure is being increased, and when the sights are correctly aligned, the rifle will be discharged more or less unexpectedly. Not knowing exactly when it was going off you didn't set your muscles against the kick, didn't flinch, and the rifle wasn't disturbed in its alignment at the critical instant just before the discharge. Then, if the sights were correctly adjusted for range and wind, your target will surely be struck.

Sure and fast functioning of the rifle, cocking it or throwing off the safety, throwing it to the shoulder, aligning the sights on the vital area without looking at the rifle, and keeping the eyes on the game, are highly important in game shooting. Actually, aiming, holding and trigger squeezing can be practiced with an unloaded gun. However, the trigger of an empty gun should never be squeezed, for fear of damaging the firing pin. Slip an empty cartridge, plugged with wood, into the breach of the gun for practice purposes. Or use a hard rubber plug.

SHOOTING AT RUNNING GAME

Up to now we have been considering shots when the game has been in a standing or stationary position. While you'll get plenty of these shots while hunting, especially for big game, you'll also get some when the animals are on the move. To hit running game at close range is largely a matter of precision and speed, with little lead being needed. On the other hand, to hit running game at longer ranges on the plains and in the mountains, precision and proper lead are more important than speed since the game is usually in sight for some time. But under both conditions you will note that precision is necessary because one shot that hits in a vital spot is worth any number of shots that don't hit at all.

Just as in shotgun shooting, there are two methods of leading with a rifle. The first is the fast swing—this is very similar to the pointing-out method for shotguns described in Chapter 1. In this method, you start the swing behind the animal, swing ahead of him with a rapidly moving rifle, and then squeeze the trigger without stopping or slowing the speed of the swing as the rifle moves on ahead of its mark.

The faster the rifle is swung the more the lead can be cut down. The faster the game is moving the faster the rifle must be swung to overtake and pass it. In other words, the forward allowance or lead of the rifle consists only of the distance the target will move during the time of the bullet and in some respects the lead could be said to be self-correcting. In a few cases when shooting at moving game, particularly at deer on the jump, you just throw your rifle to your shoulder so the sights settle on the vital area instantly. If necessary swing with it, and squeeze the trigger practically at the same instant, like a snap shot.

The second is known as the sustain lead and, in theory, is the same as the shotgun's swinging-past method. With this method, you decide how far you must lead your game, then swing your rifle with the animal, making sure to keep the sights the same distance ahead as you squeeze the trigger. This system of shooting is accurate, of course, but it is much slower than the fast swing, and for this reason the sustain lead method isn't employed as often while in the field.

As is the case of bird shooting with a shotgun, all running game shots are not crossing ones and thus you don't need to swing your rifle. When an animal is running straight up a hill, for instance, you should simply aim and hold a slight bit higher and let him run into the bullet. The same is true of the slightly quartering shot on running game, just as it is true in the case of slightly quartering pheasants.

HITTING VITAL AREAS

Killing any hoofed game—deer, moose, elk, antelope, etc.—involves either destruction of vital organs or extreme shock to the nervous system, or both. The anatomy of these big game animals is exactly the same, so to kill any of them cleanly and quickly the bullet must enter the chest cavity or pierce the spine. An experienced hunter, when sighting his game, instantly forms a mental picture of the location his bullet will reach, that small package of heart, lungs and nerves where his game "lives." It's not so large an area as you might think. In deer species the chest cavity extends from the last rib forward to the brisket in the lower two-thirds of the body. Both the heart and lungs lie low in this cavity, usually in the lower third, and thus the shot into this cavity should be held low enough to strike this lower third. Most fluke hits (which often lose the game) occur in the middle or rear half of the body; such hits effect little shock and cause poor bleeding unless an extremely high-velocity bullet is employed.

If you try to visualize that the deer (or other hoofed game) carries its "life" in a small bundle just between and behind its front legs and if you can pierce this bundle, from whatever angle, you won't have any trouble in killing one. The confusing aspect of all hunting is that the game presents so many different angles to the hunter. Seldom are any two shots exactly alike. The broadside shot is relatively simple. If the bullet is placed right at the point of the foreleg, the game is as good as tagged. However,

deer hunters get more angle shots than broadsides and this changes the point of bullet entry.

On quartering-away shots the hunter should visualize that his target is the far or offside shoulder. If his bullet drives through to that far shoulder it will clean house in the chest cavity. On incoming quartering shots the aiming point is just ahead of the near shoulder. This shot, too, will usually emerge or stop in or near the far shoulder depending on the angle. There are no fixed rules for hitting this vital spot but a good plan of action is to try to keep the bullet always ahead of the animal's middle and held low enough to enter the lower half of the body.

On dangerous game such as grizzly and Alaskan brown bear the chest cavity shot is equally good but the major effort here should be to anchor the animal as quickly as possible to avoid a charge. Bear anatomy differs from hoofed game in that the high shoulder shot will usually break him down quickly and permit a follow-up finishing shot at a safe distance.

You can develop all these skills in marksmanship and in handling your rifle, if you'll keep it in your bedroom, and every day take it in hand for a few dry shots at the picture of a deer on the wall. For every such shot use the utmost pains to hold steady, aim accurately and get a good squeeze—then quick manipulation of the mechanism, and another shot with quick aim. It is wonderful what skill you will acquire in a few weeks. And then, of course, a little range practice, and the sighting-in of the rifle. Further information on rifle shooting for various game species can be found in Chapters 5 through 7. But remember that as you increase in rifle skill and experience, you'll find that your reactions become faster and surer, so that shots which in the past would have seemed impossible, now are actually easy.

Care of the Rifle

A rifle needs daily cleaning and attention when in use, and proper storage when not in use, or its accuracy and effectiveness will deteriorate rapidly; but if properly taken care of, a rifle will last you a lifetime, as it practically never wears out from firing alone.

You should understand clearly the effect of rust. Many people think that rust can be removed. Red rust is evidence of the eating away of the surface of the metal. Even if you remove the red evidence you can never repair the damage the rusting has caused. Rust is always the result of neglect or ignorance. A clean steel surface oiled to protect from moisture doesn't rust. Never allow even a suspicion of rust to appear on or in your rifle. It won't appear if you'll care for your rifle as described here.

Cartridges loaded with non-corrosive priming, smokeless powder, and lubricated or film-coated lead bullets leave a fouling in the bore which is both non-corrosive and rust preventing. It's very easy to keep the bore in condition when such ammunition is used. Ordinarily, if this type of cartridge is used exclusively the bore need not be cleaned from day to day while the rifle is in continued use, although there is no objection to cleaning it. But the bore should be cleaned when the rifle is put away for a long period, or in localities where the air is excessively damp.

Cartridges loaded with non-corrosive priming, smokeless powder, and copper or cadmium-plated bullets give a non-corrosive but not a rust-preventing fouling. On rare occasions after such cartridges have been fired the bore might rust from moisture in the air, particularly damp night air. It is therefore safest to clean the bore not later than the evening of the day on which it was fired.

Usually, fouling doesn't accumulate in a good barrel during a day's firing to an extent that would interfere with accuracy unless the atmosphere is very hot and devoid of moisture, when cleaning between strings is recommended. Therefore, there is no advantage in cleaning in the middle of the day's firing or between scores. Clean before evening when the air becomes damp.

For cleaning you need a steel cleaning rod, a supply of Canton flannel cleaning patches, and a can of gun oil. Patches should be cut from a medium weight Canton flannel, about three-quarters of an inch square, so that when centered with the tip of the cleaning rod and pushed into the bore, they will make a snug fit in the bore, but not so tight that the patch might be punctured by the rod, or that the rod and patch might get stuck in the bore. Clean from the breech of the barrel if possible, but if the mechanism of the rifle won't permit this, then clean from the muzzle and use fingers as a guide to prevent the cleaning rod rubbing and wearing the muzzle.

1. Wet a flannel patch with water, powder solvent, or light oil, lay it over the breech or muzzle, center it with the tip of the cleaning rod, and push it straight through the bore and out the other end. This pushes out the bulk of the fouling.

2. Swab the bore with two or three patches wet with water, powder solvent, or light oil. To swab: place a piece of paper on the floor, rest the muzzle on it, push the patch down to the paper, and pull it back to the chamber a dozen times, thus swabbing the bore thoroughly from end to end with each patch.

3. Dry the rod. Then swab again with about half a dozen clean, dry patches so that the bore is thoroughly dried and cleaned out, and becomes slightly warm from friction.

4. Saturate a patch with gun oil and swab the bore with it, and leave the bore in this condition. The bore is now clean and protected and won't rust. If you're putting the rifle away for over a week, the next day wipe out the oil and swab with a patch heavily coated with gun grease. Don't use powder solvent for this last swabbing. It is a cleaner only, and not a good rust preventative.

5. Wipe the exterior of the rifle and all parts of the mechanism that can be reached with a dry rag and then with an oily one.

6. Before starting to fire, always push a clean, dry patch through the bore to wipe out the film of oil or grease. Oil in the bore and chamber will cause the first few shots to fly slightly wild until the oil is shot out. Grease in the bore may cause serious injury to the barrel if the rifle is fired without its being removed. Gasoline on a patch will facilitate the removal of grease.

Sometimes an automatic rifle that is fired very rapidly for some time, so that the barrel gets very hot, will have lead or copper deposited in the bore. To remove this, screw a brass bristle brush on the rod, dip the brush in kerosene and swab the bore with it, pushing the brush all the way through the bore, and then pulling it all the way back, without reversing it in the bore.

The above cleaning is all that is necessary to preserve the rifle in first-class condition indefinitely. It is the one best way. Other methods may or may not be efficient. Note also the following:

The bolt, particularly its interior mechanism, should merely be wiped dry and then wiped with a slightly oily rag. Any quantity of oil or grease on the interior mechanism of a bolt may cause poor accuracy by interfering with perfect ignition.

On a sandy or dusty location pay particular attention to keeping the action clean during use. The cutting effect of sand or dust on the moving parts may cause wear which eventually results in the rifle not breeching up tightly enough for accuracy or safety.

Perspiration is a great promoter of rust, so after use, wipe the exterior of the rifle with a dry rag and then with an oily one. Occasionally rub raw linseed oil into the stock, and neatsfoot oil into the gunsling. Don't lay the rifle on damp ground or grass as it might warp the stock—use your forked rifle rest. After a rifle has been wet from rain wipe it off dry, oil the metal parts, and apply linseed oil to the stock. Constantly guard the rifle and its sights against blows and falls.

Chapter Three

LEARNING UPLAND GAME BIRD GUNNING

THE VAST MAJORITY of hunters in the United States can be classed as "upland game bird gunners." There are two good reasons for the popularity of this phase of the sport of hunting. First, upland wingshooting is probably the most varied and tricky of all hunting endeavors, and possesses the maximum number of thrills while requiring, undoubtedly, the minimum amount of equipment and expense. Second, it requires the least amount of knowledge, technically, about the hunting of each individual species of game bird. If you know how to handle your gun properly, are able to identify the various upland game birds, know their general habitats and their special habits, you have only to go to their covers and begin your hunting. In other words, upland game bird gunning is the ideal starting point to begin to teach yourself how to hunt.

General Upland Game Bird Techniques

One of the major "sicknesses" any beginning hunter has is the ailment called "buck fever." Its cure is simple but is strictly up to the shooter and to nobody else.

Buck fever ordinarily is diagnosed as overanxiety in the presence of game. Overanxiety, that is, to bag the flying game before it gets away. In reality, buck fever is deeper-seated than a mere case of the jitters. It should be described more properly as a shooter's inferiority complex—distrust of his own ability to pull off the shot when the emergency confronts him. As a result of his buck-fevered state of mind, he either freezes his eyes and body muscles and fires too slowly, or else hurries the shot and bangs a hole in the air.

There is no denying the fact that the whir of a rising covey of quail, or the seeming explosion of a grouse in the dry leaves, is calculated to unnerve any gunner. The word "calculated" was used advisedly,

since Nature intentionally equipped most game birds with this protection against their natural enemies. Yet this same surprise as game takes wing is the real thrill of upland game shooting.

Perhaps the jittery shooter will take heart at the experience of an old-time quail hunter who once made camp near a little village whose inhabitants had offered to share their game supply with the old-timer and his party. Camp was made in the early evening, and the old-timer spent several hours talking to the boys in the back room of the general store. Along toward midnight he retraced his steps toward camp. It was necessary that he pass along one side of the village graveyard. Ordinarily not superstitious, and on this occasion doubly armed with the warm glow of hard cider, he swung along the path with no thought of ghosts.

Suddenly an old, grass-tufted grave almost in his path exploded into myriad flying meteors that lashed out for his head, fanning his neck with the miniature hurricanes of their passing, deafening his ears with the thunder of their flight. Stark terror took control. The old-timer had only one thought, and that was to scram! A hundred yards down the path he came to his senses, sat down on a convenient stump, and laughed until he cried.

Few shooters will ever experience such an ordeal in these modern days—that of walking into a big covey of quail on their roost in a country graveyard at the hour of midnight. Yet it might be well if every upland gunner had such an experience at the very outset of his shooting career. Now, every time a covey breaks cover in front of this old-timer, he laughs. Sometimes his mirth so convulses him that the birds fly away unharmed—that is, all except two or three of the stragglers. The whir of a covey no longer holds any terror for him in broad daylight.

Summing up the many reams and volumes that have been written on upland game shooting, it seems

Fig. 3.1 Typical upland game bird shots. (Both photos courtesy of Pennsylvania Game Commission)

that the noise of the fanning wings creates the impression in the gunner's mind that the game is going places, and that he must hurry, hurry, hurry! Well, so what? You, indeed, must hurry, but not to the point where you bang an unaimed shot in the general direction of the speeding game. You *must* take time to do these three things:

1. Advance the pivot foot in the direction of the flying target or targets, at the same time selecting *one* bird—if more than one has flushed—at which to direct your first shot.

2. Mount the gun quickly and press your cheek to the stock, covering with the sighting plane the theoretical zero point of your imaginary vertical clock, which will be that point on or near the path of the target which the target occupied when so identified.

3. Estimate the angle with the sighting plane of the gun formed by the continuation of the flight of the target, and *swing* along the arc between the gun muzzle and the actual target, firing the shot as the target is passed by the muzzle.

The foregoing rules merely are repetitions of what was stated in Chapter 1. If you experience difficulty with your footwork, with your estimation of direction of the target, with the releasing of the trigger, with any single operation of the entire sequence, then you should take out your pencil and paper when you get home, sketch the situations where shots were missed, and from a study of these actual situations, evolve a remedy that will suit your case.

Remember: if you merely learn to follow the target with the sighting plane of your gun, you'll take a lot of game, whether you do anything else correctly or not. Certain of your errors will compensate for certain other errors, and an occasional quail, grouse or pheasant will come to bag. It will help a great deal if you learn to keep your head down, if you keep your eyes open and at universal focus, and if you pull or slap the trigger firmly but not roughly. Right at this point, it would be wise to review the subjects treated in Chapter 1.

Suggestions given here apply particularly to the hunting of upland game birds in ordinary cover, with or without a dog. Most upland gunning is accomplished without the services of man's best friend— and the shooting is just so much harder because the game must be located in air after it has flushed, rather than located as to general whereabouts before it takes wing. But whether a dog is used or not, the upland gunner should bring all his shrewdness into play in the way he quarters his ground, particularly in the matter of approaching shots which he may suspect will spring from the next corn row or the nearest hillock.

Most game birds, when flushed, make for the nearest heavy protective cover with which they are familiar—cover which lies on their own covey range, in the case of quail, or which offers particularly attractive shelter, in the case of grouse. Experience will teach you that quail in the open should always be flushed *toward* the nearest heavy cover, rather than to attempt to drive the game farther out into the open. The result of such amateurish tactics will be an immediate zooming of the birds back over your head and they'll go to the woods anyway, so it's better to have two straightaway shots than only one at a target curving back over the peak of your cap.

In hunting any game bird in the open fields or in semi-wooded territory, you should cut up your ground so as to work parallel with the edge of the nearest heavy cover and not back and forth toward it and away from it. This system will result in almost 100 per cent quartering shots as the birds break for cover and not 50 per cent straightaways and 50 per cent overheads, which will be about the normal percentage if the ground is not worked properly.

These hints are given with only one object in view —to help you in so placing yourself that you can make every shot count. Game that offers no worse than a right-angle shot offers a fair chance to you. Towering, gyrating birds don't offer a fair chance to apply either the "swinging-past" or the "pointing-out" method of gun pointing. They require downright snap-shooting and you have worked out the chances against scoring a hit under this system. Yet there is a real place for snap-shooting in the bag of tricks of the real hunter and particularly the grouse hunter. It will sometimes grass a bird that otherwise would have escaped. The really expert gunner must be able to apply any one of the three methods, instantly, before he has earned the right to wear a feather in his cap.

Remember that the upland shooter's job is to hit, not to hit far out. You want the widest spread of pellets that will still be dense enough to down your bird at normal distance, at about twenty to forty paces. You'll shoot the smaller shot sizes (rarely pellets as large as 4's) and need the multiple shock (killing effect) of many small shots closer in, rather than the punch of a few big pellets far out, as is the case of waterfowl hunting. Actually, the secret of successful upland shooting is more scattergun handling than shotgun ballistics, a fast but sure gun-swinging. Taking upland game birds on the flush calls for cool-nerved application of basic principles discussed in Chapter 1: proper footwork, close coordination of hand and eye and a smooth swing for the lead—the wingshot's art.

Modern firearms, even the inexpensive kind, are so efficient that any gun with smokeless shot shells will kill plenty of game if you take your shots properly. On the other hand, there is that growing tendency on the part of the American sportsman to take pride in the tools of his hobby, and his own technique with those tools. This tendency is responsible for the increasing popularity of small-gauge guns, particularly the light 16's and 20's, for upland game shooting. Even hardy old grouse and pheasants will succumb readily to a full ounce of chilled 6's from a light 20-gauge and these slim, beautiful little weapons are a joy to carry in comparison to the greater weight of the old American standard, the 12-gauge.

Actually, hunting conditions in your section of the country should dictate the choice of a gun for upland shooting. If you will do any gunning for grouse in heavy cover, if you intend to shoot pheasants in the Great Plains area, or quail in the timbered Ozarks, then indeed your field gun may well be a 12-gauge, preferably a double with its choice of one open and one tight barrel. The choice of a 12-gauge is particularly happy if you intend to hunt waterfowl with the same gun. If you are just embarking upon a shooting career, by all means let your dealer or some trade representative advise you.

Your choice of clothing, shoes and other equipment will have a great deal to do with your enjoyment of upland gunning. By all means avoid tightly laced knee boots, breeches which bind the knees, and great, stiff hunting coats that bind your arms and catch on all the twigs and wire fences in your immediate vicinity. Adopt short, easy boots; wool trousers that will resist briers and yet not bind the knees; and a wool shirt to suit your climate, topping off with a combination game pocket and shell belt, or a light hunting coat that will conform to your body and not bind the arms.

Since most upland game bird hunting is done on or near farm areas, always be sure to get the owner's permission to hunt on his property. Also always try to make the farmer your friend. Share your game with him and leave him a few dollars after your hunt. Don't forget him at Christmas, even if it is only a letter or postcard, and invite him to visit you when he comes to town.

Upland game shooting isn't only one of the finest sports on earth—it is the heritage of the true American. It should be enjoyed leisurely, and not ridden like a wooden hobby. When you have made of it a pastime of really controlled relaxation, then indeed you will have achieved the goal of every true sportsman who aspires to honest enjoyment of the better things of life.

How to Hunt Quail

There are several species of American quail, varying in length from 9½ to 11 inches. The most familiar is the bird known in the North as the bobwhite and in the South as the partridge. It earned its name with its questioning call, *bob, bobwhite?* It breeds eastward from the Rockies and from Canada to northern Texas and Florida. In the arid Southwest there are valley, Gambel's, scaled and Mearns's quail. Mountain and California quail are found in the humid districts of the Pacific coast. Although quail are small targets, they travel in sizable coveys of from six to twenty or more birds, have a rather straight flight, and therefore are extremely popular with beginning hunters.

BOBWHITE QUAIL

More bobwhite quail are taken by hunters in the United States each year than any other species of upland game birds. They are found throughout much of the agricultural belt where sufficient cover is present to furnish them food and protection. The southern and southeastern states provide the best quail shooting. Extreme cold or dry areas aren't favorable for this popular game bird.

Fig. 3.2 Be sure to get owner's permission and be sure to obey all his requests. (Courtesy of Wisconsin Conservation Department)

Fig. 3.3 The bobwhite quail. (Courtesy of Florida Game & Fresh Water Fish Commission)

The plumage of the bobwhites—a mixture of mottled brown and buff-gray and white—makes them almost invisible when they lie quietly in fields or woods. They often squat motionless until one is on the point of stepping on them. Then they take wing explosively.

Bobwhites aren't wilderness birds. To seek quail in deep woods far in from fields and openings would be foolish. Old hedgerows, multiflora rose fences and fields of farm crops with bordering fences grown up to weeds and briers are ideal places for bobwhite shooting. Quail are early and late feeders. Cornfields, soy bean patches, lespedeza pastures, or ragweed thickets are the best places to find them during early morning hours or in late afternoon. If these areas are bordered with heavy escape cover, you can look for your birds in such places during the midday hours. During inclement weather, like most upland game birds, bobwhites will stay closer to cover, and won't be inclined to be out quite so early, nor will they be so easy to locate.

No upland game bird is so ideal to hunt with dogs as the bobwhite. Dogs are almost a necessity, and handling your own pointer or setter is actually the major part of your hunting (see Chapter 8 for details on dogs). The whir of wings as a covey breaks cover and two well-placed shots on the fleeting brown rockets is the end result of good dog work.

Successful quail hunters usually know intimately the terrain where they shoot. Bobwhites range very closely to the place where they were hatched. The same hedgerow, brier thicket or weedy draw usually produces a covey of birds each year. If you're shooting with a guide or a friend who knows the area, it's well to let him direct the activities of the hunt and give the word to shoot when the birds have been pointed. Remember that in walking up a covey of quail or a single, the pivot foot must be kept advanced in order that perfect balance may be maintained while making the shot. Guns must be at ready and a previous survey of the situation determines whether there might be domestic animals or other hunters in the line of fire.

In the South on large estates, where there are few fences, dogs are usually followed on horseback or in a jeep. Corn patches and bean fields adjacent to heavy cover make ideal shooting places. Dogs are worked crosswind, or directly against the wind if possible, and parallel to the heavy escape cover. When a point is made the hunters dismount, load their guns and step in for the shot. Care should be taken in approaching the dog. The quail will almost certainly head for the nearest escape cover. If the gunner is between the rising birds and the safety they seek, a difficult overhead shot will result. Better to approach the point as you have been in hunting—parallel to the cover. A right or left angle shot then will result.

Bobwhites are shot at relatively close range. Balance for shooting and readiness have been stressed. The sudden whir of wings often confuses gunners, causing them to shoot hastily in the belief that the birds are getting away much faster than they really are. A quail flies fairly fast, to be sure—maybe forty miles an hour. But in reasonably open shooting you still have plenty of time. Shooting too quickly on the covey rise means shooting while the birds are still going up. Most such shots go under. One successful quail hunter once said to count three, when a covey flushes, before firing a shot. This interval may be a bit too long, but you should *not* hurry with your shooting. There will be sufficient time for two or more well-aimed shots.

Another good rule of successful quail shooting to follow is to forget the covey. As the birds rise, get your eye on *one bird*—the first one that registers. If it's a difficult shot, never mind. Stick with that one Don't take your eye off it. Remember that you can only shoot one at a time. Shoot at that bird. If you hit it, pick another target—the next bird your eye registers—and shoot at that one. Also train yourself to have a kind of "second sight" in marking down where the scattered escaping bobwhites drop while you're shooting at your birds. Hunting down singles can be one of the enjoyable and exciting phases of quail shooting. Don't, however, hunt down a covey too closely. Three or four birds taken out of a dozen-bird covey should be the limit. Then leave the singles and go after another covey.

Selection of guns for this close work is a matter

Fig. 3.4 Quail are shot at relatively close range, as you can see by the illustration, and when a covey takes off, it can confuse both hunters and dogs. (Courtesy of North Carolina Department of Conservation & Development)

of preference. It is obvious that the boring must be rather open, as most quail are killed within 30 yards. In a double gun, improved cylinder and modified choke make an ideal combination. Gauge is a matter of choice. The 20 is preferred by many because of its light weight and resultant quick pointing. Repeating guns and autoloaders are very popular with quail hunters. Not only is a third shot made possible, but the single sighting plane is preferred by many. Formerly, 12-gauge cylinder-bore guns were quite popular in the South, but the trend today is in favor of an improved cylinder bore, or the attaching of an adjustable choke device. In extremely heavy cover, the choke may be opened to full cylinder. In more open terrain, the choke may be closed somewhat, in preparation for the longer shots that can be expected.

Quail are not hard to kill, and No. 7½ or No. 8 shot are adequate in size. It is an ill-conceived theory that No. 9 are even better because the pattern is more dense with the smaller shot. The velocity of No. 9 shot falls off rapidly and so does remaining pellet energy. Though quail have a light coating of feathers compared with some game birds, cripple losses will be kept to a minimum with the larger shot. High-velocity loads, with their greater shot content,

are used by many hunters in 16- and 20-gauge guns.

In the early days, with the clearing of the forests by homesteaders, quail habitat in some parts of the country was actually increased. Small farms bordered with cut-over land and weedy growths made ideal cover. But with an increasing human population, more land was cleared. "Clean" farming practices were instituted and quail all but disappeared in many fine areas. Today, sportsmen are planting their own places or encouraging farmers to restore cover, food and water. This entails the planting of lespedeza, multiflora rose, building of fenced farm ponds and following agricultural practices which encourage the growth of shrubs, trees and grasses to check erosion. This procedure not only has restored the population of quail and other upland game in many areas, but the value of the soil has been greatly increased and larger crops are being produced.

OTHER QUAIL SHOOTING

Desert, mountain, valley and other species of quail are found principally in the southwestern states and the lower Pacific coastal area. As a rule, they frequent the semi-arid or arid regions. They favor habitat along small streams where green thickets and grasses are to be found, or adjacent to waterholes in the desert.

Practically all of these species work poorly to dogs. Not only are they habitual runners and refuse to hold well to a pointing dog, but at the longer ranges at which they are shot, they are much harder to kill than bobwhite quail. Usually vegetation is sparse in the Southwest, and often there is little ground cover in which a bird may hide.

Along the arid river valleys where heavy grasses are found, hunters can sometimes have a good shoot on these birds. One hunter circles widely and heads off a running covey, driving them back toward his companion. One or the other usually gets a bit of shooting. In such instances the birds will flush and fly. Once on the wing they are fast and difficult targets. In river bottoms heavily overgrown with mesquite, dogs are often used. A careful dog with years of experience can sometimes handle birds in such cover to advantage.

Shotguns with rather tight boring are required for this shooting. A 12-gauge full choke is preferred by most hunters for these tough, running, large-range birds. Also, shot sizes seldom run as small as No. 7½, No. 6 being greatly preferred by many hunters.

How to Hunt Pheasants

The first successful planting of ringneck pheasants was about seventy-five years ago, in Oregon. They came from China. Today, the ringneck of the United States isn't a Chinese pheasant. Rather, he is a cross of various strains, the stock being Chinese ringneck, English ringneck and the Mongolian pheasant. So widely has this hardy bird spread his kind that in

Fig. 3.5 Ringneck pheasants. (Courtesy of U.S. Fish and Wildlife Service)

many northern and central states pheasants furnish the major part of upland gunning.

The male ringneck is about three feet long, including the tail. The head and neck are metallic green and purple, with a white ring about the neck. The chest is the color of burnished copper. The back is reddish brown, the underparts golden umber, stippled with black crescents. The females are a mottled brown and black, with a whitish breast. It's important that you be able to identify the difference between the pheasant hen and cock at a quick glance, for shooting the female is prohibited in most states.

The pheasant isn't usually a woods bird. He generally prefers farm country, provided the farming area isn't too "clean"—a condition which doesn't give him his desired cover. While he likes corn country for both cover and food, few birds feel at home in tangled briers, deep swamp bogs and thick stands of cattails as do ringnecks. When heavily pressured by hunters, he takes out for this kind of cover and usually succeeds in outwitting both hunter and dog.

Knowing the regular habits of pheasants you will have a better chance to find them. As a rule, they feed in the morning and retire to the weed patches and cover during midday. In the middle of the afternoon the birds begin to come out of cover for water and feed. Toward sundown the birds seek gravel along the roadsides and head for the roosting cover just before sundown. In country where shooting is permitted in the forenoon, hunt the cornfields in the morning, then work the slough bottoms and weed patches as noon approaches. Creek bottoms, ditches and wet spots are always good for birds in midafternoon, while the edges along the gravel byroads can produce around quitting time. If the district is hunted hard at the opening of the season, you can always be sure that the majority of the hunters will work the cornfields. This is a tip-off to the hunter who is willing to work, for he will find plenty of birds in the heavy slough grass adjoining the big cornfield. Hunting this heavy cover is rugged work. You know the birds are there, but flushing them can sometimes be rather difficult. Remember that where hunter pressure is quite heavy, ringnecks develop great sagacity. They may lie tight and permit you to pass within a few feet of them. For such shooting, good bird dogs are a great asset and frequently they will hold pheasants as tightly as they do bobwhite quail. Dogs for pheasant hunting of any type should be taught to work quite closely to the gunner. Sometimes running birds can be pursued by good dogs for some distance and made to hold. In general, however, dogs should be kept in close.

In the flat states, such as the Dakotas, pheasants are commonly hunted by driving large cornfields or cover along sloughs and potholes by five to a dozen gunners. Hunters—called the drivers or beaters—walk slowly abreast a gunshot apart, within easy view of each other. Birds are driven ahead where other gunners—called the blockers—have posted themselves to take shots at any driven game which comes overhead. But if the drivers walk slowly and don't permit the birds to double back, there are generally some big cocks that can't stand the nervous strain and decide their best strategy is to take to the air. It's essential to walk to the very end of the field and then work the cover hard at the end of the field with every available man, as it is surprising how one of these big birds can hide within a few feet of a hunter who has already started to unload his gun. Frequently, retrieving dogs are used to find the fallen birds, as ringnecks are difficult to kill and, even when mortally wounded, can conceal themselves or escape by running.

Fig. 3.6 Hunters on a drive hope that a pheasant will be jumped (above); then one goes up and the hunter has a shot. (Both photos courtesy of Wisconsin Conservation Department)

Remember that pheasants usually prefer to run and hide rather than taking to the air. Where there is favorable cover it's not uncommon for a bird to run half a mile or more in front of a halting pointer if the dog isn't smart enough to circle, in order to cut him off and hold him in a tight point for the gunner. Pheasants can give plenty of trouble to good bird dogs simply because of their habit of moving constantly, rather than lying tight to be flushed. However, a pair of smart bird dogs can usually trap a wise pheasant quickly by one trailing and the other circling ahead to cut him off.

When a ringneck flushes, he does so, as do most upland birds, into the wind. When driving into the wind, he will frequently flush into the wind and turn downwind and back over the drivers, presenting a difficult target, since he has the wind behind him and has towered to considerable height. When driving into the wind, the drivers usually get most of the shooting. Upwind driving is generally the safest method, as the shot charge is directed at a higher elevation when shooting towering birds. Driving downwind should be done in short drives, as the pheasant is always aware of the whereabouts of the driver, and will hide and take wing after you have gone by his hiding place. In downwind the drivers should be spaced not over 12 corn rows apart, to assure a successful drive. If crosswind driving is required, the birds will flush into the wind and then quarter down the wind. Therefore it's well to place a driver on the upwind side, 60 to 80 yards in advance of the drivers, to take care of the birds leaving the field and to attempt to keep the birds in the

field until they're in range of the blockers. In rainy weather pheasants are sometimes extremely determined not to be flushed.

Drive shooting calls for good coordination of the gunners. Wild shooting can't be tolerated, and birds must be shot only when in the sector of the individual gunner. Shooting glasses are recommended to prevent possible injury to the eyes by stray shot from the guns of other hunters.

The use of pointing dogs is often a disappointment in areas where pheasants are plentiful. They're often so abundant that the dog can't point a given bird, since the scent of pheasants is everywhere. One of the retriever breeds or a springer spaniel may be a better choice, as they not only will point out many birds, but are better fitted for retrieving cripples.

In much of the wooded areas of New England and the northern states, pheasants aren't so abundant, and are found in much rougher and denser habitat. Here, pointers and setters do excellent work.

Always remember that ringnecks are tough birds to kill. When first flushed from heavy cover, they may be quite close and their flight is a climbing one until they have gained sufficient height to level off. Such climbing shots are relatively easy and the gunner needs only to take a high hold on the bird. Once off on level flight the pheasant is quite fast. Here the gunner may find that he isn't taking sufficient lead. The long tail feathers of the cock bird exaggerate the size of the target and frequently the shot charge will hit too far back for effective kills. Long leads on ringnecks should be the rule lest tail feathers floating in the air be the hunter's only reward.

Guns smaller than 20-gauge are inadequate for clean kills on ringnecks. Doubles, bored modified and full, are favored in open prairie shooting where long shots may be common. Repeaters and auto-loaders should be modified or full choked. Adjustable choke devices are practical for pheasant shooting, where ranges may vary with different types of cover.

Shot shells should be high velocity, and No. 6 shot is recommended for clean kills. Hunters should give due consideration to the maximum range of their guns and loads, for there is no upland game that requires harder hitting than the ringneck. In some coverts, woodcock and ruffed grouse hunters may at times flush ringnecks. They can be readily taken at close range with the more open guns and lighter shot loads used for this type of hunting, but light shot and open guns definitely aren't good ringneck equipment under most conditions.

How to Hunt Grouse

Of the eight principal species of grouse found in America, sportsmen are more concerned with only three—the pinnated or prairie chicken, the sharptail and the ruffed grouse. Other members include the Dusky, Franklin's Hudsonian, spruce and sooty grouse. Sage hens also belong to this great family.

PINNATED AND SHARPTAIL GROUSE

In early days, before the prairie sod was broken, prairie chickens usually were hunted from horse-drawn buckboards, and offered one of the finest forms of American upland game shooting. While about the size of a bantam chicken, the pinnated grouse is buff in plumage, heavily overlaid with bars of black. When the bird displays he erects a tuft of

Fig. 3.7 A pair of sage grouse or—as they are better known—sage hens. (Courtesy of U.S. Fish and Wildlife Service)

long, stiff feathers at the back of the neck. Young birds work fully as well as bobwhite quail to pointing dogs. The fenceless plains permitted driving almost anywhere, following the working dogs ahead. This era can never return and it's even questionable whether prairie chickens will long be with us as a game bird because of continued shrinking of their habitat.

The sharptail, close cousin of the prairie chicken, is holding up in larger numbers. (They can be easily distinguished by their longer, more pointed tails, the absence of the crest and the pale purple color of their neck sacs.) They, too, work well to dogs and, as they frequent the brushy thickets of the plains states, their nesting and feeding grounds haven't been disturbed to such a great extent by the breaking of the virgin prairie sod. Cornfields harbor them

Fig. 3.8 A sharptail grouse will sharpen any gunner's shooting. (Courtesy of Bill Browning, Montana Chamber of Commerce)

in good numbers and they frequently are taken in conjunction with pheasants and Hungarian partridges.

Along shrubby ravines on the prairies, sharptails work quite well to bird dogs. In the more open cornfields they're usually driven in connection with pheasant shooting. Here, retriever dogs are widely used. It is seldom that escape cover is so heavy that one need hunt sharptails parallel to such growths. Such a condition does exist along the brakes of the Missouri River and in South Dakota; it's also encountered in some of the prairie provinces of Canada. Often islands of poplars may harbor a dozen or more of these birds.

Shotguns for pinnated and sharptail grouse should be of 20-gauge or larger. Boring is recommended as modified and full for doubles, and modified or full in the case of repeaters and autoloaders. As a rule, high-velocity shot shells are most practical, as often these birds are taken at rather long yardages and pheasants are also found on the same range. No. 6 shot is the ideal size.

During warm fall days in broken prairie country, it's well to wear high-topped leather boots or shoe-pacs. Prairie rattlesnakes seem to be most abundant in good sharptail country and on warm fall days are still active.

If possible, drives for sharptails should be made in cornfields at early and late hours. They feed in the fields at such times and are inclined to seek heavier cover during the heat of the day. Many of these birds may be bagged on drives without the aid of dogs, as are pheasants. To aid in retrieving and cutting down the possible loss of cripples, dogs are recommended. Hunting into the wind or cross-wind allows better dog work and also permits hunters to more closely approach the sharptails in the event dogs are not used.

RUFFED GROUSE

The ruffed grouse or partridge, as he is often called, is one of the grandest of upland game birds. Found throughout the wooded parts of many of our states, they're birds of strong flight and considerable sagacity. In their native cover of beeches, alders and cut-over timbered areas, they are more than a match for any except the experienced.

The ruffed grouse is about the same size as a prairie chicken, but his head, nape and back are reddish brown with generous flecks of gray, black, white and yellow-red. The iridescent collar, or ruff, is formed by the tufts of long feathers at the base of the neck. The breast of ruffed grouse is brownish white, crossed with dark-brown bars. The semi-circular fan of tail is banded by narrow stripes of tan and black. While the plumage varies slightly in detail from bird to bird, you can't mistake the ruffed grouse for other upland game.

The hunter who knows where to look usually is able to find birds without much difficulty, although grouse are normally scattered over wider terrain than the majority of upland game birds. The best place to seek them is always in areas where the food they prefer is to be found. In the fall the various types of food vary with the season. Early October may find them among the wild grapes but November may find them in the beech groves. Old orchards, grapevine tangles, sumac clumps, wild cranberry bogs, hawthorn thickets, clusters of hemlocks or other conifers, alder thickets and multiflora rose covers all other possibilities.

Ruffed grouse may be hunted with pointers or setters and, as mentioned in discussing woodcock shooting, these two birds are often found on the same range. The custom of putting a bell on a dog in heavy cover for grouse hunting is quite practical. Grouse, however, can be hunted without canine help, and some skilled shooters prefer this method. The sudden nerve-shattering whir as a grouse flushes calls for steady nerves and quick gun pointing.

Good grouse dogs are rare. They should hunt in close and almost creep to point on their bellies, for the bird is easily alarmed. In hunting without dogs, it's well to hunt parallel to very heavy cover along winding streams or ravines, or old wood roads. These birds have the faculty of always flushing when one least expects them to, and they are most adept at putting trees between the gunner and themselves.

Fig. 3.9 The ruffed grouse. (Courtesy of U.S. Fish and Wildlife Service)

When hunters are stepping over logs or windfalls, or stooping to go beneath low branches, grouse seem to recognize an opportune time to break cover. They may rocket high into dense foliage, or dive low into dark cover, placing all possible obstacles between themselves and the shooter. Therefore, move slowly when hunting grouse. If you walk too fast, you'll pass up more birds than you'll ever see. Halt now and then and look around you. Many a hunter has been surprised to find a ruffed grouse practically in his lap.

Grouse flush farther ahead of the hunter on some days than on others. Most of them may flush far out of range when it is windy, or the leaves are exceptionally dry or the snow is crusted. And it often happens that the more they're hunted the wilder they get. Usually, however, many of them will flush within 50 feet. Sometimes you'll get considerably closer. Where the cover is open enough you can often mark them down and flush them a second time. The distance they'll fly when flushed varies considerably but is usually between 100 and 300 yards. It's usually wise to mark the bird's flight and follow him rather than look for another.

When grouse are flushed from among big trees chances are that they'll angle off into still deeper woods. There are times you'll find them loafing around the tops of fallen trees or brush piles. Work in carefully on such locations. The birds will quite often move through the cover and flush from the far side. This is a very common trick of grouse and one that works very well on all but the more experienced shooters. If you can surprise grouse on the edge of a clearing, they are apt to head straight out into the clearing. Their location, before they are flushed, will generally dictate the direction of their flight. But in rough mountain country, no one can tell how grouse will flush or in what direction. The best tip is to go slowly and as quietly as possible. Also, never relax while on the hunt itself. Just when your senses are least alert, the grouse will explode from a tiny stretch of brush you didn't even notice. The resulting confusion isn't calculated to increase your "hitting" percentage.

Experienced hunters sometimes snap-shoot at the sound of a grouse's wings, and such quick shots are often successful. Guns for such fast work, however, must be light and fast pointing. Barrels of 26 or 28 inches and small gauges are preferred. Boring should be improved cylinder and modified in double guns, and improved cylinder in pumps or autoloaders.

Snap-shooting at the sound of a grouse's wings, or through the branches of a tree behind which the grouse has disappeared, offers the best example of true snap-shooting in American upland gunning. Most practical snap-shooting, as previously has been described, in reality is a rapid execution of the swinging-past method, the initial pointing of the gun being corrected by a brisk swing as the trigger is pulled.

No such correction is possible in snap-shooting at invisible game, so this shot remains a true snap. The discharge of the gun is timed to occur as the muzzle covers the supposed location of the target, this being accomplished by pulling the trigger as the gun is mounted. You have time only to "will the shot" and to score regularly with this technique you must have trained yourself to do *three things* at once—face the shot, mount the gun and pull the trigger—during a single reaction time period.

The faster your reaction time, the more accurate the shot, since the flying target will have had less time to move along its course. If that course happens to be directly away from you, rapid reaction time isn't too important. If the bird is moving at an angle, however, a reaction period too long by one-tenth of a second may mean a miss. Since you can't see the direction the target is moving in, you must always strive for the utmost speed in your gun handling.

Many experienced hunters execute the "blind" snap shot as a two-handed gun-pointing operation, like the pointing of the proverbial broomstick. Often the stock doesn't touch the shoulder, nor does the cheek touch the stock. It might be called "instinctive" gun pointing—if a man may be said to do anything with a gun instinctively.

Because the "blind" snap shot is always directed into heavy cover, it should *never* be attempted with the muzzle of the gun at or below eye level. It is safe *only* if the muzzle is directed upward at an angle of 30 degrees or more from the horizontal. Otherwise, a human being or a valuable hunting dog may get shot. The best rule is to *play safe!* If there is the slightest chance that anyone may be in the line of fire, simply don't shoot. There will be another chance in the immediate future, perhaps at the same bird.

A light 20-gauge is ideal for ruffed grouse hunting, although larger bores are used by practiced hunters who do not object to the added weight. Shot size is important. No. 7½ is very satisfactory and No. 8 is sometimes used with success. Like most upland game birds, ruffed grouse feed early and late, and utilize the midday for resting. At that time they are probably in very heavy cover unless sunning or dusting themselves in an open glade.

How to Hunt Partridge

HUNGARIAN PARTRIDGE

The true partridges—the chukar partridge and Hungarian partridge—are not native to North America. The Hungarian partridge was imported to the United States over fifty-five years ago. In much of the wheat land of the West and Midwest and the Canadian provinces, it furnishes considerable upland shooting. Prone to be cyclic, the abundance of Huns varies considerably from year to year.

Slightly smaller than a grouse, the Hungarian partridge has grayish upper parts and white underbelly. This grayish portion of his body is mottled with brown, white and greenish spots of iridescence. The Hun's sides and breast—there's a large red-brown patch near the chest—are grayish white and stippled with black vermiculations. Also seven rather conspicuous red-brown stripes radiate from the shoulder area and curve back along the sides. The throat and face are a pastel ochre. The Huns fly faster than quail, run faster than a pheasant and can outsmart all but the best of bird dogs.

Speaking of dogs, Huns can be worked with pointer or setter dogs. They aren't so easy to hold as bobwhite quail and often choose to run in more open areas. Also, they rise much farther from the gun and are tougher, harder birds to bring down. Experienced dogs learn to circle coveys of Huns and get ahead of them. When this is done, excellent shooting may be had.

The Hungarian partridge is a natural grass-seed eater and where they have flourished best, such as the northern plains region, the preferred seed is from man-cultivated grasses or grain. They like huge stubble fields and, frequently, in driving cornfields for pheasants or sharptails the Hungarian is flushed. Gunners who are alert frequently succeed in taking advantage of these unexpected shots.

Shotguns for Huns should be bored modified and full in the case of doubles. In pumps or autoloaders, modified barrels are good, though both pheasants and Huns often are taken with full-choked equipment. Adjustable choke devices lend themselves well to this shooting. Shotguns smaller than 20-gauge should not be used. Shot sizes should be big enough for shots out to 45 yards. No. 7½ is about the minimum recommended, and unexpected rises of Huns are taken most successfully with No. 6 shot. Because of pheasant and sharptail possibilities in the Hungarian coverts, high-velocity shells are most practical.

Fig. 3.10 (Above) A brace of Hungarian partridge. (Courtesy of Bill Browning, Montana Chamber of Commerce) (Below) A pair of chukar partridges. (Courtesy of U.S. Fish and Wildlife Service)

CHUKAR PARTRIDGE

This recent immigrant to our shores from the foothills of the Himalayas is a rather tough customer, already shaping up as one of the most difficult to hunt of all our upland birds, which is exactly the challenge that shotgunners welcome. This is why this bird has become so popular at many shooting preserves (see Chapter 10).

The chukar, slightly larger than the Hungarian partridge, has rather bold markings when viewed close up: the black eye-stripe running down the neck and joining beneath the throat to form a bib, the heavy black bars alongside the breast, touches of rich chestnut on the tail, crown, and underparts and bright-red bill and feet; yet, when seen from a short distance away, he isn't the least bit conspicuous. In the "wild" state chukars do best in the West, where they find environments quite similar to their original Asian habitat—dry stubble fields, open prairie, arid semi-desert flats and barren hills.

The methods of hunting chukar are quite similar to those used in the taking of Hungarian partridges. Shotgun loads and boring are also identical.

How to Hunt Woodcock

The woodcock is considered an upland bird though in reality he belongs to the shore bird family. Frequenting the heavy growths of black alders, sycamores, birches, willows and the thickets of mountain slopes of the northeastern states, his range often is almost identical with that of the ruffed grouse. Very frequently these two birds are bagged during the same hunt. In the South, on their wintering grounds, woodcock may be found along small streams in the pine woods and in the tupelo gum swamps. Here the bobwhite hunter often finds the "timber-doodle" with his pointers or setters.

The woodcock, except for the coloration and shorter legs, looks a great deal like his beachfront cousins, the snipes. His breast and belly are a rich cinnamon, while his back and wings are stippled with alternating bands of black and brown. The somewhat large head of this bird is marked with black bars on top and down the back of his neck. The eyes are set high and to the rear of the head. The woodcock's bill is extremely long—about twice the length of his head. The tail is almost nonexistent, being comprised of a short tuft of white-tipped feathers. His coloration matches his cover so perfectly you can almost step on him and never know it. This is why it's so difficult to find a downed bird; that is, of course, unless you have a dog.

Woodcock are nocturnal feeders and, as a result, lie close in heavy cover during daylight. While they can be walked up, the use of pointers or setters is recommended. Even retrievers can be trained to be excellent animals for this hunting. The practice of putting bells on the dogs has proved most helpful. Usually the cover is so dense the hunter has difficulty in keeping track of his dog. The bell is a good indicator that no game has been found so long as its merry jingle is ahead. Once the bell stops, the hunter may be reasonably certain that a point has been made and can walk to his dog for the shot.

In deep, tangled cover, it's often most difficult to take a shot with the pivot foot forward and body in perfect balance. Vines and sweeping limbs in combination with poor footing cause more misses in woodcock shooting than the erratic flight of the bird. Woodcock do fly with a bat-like beat of wings that is confusing and causes the shooter to think them a very difficult target. In reality, their flight is slow, but, dodging through the heavy cover, they are easily missed.

The woodcock usually flushes straight up, soaring above the undergrowth and trees before leveling off, and then he flies in a rather erratic course. When he flushes, don't rush your shot. Wait until the bird hits the top of his rise or until it starts a general flight pattern. This will give you a clearer and better shot. Keep your eye on the bird and no matter how screened by brush he seems, squeeze the trigger when you're definitely on him. But remember that once

Fig. 3.11 The woodcock. (Courtesy of U.S. Fish and Wildlife Service)

you have downed a woodcock, he is among one of the most difficult of all birds to find—that's why a dog is so necessary when woodcock hunting. If you don't have a dog, make it a point to always mark your bird down to a pinpoint. It's better to pass up a chance for a double than to fail to mark down number one—and discover you have neither woodcock.

Guns for woodcock should be light, short-barreled and easily maneuvered in heavy cover. The light 20-gauge double bored improved cylinder and modified is ideal. In pumps and autoloaders, the 20-gauge with improved cylinder or adjustable choke device is excellent.

While a few gunners use No. 9 shot in skeet loads for this bird, this practice can result in crippled birds. Also, because ruffed grouse or bobwhites are taken frequently on woodcock hunts, it's recommended that No. 7½ or No. 8 shot be used. With the shortness of ranges encountered in hunting this bird, extremely small shot are of no advantage, as the extra density of pattern is not needed. Also, in heavy cover the larger shot will bore through leaves and twigs and retain sufficient velocity to make clean kills.

As has been stressed in hunting other upland game, it's of great advantage to know the terrain one is hunting. Woodcock have definite areas where they stop off on their migration. One day may prove fruitless in good woodcock cover, but overnight a new flight of birds may come in and give excellent shooting the next day. The skilled hunter seeks soft, boggy places and searches for the white splashes or droppings of woodcock. Holes bored into the soft earth by these long-billed birds in their search for earthworms—their favorite food—is also a good indication that they're present.

It will bear repetition that any shotgun with rather open boring will suffice for woodcock hunting. Many prefer the 12-gauge, but because of the difficult terrain one encounters, light guns are usually most practical. This hunting is strenuous, and light clothing that doesn't snag easily is recommended. Rubber-soled shoepacs make ideal footgear, as muddy footing is frequently encountered.

Unlike bobwhites and pheasants, one can rarely be successful in hunting parallel to edges of heavy cover for woodcock. They invariably will be in the thickest of the alders and must be hunted where they are found. Sometimes on brisk days, when the dark cover is cold, they do frequent more open hillsides or spots where the warm sun may be more to their liking.

How to Hunt Doves and Wild Pigeons

MOURNING DOVES

Mourning doves furnish shooting in some 25 of our 50 states. Though considered migratory birds they nest in every one of our states except Alaska and Hawaii. In the early days of our country, they were possibly the most plentiful of all game birds. But their numbers have since been drastically reduced, particularly in the northeastern portion of the United States. Today, most of the New England and Middle Atlantic states prohibit the shooting of doves, which is the reason for the good comeback of these birds in recent years.

There are two species of mourning doves, eastern and western. Small in size, doves weigh about 4 ounces, the western ones running somewhat larger. The dove's upper parts are gray; below, a pale pinkish buff finishes off with puny pink feet.

Fast, erratic-flying birds of considerable speed, mourning doves are often said to be the most difficult targets in upland shooting. They don't, as a rule, rely upon thick cover for their protection from hunters. Rather, their dodging flight and sheer speed serve as their protection. Their small body size, with a heavy breast protecting their vital organs in overhead shooting, requires shotguns giving dense patterns.

Doves are creatures of habit. Each day they follow almost the same routine. That is, shortly after sunup, they fly from their roost to feed, which occu-

Fig. 3.12 The eastern mourning dove. (Courtesy of U.S. Fish and Wildlife Service)

pies them until nine or ten a.m. Then they have a drink, and drift off to laze about in leafless or lightly foliated trees, or on the ground in the sparse shade of high weeds, until midafternoon. Now they fly off to feed again. Toward dusk they go for another drink or for a bit of gravel, and then to roost for the night. Roosts are likely to be in high shrubbery; not often in extremely tall, open woods. Doves are seed- and grain-eaters. But they don't scratch for feed or eat it from the stalk. Thus, harvested or hogged-down cornfields, cut-over sorghum or other grain, stands of ripened weeds and grasses with dropping seeds all make good shooting sites.

Dove hunting is a gregarious pursuit; it isn't a sport for the lone hunter unless he happens to have located a roost or waterhole frequented by the birds. A good shoot calls for anything from six to twenty hunters for in this way it is possible to keep the birds moving inside the margins of the field. Once a field being used by the birds has been located, a half-dozen shooters usually can get a good bag.

For the lone hunter, as just stated, dove shooting is usually not a walking proposition. On lines of flight between timbered areas and grain fields you may take your stand and enjoy pass shooting. (See Chapter 4 for details on how to pass shoot.) Timbered fringes adjacent to pea fields or stubble often provide good spots for you to take coursing birds coming to the feed. Conceal yourself by a fencerow, a bush beneath a tree, or a clump of high grass. Dove decoys staked out on the ground and placed sparingly in trees often help to bring these birds in close to you. But be sure to wear modestly drab clothing in order to be reasonably inconspicuous.

Water holes and small lakes, if they're the ones used by the doves, are possibly the best location since they are heavily utilized by doves in late afternoon, and you can take advantage of this by taking a stand between the water and the fields where doves have been feeding. Shooting too close to watering places isn't particularly sporting, because incoming birds have slowed down in flight and often may be actually alighting. If you will stay back from such places, then strong-flying birds present ideal shooting.

The practice of shooting along dove roosts is highly productive, but should be discouraged. Birds returning from feeding or watering slow down as they approach the roosts—such as hedge fences or fencerows—presenting relatively easy and close shots. Even legal shooting along the roosts during shooting hours hastens the departure of doves for other climes. Cool nights are another factor responsible for doves moving out of given areas for warmer climates.

Shotgun sizes and barrel boring for doves are determined considerably by the type of shooting to be done. On flight shooting where high overhead birds are the rule, double guns should be bored modified and full. Repeaters and autoloaders, unless equipped with adjustable choke devices, should be modified or full.

Ideal shot shells for doves are in sizes No. 7½ or No. 8. In 16- or 20-gauge, high-velocity loads can be used on these small-bodied birds to good advantage, for they often are at considerable yardage and are quite hard to drop unless well hit.

WHITE-WINGED DOVES
These birds, somewhat larger than the mourning doves, are found in the southwestern United States. The male whitewing is brownish gray. It sports a dark blue patch on the side of the head. Near this patch is a glossy golden brown spot. Its white wing-markings are easily seen in flight. The whitewing is even warier than the shy mourning dove. Whether feeding, roosting or nesting, whitewings keep together in large flocks. The methods of hunting them are quite similar to those used in the taking of mourning doves. Shotgun loads and boring are identical.

BAND-TAILED PIGEONS
These pigeons, often called wild pigeons, are a popular game in some of the mountain states of the West. They are larger than the domestic species, but are similar in general appearance. Their over-all coloration is brownish or bluish gray. A conspicuous band separates the squared-off tail into lighter and darker portions. A white marking on the nape of the neck gives it a third common name of white-collared pigeon. Like its domesticated cousin, the wild pigeon is gregarious and congregates in thick flocks, roosting on top of tall trees between feedings. Usually taken on flyways between timbered ridges and valleys, where it feeds upon acorn mast, it offers very sporty pass shooting.

Considerably larger than doves, wild pigeons have the same body characteristics of heavy breast and hard-to-penetrate vital parts. Shooting ranges are longer and high-velocity loads with No. 6 shot are recommended for this shooting. Shotguns should be 20-gauge or larger and double-gun boring of modified and full is ideal. In pumps or autoloaders, the boring should be at least modified.

How to Hunt Wild Turkey
The wild turkey, also called the bronzeback, is the largest and perhaps the most noble of all our upland

Fig. 3.13 A pair of wild turkeys. (Courtesy of Florida Game & Fresh Water Fish Commission)

game birds. Actually, there are six recognized species of wild turkey on the North American continent. The eastern wild turkey originally had the largest range by far, for once it lived from the Ätlantic seaboard westward more than halfway across the continent and from the Great Lakes to the Gulf. The next race westward is known as Merriam's turkey. It's still found from Colorado to western Arizona and south to Mexico. Then there are the Rio Grande turkey, which extends from central Texas to northern Mexico, and the Mexican turkey of northeastern Mexico, and from the latter our domestic turkey is directly descended. The Florida wild turkey inhabits the peninsula of that state. While twenty states currently have a wild turkey season, Florida and Pennsylvania together account for a larger kill than the other eighteen states put together. But the remaining turkey states seem to be continually increasing their numbers of these birds, as are several states which don't as yet conduct an open season. Intimate acquaintance with the hunting area is a must if the hunter is to be successful, unless he has a guide who knows the likely places.

Possessed of extraordinary hearing and eyesight, the seemingly huge birds have much cunning and wisdom in their small bald heads. During their relatively short life-spans, seldom exceeding five years, they rarely relax guard. Stalking them for close range shotgun shooting is next to impossible. While there are a number of hunters who claim to be able to perform that feat, investigation usually brings out the fact that stalking a turkey means something else altogether—usually calling one within range, locating a roost prior to daylight or making a long shot with a scope-sight-equipped rifle at a bird perched in

a distant pine, or accidentally flushing a flock ahead of one's gun while walking. There *is* a difference!

Wild turkeys are extremely gregarious: they remain flocked together all winter either in mixed or family groups. That's the way they're found during most open hunting seasons. Except after very heavy hunting, single birds are seldom seen. Occasionally several large toms will band together, but this isn't especially common. The birds roost in trees at night and fly down each morning to feed. Like most gallinaceous (scratching) birds, they feed all day but concentrate on two major "meals." The first is right after flying from the roost each morning and the second is just before returning to the roost each evening. Usually they'll use the same roost until they're disturbed or until a scarcity of food draws them to greener pastures. In extremely bad weather, as during heavy snowstorms, a flock may huddle on the roosts for several days without leaving.

It's of great advantage for the flock of birds to be scattered early in the morning. This can be done by deliberately flushing them as they leave the roost. The dispersed birds will remain silent for some time, and so should the caller. After possibly half an hour, the concealed gunner may sound his call. The turkey, anxious to assemble again, will answer if the calling is very good. Birds frequently run directly to the caller, or fly close to him. The least movement by the concealed hunter will be detected by the sharp-eyed birds, and the shot will be lost.

Some states have spring gobbler seasons. During this mating time, these big birds may be called more easily. The flocks break up into breeding harems for the breeding season because the birds are polygamous. The activity of courting and breeding is nourished by the increased light of each spring day, rather than by warmth, because turkeys breed about the same time every year whether the weather is warm or snow still lies on the ground.

Wild turkeys are more slender and sleeker of body than the common Thanksgiving variety, but not necessarily less meaty. The average tom weighs around 14 pounds, although some have gone as high as 40 pounds. The females, which aren't permitted to be shot in most states, are smaller and lighter, from six to 12 pounds. Despite their size, wild turkeys can slip quietly through dense brush or run at an average speed of 15 to 18 miles an hour and even hit 30 for short spurts.

Turkeys possess hair-trigger temperaments. For seemingly no reason at all habit patterns will be altered, feeding ranges changed, flocks divided or merged and other strange whims of wild-turkey brains given concrete expression. To bag wild turkeys consistently takes considerable know-how and usually more patience than the average hunter can muster. To the latter's advantage, however, is the wild turkey's gregarious instinct and his likely response to an expertly operated call in the hands of a patient hunter exercising good sense.

Expert turkey hunters usually plan their hunts and choose one of three recognized methods: still-hunting from an improvised blind; covering the hunted area in company with a foraging dog until a flock is located and scattered, then silently occupying a blind until one or more birds respond to your own imitations of turkey talk; and drive hunting, a method by which noisy beaters cause the turkeys to move ahead in the general direction of other hunters quietly occupying selected stands.

First, however, the methodical, serious, lone hunter who really wants to bring home a wild turkey will thoroughly familiarize himself with the geographical features of the country he intends to hunt and will locate favorite routes of travel and feeding spots of the big birds. Fortunately for the hunter, the wild turkey leaves considerable signs of his passage. Scratches in soft earth, dust wallows, clearly defined tracks made during cautious travel through the woods and shed feathers all indicate use of an area by wild turkeys. An experienced reader of "sign" can often determine both the number of birds in a flock and the approximate hour of their passing. A fortunate find is where a flock of turkeys seek their water for, if previously undisturbed, they frequently will visit the same spot at the same time each day. The exact hours the hunter must figure out for himself. Cooling-off time may be early morning or late afternoon. Once disturbed, however, they are pretty sure to change watering places. The same holds true of located roosts. The lone hunter has to quietly enter the immediate area long before daylight so as to be on hand when the unsuspecting turkeys begin to fly down. He dare not give voice to his turkey call until sure that some of the hens have left the roost and he also can't wait too long to begin calling, or the flock will have already reassembled and started their day on the ground. In the latter event he must locate and scatter the flock or try another spot and technique or return another day.

Various types of artificial callers are utilized to induce scattered birds to congregate. Some are amazingly natural and effective in skilled hands; others are more apt to alarm the wary, sagacious birds than to decoy them, and are best left at home. One of the best—when you can get and master it—is a yelper made from the wing-bone of a turkey that has al-

ready been given dinner-table attention. In using this style call, try giving three short yelps, followed by long intervals of unbroken silence. Box calls of two closely-related scraper types are also popular. One involves scraping the edge of a curved box across a piece of chalked slate or the chalked, curved area of a gunstock. Another style of box call is a hollow, coffin-like, small sounding box with a lid bevelled on the underside and fastened at one end. This style is probably the most common type of turkey call and is usually made of cedar. Some makers prefer to make the box section of well-seasoned basswood or yellow willow, with the cover portion of locust or mahogany, claiming that these woods produce more natural tones in the finished products. But whatever their materials, for maximum effectiveness the box-style callers must be kept dry.

Regardless of type of turkey call used, your broadcasts must be natural in tone and of appropriate meaning. Especially is this true if a turkey responds to your first call: succeeding calls must be perfectly natural with emphasis on the get-together notes only.

Expert calling will definitely get you shots at turkeys, provided you have the patience to remain glued to one spot until one or more birds have been decoyed within sure killing range. The drawback to being a perfectionist is that the more natural your turkey talk, the greater your risk of being fired on by another hunter!

Anyone who has successfully hunted wild turkey over a period of time recognizes the different calls used by the birds during different situations. To him, the throaty "gil-obble-obble-obble" is the courting note of a male gobbler and "keow, keow, keow" is the gentle answering call of a flirting hen. Equally familiar is the assembly call, or yelp—"heoh, heoh, heoh"—which the serious turkey hunter attempts to duplicate to perfection. The turkey language that most threatens his chances, he knows, is the drawn-out alarm call of a hen—"kwa-a-ah!"—and the "purt" danger call of the bronzebacks. Probably the most soul satisfying to the hunter is the predominant "yedle, yedle, yedle" turkey talk that is indulged in by a feeding, undisturbed flock heading in the direction of his blind. Practice, therefore, should be centered on the get-together notes alone; should a "purt" be inadvertently inserted, the hunter might as well return home. In calling, never yelp more than four times and not at all if a bird has already answered twice and is estimated to be within 100 yards of your stand.

Even when calling brings no encouraging answer, don't make the mistake of temporarily moving from your blind. Turkeys sometimes don't answer as-

Fig. 3.14 (Above) The desired result of any turkey hunt. (Courtesy of Florida Game & Fresh Water Fish Commission) (Below) Can you find the camouflaged turkey hunter?

sembly calls at all, but cautiously approach the spot from which your plaintive yelps emanated. Merely getting up momentarily to silently stretch cramped muscles can quickly cancel out your chances of getting a shot! As one veteran turkey hunter so aptly expressed it, a really alarmed turkey who has glimpsed the waiting hunter "not only quits the country, he quits the world."

An ideal hunting situation, and one of much promise, is when two birds in opposite directions answer to a hunter's first call. Thereafter, he can let the separated birds do most of his calling for him, so long as they continue to progress in his general direction and gun range.

As to what constitutes killing ranges and killing shots, there is much difference of opinion. Forty yards is just about the maximum killing distance for shotguns loaded with No. 4 or No. 6 shot. A load of high-velocity small shot that patterns tightly around a turkey's head is usually a killing load. Although buckshot carry much farther, turkeys are generally hard to kill with such shell loadings. It isn't that buckshot won't kill at fairly long ranges, but they characteristically fly wide, especially when they are fired from double-barrel guns. In like vein, the load of small shot that proves to be a killing pattern for head shots frequenty results in merely wounding birds when centered on a turkey's well-feathered body. In selection of shotguns, one of 12 gauge and full choke boring is preferred.

Fortunately, and to the delight of deer hunters who wish to put big-game guns to dual use, a rifle can be used very successfully on wild turkey. Potential killing range is greatly extended, making possible long shots that develop either from skillful calling or accidental sighting of the wily birds. But some of the large caliber, mushroom bullet loads popular with deer hunters—like the 180 grain .30-06 soft-point and the same bullet weight in .300 and .308 calibers—are too destructive of flesh to be desirable turkey killers. Light loads or full-patch, hard-nosed bullet styles can be carried and quickly substituted when chances for a shot at a wild turkey are good. These chance encounters constitute a fourth method of hunting the big birds. Still better as turkey killers are rifles chambered for center-fire .22 cartridge calibers.

Adjust rifle sights to hit the exact point of aim at 100 yards and, for still shots, aim at the turkey's back or the butt joint of a wing, preferably. With sights so adjusted, killing shots can be made as close as 30 yards and as far out as 150, if shooting position and aim are normal. Head shots, while desirable, are difficult to make with a rifle unless visibility and shooting conditions are right and the hunter holds hard and feels lucky. The head of a turkey is a small target.

In the matter of hunting clothing, neutral and subdued colors are to be preferred. The usual red worn by deer hunters is a sure give-away to a wild turkey; so are light-reflecting wrist watches and bands, belt buckles and gun barrels that have not been smoked to kill their glare. Excellent for turkey hunting are the lightweight cotton camouflage suits. As a matter of fact, camouflage and concealment play major roles in consistently successful turkey hunting. Merely remaining motionless, a trick that can sometimes make a deer think the hunter is a harmless object, isn't enough when still-hunting turkeys. Unlike a deer, the wild turkey isn't going to be easily fooled into mistaking the motionless hunter for a tree or stump!

When a bird is near the hunter's gun, yet cannot be definitely located for a shot, continued concealment as well as absolute immobility is definitely in order. Should it develop into a contest to determine which principal can remain motionless the longest, the safest bet is one placed on the turkey. Cautious birds have been known to remain absolutely motionless for minutes on end, even when sudden awareness of danger has brought about cessation of motion while still in an unbalanced position or with uplifted but unplaced foot! In a waiting game, a wild turkey can usually outwait his hunter.

Occasionally, while hunting other game, a hunter will spot a turkey in the top of a distant tree, well out of shotgun range. Should an approach be attempted, some professional guides advocate walking boldly toward the perched bird until within killing range. Trying to sneak up on it will surely cause the bronzeback to take flight, they say. Especially is this true in cases where the gobbler has already been flushed and is using his high vantage point for a comprehensive survey of area conditions of the moment. Generally, however, shots won't come easy. To really take turkeys with any degree of regularity, you will have to be like a certain Southern Negro, wise in the ways of wild turkeys, who, when queried as to the secret of his conquests, confided, "I first finds Mistuh Gobbler, then I out-waits him!" It seems such an easy accomplishment—until you try it.

Chapter Four

LEARNING WATERFOWL SHOOTING

WATERFOWLING IS A strange and wonderful hunting sport. There is apparently no organic disorder causing a normally sane man to go forth on a perfectly miserable day, sit with both back pockets awash in a bulrush barricade and attempt, through half-frozen lips, to lure a passing flight of wild ducks or geese within range of a shotgun. Remember that the pleasant days that fall during the duck season are ruefully referred to as "bluebird days" and only the novice duck hunters go forth. The novices are the ones who haven't as yet learned that raw winds, driving rain, sleet and snow are necessary ingredients to a good shoot.

Types of Ducks

While there are nearly sixty native species of ducks living on the North American continent, there are only two distinct types or classes. They are the shallow-water feeders—dabbling, or puddle ducks—and the deep-water feeders, or divers. Shallow-water puddlers can best be hunted in sloughs, timbered river bottoms and shallow coastal or inland marshes. Divers are most frequently taken on deep lakes, rivers and coastal bays and shorelines. Methods of hunting these different types of birds vary considerably with the location and the species hunted.

PUDDLE DUCKS

The puddle, dabbling, or pond ducks receive their name because as a class they do their feeding in shallow water, either dabbling or wading and scooping up food from the weeds and mud. In shallow water, as a rule, they eat by standing on their heads with their tails tipped up in the air. They rarely dive except when they are in danger or when wounded, and in such cases they can swim excellently under water It is these ducks which are most commonly shot at throughout the U. S. since they will most often come within your gun range as you

wait on the edge of pond or pothole, riverbank, marsh or lake shore.

The one habit common to all members of this group is that when taking off from the water they leap straight up into the air and get under way by sheer wing power. Every hunter should know this spring-up habit of puddle ducks, especially if he intends to try jump-shooting—that is, stalking. Members of this class are among the finest table birds, especially since they will, whenever possible, feed from inland grainfields. The only exception to this is ducks that have been eating crustaceans, duck clams, mollusks, etc.

Ducks of this group can also be identified by their feet. All ducks have four toes: three forward, which are webbed, and one small toe aft. The hind toe on this class of ducks has no web or lobe to it. The feet of puddle ducks are smaller than those of the diving ducks. The legs are placed near the center of the body, and the bird usually swims with the tail held clear of the water.

Mallards, black ducks, pintails, shovelers, baldpates, gadwalls, wood ducks and teal are the better known puddle ducks.

DIVING DUCKS

The diving or deep-water ducks are, as their class name implies, birds that like open or deep water and do their feeding almost entirely by diving beneath the surface for underwater vegetation and shellfish. Most are inclined to gather in large flocks or rafts along the seacoasts and on large lakes.

The major difference in habit between these and the puddle ducks is that instead of springing straight up into flight, the divers take a half-running, half-flying start along the water's surface for quite some distance, then lift themselves into the air much as an airplane does on take-off. This difference of taking off from the water is very important for the duck gunner to know, for it makes for quite radical

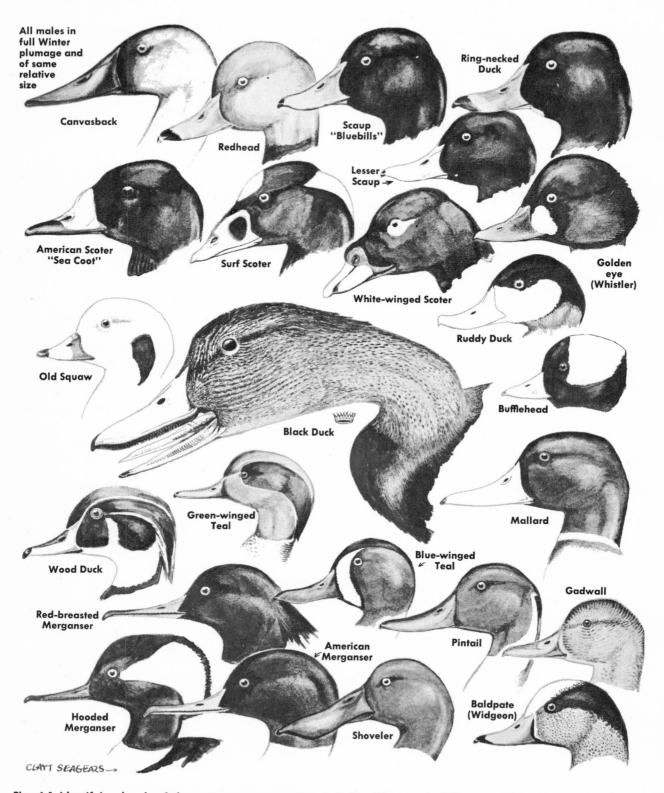

All males in full Winter plumage and of same relative size

Canvasback

Redhead

Scaup "Bluebills"

Ring-necked Duck

Lesser Scaup →

American Scoter "Sea Coot"

Surf Scoter

White-winged Scoter

Golden eye (Whistler)

Ruddy Duck

Old Squaw

Black Duck

Bufflehead

Green-winged Teal

Mallard

Wood Duck

Blue-winged Teal

Gadwall

Red-breasted Merganser

American Merganser

Pintail

Hooded Merganser

Shoveler

Baldpate (Widgeon)

CLAYT SEAGEARS →

Fig. 4.1 Identifying heads of the more common species of ducks. All males in full winter plumage and of same relative size. (Courtesy of N. Y. State Conservation Department)

differences in shooting angles and ranges between the two classes when they are flushed. Another major characteristic difference between the two is that the hind toes of diving ducks have a rather broad lobe. The legs are set near the rear of the body, and the birds usually swim with the tail held close to the water.

In addition, as a class, the diving ducks might be spoken of as hardier. This is because most of them generally nest much farther north than the puddle ducks, and they do not migrate in force as quickly as their pond cousins. They usually wait in the Far North until snow and cold temperatures force them on their way south. Thus the hunting for these deep-water species is likely to be best during the middle or late portions of the season. The shooting for ducks of this class differs from that for the puddle ducks mainly in taking place over open water or tidal waters or along the edges of large marshes giving onto open water, rather than in the marsh ponds, lakes, rivers, or potholes. Most divers decoy well.

Scaups, redheads, canvasbacks, goldeneyes, ring-necked ducks, buffleheads, old squaws, harlequin ducks, eiders, scoters and mergansers are the better known divers.

Methods of Duck Shooting

Generally speaking, there are three types of duck shooting: jump-shooting, pass-shooting, and shooting over decoys. All three kinds of shooting have different techniques and must be studied in detail.

JUMP-SHOOTING

Only in jump-shooting are ducks flushed in the manner of upland birds. This shooting is an interesting and popular sport, and it is the method followed by a great many hunters who aren't keen waterfowl enthusiasts but who try to get in a day or so of this sport, and a bird or two, each year. This type of hunting is almost entirely for the puddle ducks, and the best of it occurs during the first half of the season, before hard frosts have laid the marsh grass, rushes, reeds and other vegetation low. The shooter simply slips on a pair of hip-boot waders and enters a marsh, walking into the wind if at all possible, covering the marsh carefully and slowly, and being ever alert.

Mallards, teal, pintails, black ducks and similar puddle ducks will often be found feeding and hiding in the deep vegetation, usually where there is enough water to at least float them, but sometimes where the ground is only wet. By cautious movement, the hunter comes upon the birds unaware of his presence. They flush quickly the minute they see or hear him, and he gets shooting much like upland shooting. This same jump or "sneak" method of stalking is used around the small ponds—or as they are better known, "potholes"—where the puddle ducks consort. While this type of shooting is fairly easy to do, it is difficult to do alone. Depending upon the lie of the land and the shape and size of the area planned to hunt, it is advisable to have anywhere from two to five shooters along. Experience with each location will teach you which way the flushed ducks will fly out on which wind. While they may follow a land route, the flushed birds will usually attempt their escape in the air above a brook or water running out or into the marsh, lake, or pond.

If a group—three to five hunters—are jump-shooting together, it is wise to use an old deer-hunting technique. That is, all of the hunters—except the "beater"—make their respective ways quietly to spots along the probable flyways from the pothole and conceal themselves as well as possible from any bird flying away. When each man is in position, the beater proceeds cautiously and as quietly as possible to the pothole. He generally gets the first shot, but the rest of them usually get shots, too.

There's a lot more to good jump-duck hunting than the actual scaring out and shooting. It's a lot of fun, even legal, to start before the season opens. Just leave your shooting iron at home and take a pair of binoculars instead. Methodically, whenever there's a little spare time, reconnoiter every patch of water in your neighborhood where this type of shooting might be permitted. Some flights usually arrive in every region before opening day, so make it a point to know just where they are and what they're doing. Check all the inconsequential marshes, potholes, sloughs, creeks, lakes, rivers—the works. Visit some farmers and inquire about hunting on their ponds. Get a county map (most county engineers have them available), if necessary, to locate waters you've never known about. Look especially for newly flooded woods and croplands; these are terrific. By following these suggestions, you know where the most ducks are loitering on opening day. You know which place is the easiest to approach.

Shotguns of 20-gauge or larger with full-choked barrels are recommended for this type of hunting. Shot size should be No. 6, except in taking smaller species such as the teal. Here No. 7½ shot is adequate. Jump-shooting requires speed and a fast snap shot, just as the grouse shooters teach themselves to deliver before the bird is out of range or hidden behind a tree (see Chapter 3).

PASS-SHOOTING

Of all duck hunting, pass-shooting provides the most difficult and the most thrilling sport. The term is actually used because the ducks always seem to be passing—usually from one body of water to another to rest or feed. They need not be moving from water to water. It could be that they are going to or from a field of wheat, corn or rice. In any case, they are going someplace nearby and are flying at low altitude, but remember that what is low for a waterfowl may be high for a shotgun. For this reason, when doing this type of shooting, full-choked guns of 12-gauge and No. 4 shot are recommended. Many gunners prefer the 12-gauge Magnum with three-inch shell for such work.

Pass-shooting requires no more equipment than that for jump-shooting, except that a blind is needed. But it does require a good knowledge of the area in which the shooting is to be done, and of course not all areas provide it. Animals have their game trails, and ducks develop regular feed routes or flyways. Thus, if a gunner knows of such a flyway, he locates himself advantageously somewhere along it, well concealed in a suitable blind, and proceeds to try to prevent a certain number of ducks from passing. The same type of shooting may often be had along rivers, where the ducks tend to trade back and forth, flying up and down the stream perhaps all day, especially if the weather is bad or if many hunters are out and the constant barrage tends to keep them on the wing. It should be obvious that, as usual, a good retriever is very important to this operation.

Pass-shooting might involve puddle ducks or divers. The essential techniques of this type of shooting—judging distance, lead timing, swing, etc.—are discussed in detail later in this chapter.

SHOOTING OVER DECOYS

Since jump- and pass-shooting are both somewhat of a gamble in most instances, shooting waterfowl over decoys has been the standard and most popular method over the years. In many ways shooting over decoys is the easiest, since you usually have the ducks in close, and coming in to the blocks usually slows the ducks down. There are days, of course, when all your decoys will do is pull the flocks past for a look-see, and you will have to use the pass-shooting method, since the ducks will just take a look at your stool—as your arrangement of decoys is called—and keep on going.

Determining if the ducks are going to circle after passing the blocks and come back and set them-

Fig. 4.2 A sight any duck hunter longs for—a big black duck within range. (Courtesy of Graham Wilson—Leonard Ruenterprises)

Fig. 4.3 Four types of permanent blinds.

selves down, or whether they are going to wing right past you, is a matter of experience. All too often, shooters have the tendency to fire at waterfowl when still out of range, and they would do better to let the ducks decoy. It generally takes a flock some time to make up its mind that the decoys look friendly. If they're interested, it's best not to move a muscle and wait the ducks out rather than to take a long, desperate pass shot at them. You can use the same type and gauge shotgun—namely a 12-gauge—as was recommended for pass-shooting, except that No. 6 shot is usually ample.

Blinds, Boats, Decoys and Calls

Ducks are about the wariest of all game birds. Therefore, to get your limit, you must be an out-and-out opportunist. To make the most of your every chance, you must make use of all possible aids to duck hunting, even downright trickery. A distant flight of ducks on the horizon is an opportunity, but it won't do you any good unless you can bring them in.

BLINDS
With the exception of jump-shooting, all duck shoot-

Fig. 4.4 The making of a permanent blind. Note how the boat fits into the blind and becomes the floor or platform of the blind.

Fig. 4.5 Four types of portable blinds.

ing is done from blinds or some form of concealment. We must remember that the duck is a well engineered flying machine. It has eyes equipped with a goggle-like membrane that can be lowered over the eye to protect it from rain and sleet. The eyes are also capable of focusing at will on near and far objects at the same time. In other words, while the duck is keeping one eye on the bird flying next to him, he can use the orb to scan the ground below for resting places or shotgun barrels. This ability is one reason why a "natural-looking" blind is essential to conceal the shooter as he awaits a chance for a shot.

There are almost as many different types of blinds as there are species of waterfowl. In general, your choice of blind will depend on the species of birds you're shooting and the water you're hunting in. In some areas rather elaborate blinds may be necessary to hide the hunter, while in others the only requirement is that the blind merely be sufficient to eliminate his outline. In other words, they range from a boat simply pushed in among tall rushes and cattails to ingenious living quarters with benches, hinged top, peepholes and heating stove. As a rule, they all should be constructed of natural vegetation common to the area where the hunting is done. In other words, the best blind is the one you make with what is provided at the site you're hunting. It may be a pit in the sand on a sandy beach, rocks on a rocky point, willows and alders on a brushy shore, or rushes (if they're tall enough) in a rush-choked bay. The point is that whatever you employ, it should look as much like the surrounding cover as possible.

There are concerns now manufacturing portable blinds to attach to your duckboat, and these are far better than nothing when natural blind material isn't available. One such outfit weaves treated rushes and reeds into chicken wire for a roll-up blind. Another firm wires thin, wooden slats together, painting them dead-grass color on one side and bulrush green on the other. Actually, in the last few years, the floating duck blind has become increasingly popular with waterfowlers. Such a blind offers mobility in the water. You can up-anchor and shift position as the wind changes direction or birds are observed flying a route out of normal gunshot range. You also avoid the harassment of "private property" and "no trespassing" signs which have severely limited the available stationary blind locations recently.

DUCKBOATS

Boats, naturally, go with duck hunting. It enables you to get to the locations where ducks are feeding or flying, and to set up your blind in natural cover growing out of the water. When anchored properly with push poles at both ends, a duckboat provides a solid, comfortable shooting platform for the hunter.

Back when the Indians held sway on the North American continent, duckboats were hollowed out and shaped from logs. But today, they are constructed of lightweight materials—plywood, aluminum (painted an olive drab color), or fiberglass. In addition, they are available in round-bottom, flat-bottom, double-ended, and square-stern designs. Actually, the selection of a material and type of duckboat design depends on two important items: individual preference and type of water you plan to shoot on. Of course, any boat must meet three highly essential requirements: seaworthiness, maneuverability and concealment, in the order named.

A great many duck hunters use their outboard boats as substitute standard duck types with good success. But, if you choose to adapt your summer outboard for the hunting season, remember that some of those accessories for cruising may be detriments during the hunting season. A shiny metal flagstaff is a jaunty decoration during a club cruise in July, but the same bright rod is a useless appendage that must be camouflaged or removed when the ducks are flying.

A gunning boat should be provided with a quick, jam-free system for fast anchoring and up-anchoring. When you want to chase down a cripple, you'll find it is convenient to have your anchor line lashed to a buoy and secured on your bow by a simple loop.

A

B

Fig. 4.6 Steps in making a floating blind: (A) Marsh grass or bulrush native to the area makes ideal camouflage for covering outboard runabout. Cut grass near base to ensure long stalks. (B) Six frames of 1" x 2" lath are fabricated to fit topside contour of runabout. Number of frames and dimensions varies with hull designs. (C) Swamp grass is laid over frame, then held into position—"sandwich" fashion—by lath strips laid over grass and nailed into place. (D) Light frames, grass-covered, are easily carried to and stored in outboard runabout. (E) With decoy pattern laid out, boat is anchored fore-and-aft for broadside shooting. Camouflaging starts with piece of canvas rolled back on forward deck. First frames are set in place. (F) Gunny sack slipped over motor cowling completes the cover-up. Motor is then tilted forward and locked in "up" position. (G) In shallow water by blending the blind with shore line, your rig is often mistaken by ducks for a clump of swamp grass. (H) If wooden floats are attached to anchor lines, it's simple to cast-off and run at slow speed to retrieve dead birds. Frames stay in place if lashed down securely.

C

D

E

F

G

H

Fig. 4.7 (Opposite page and above) Four types of duckboats. As shown at middle left, in states where law prohibits the use of outboards, the gun must be kept unloaded and in its case. The oar is used when the motor is tilted out of place to pole the boat around to place decoys and retrieve ducks. (Credits: Above: Courtesy Virginia Commission of Game and Inland Fisheries; Top Left, Courtesy Maine Development Commission)

This makes it easy to cast loose. As the buoy bobs on the water, set broadside to the wind so decoys are to leeward, it will be easy for you to pick up these markers and re-position yourself for further shooting.

You may find it necessary to rig a covering of canvas and burlap over a pipe or chicken-wire framework to adequately camouflage your regular boat for hunting. An old gunny sack is ideal and inexpensive as a coat for your outboard. While on the subject of outboards, you must carefully observe the conservation regulations. The federal government prohibits the use of a power boat under way as a shooting platform. Under federal migratory bird regulations, such game birds may not be taken from any boat having a motor attached, unless the boat is beached, or resting at anchor, or fastened within or tied immediately alongside of any type of fixed hunting blind.

The federal government *does* allow use of an outboard to *reach* hunting country. The motor can then be rendered inoperable by detaching the fuel tank and tilting the motor up on the transom, or by dismounting it entirely and laying it on the floorboards of the boat. If the latter is done, the motor should be placed below the waterline for better camouflaging. From the standpoint of safety and the availability of power in an emergency it is best to leave the engine on the stern. In any event, be *sure* to check your local and state regulations carefully; many are more restrictive than federal regulations.

Fig. 4.8 If the decoys are to fool the ducks they must be properly placed (left) and kept in good repair by occasional painting (right).

DECOYS

Before each blind it is usually wise to place a group or stool of artificial decoys. They generally mean the difference between getting ducks in gun range and just watching them go by. Of course, there will be days when no enticement will bring a duck in. On such days they have their minds set on travel and just aren't interested in anything else. But decoys work well most of the time if you have the proper number, size and type and if the stool is properly arranged or set out.

Each decoy should have the mooring line and weight wrapped about it in such a manner that the line can be easily uncoiled and the decoy placed in the water without stopping to unravel tangled line or untie endless knots with frost-bitten fingers. Place the decoys so that they will be available as you want them. Deep water duck decoys such as scaup should be placed farthest from the blind; therefore those blocks should be loaded last so that they will be on top when making the setting. The puddle ducks, mallards, teal and so forth are found in shallower water and therefore should be placed closer to shore and nearer the blind. These decoys are the first to be loaded and the last to be placed.

Be sure to use decoys of the duck species you're after. Some blocks or decoys representing one species of diver will get good results with the rest. For instance, a canvasback stool often will draw redheads and scaups. But as a rule, they come to decoys of their own species more readily. Also, don't mix your diving- and puddle-duck decoys. Group them separately in your set. Never set your decoys so close to shore or rushes that they will blend with the back-

ground and thus be almost invisible to even low-flying ducks. Shallow-water ducks, with their long wings, can land fairly well among flocks of others. However, they much prefer to see open patches of water near the decoys to land in.

The number of decoys you will need depends on where and for what type of ducks you hope to shoot. To be properly set up for divers, which are mostly found in good-sized flocks on the more open and deeper waters, you may use anywhere from three to thirty dozen decoys—and there may still be days when you'll wish you had more. Big rigs are especially prevalent in coastal waters—from thirty-six to one hundred and twenty diver-duck blocks on lower Chesapeake Bay, up to four hundred canvasback decoys on the Susquehanna Flats, from one hundred to three hundred redhead and canvasback on North Carolina's Currituck Sound and Virginia's Back Bay, and from seventy-five to two hundred decoys for broadbills on Long Island's Great South Bay. If your blind is on the shore of a large lake or a wide river, the more decoys you have out the better. But when you shoot over a small pond or pothole, a dozen blocks will suffice. Puddle ducks generally don't travel in big flights, as do most diving ducks, and a large spread of decoys may repel rather than attract them.

Usually, if you hunt in an area where there are lots of other hunters, it's a good idea to have out more decoys than any of the other hunters. Ducks like company, both because there must be feed where flocks have congregated and because large rafts of ducks settle in only where it is safe. Your decoys should give the impression that they are the largest, most content flock in the area in which you are hunt-

Fig. 4.9 Decoy arrangements: (from left to right) V, J, triangle, and oval.

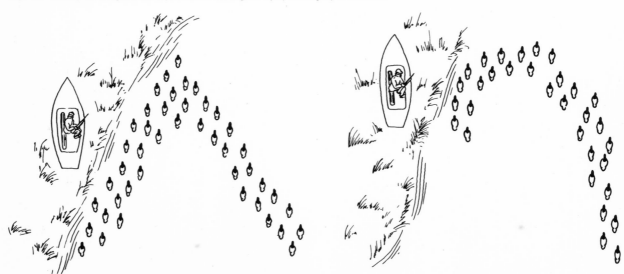

ing. Use all the decoys you can possibly get to your hunting location, and you will get ducks.

How you place your decoys is just as important as their species and size. The big thing to remember about placement is that diving ducks tend to swing outside the blocks to alight and then swim into them. Puddle ducks tend to swing inside decoys and then alight among them or just outside. In either case, all ducks alight into the wind, so this too must be taken into consideration in decoy placement.

The decoy arrangement drawing shows several of the more popular layouts. Note that in these drawings all decoys are heading in the same direction, to keep things simple. Generally, however, you may want to anchor them in some favorite layout or natural manner.

If you have a large expanse of water in front of you, the triangle and wide V-spread is usually recommended. The latter is particularly good for divers when the wind is in the hunters' faces rather than crosswise. Here two batches of decoys are set running out from the blind in a V-angle with a clear approach lane left between them. Divers invariably will choose that lane to come in and light. It's a good set for mallards, too, and best on those almost windless days when stragglers want to set right down at the point of the V.

If there isn't a great amount of water in front of your blind, and it is therefore one of limited feeding area, the fishhook or J-spread is popular. In the case of divers the bend of the hook, where most of the blocks will be, is placed upwind from the blind so ducks coming into it have to pass the shooters. Then the decoys that form the shank of the hook are set out in a string rather close to the blind so birds

alighting outside these blocks won't be out of range. For puddle ducks the bend of the hook is still placed upwind from the blind, but closer than for divers. And the shank of the hook is set far enough away from the blind so ducks can alight inside this string of decoys. The oval arrangement may also be used on smaller bodies of water.

DUCK CALLS

The art of calling ducks is one that has been long neglected by the majority of hunters. Yet to those who "know the lingo," duck calling provides a thrill that can be experienced in no other way. Sport such as most hunters have never experienced awaits the sportsman who attempts to "talk his ducks into the bag."

While it is an art to call ducks, it is one that can be learned. Just two basic calls will do the job for you. One is the "come-in" call, the other the "feed" chuckle. The come-in is used on distant flocks when you want them to head into your decoys. It starts with one or two rather high-pitched, dragged-out notes, then a series of shorter quacks, running down the scale. As the birds approach, this call is speeded up a little for its excitement-producing effect. When the game is almost in gun range, start the feed chuckle—a series of rapidly repeated grunts, like triple-tonguing on a trumpet.

Surprisingly enough, the task is easy, requiring only some practice, and the thrill of coming in with ducks literally talked into the bag more than compensates for the time spent in learning the lingo. The first task is the selection of a duck call.

There are a great variety of duck calls on the market. Some aren't too bad, but the best of them

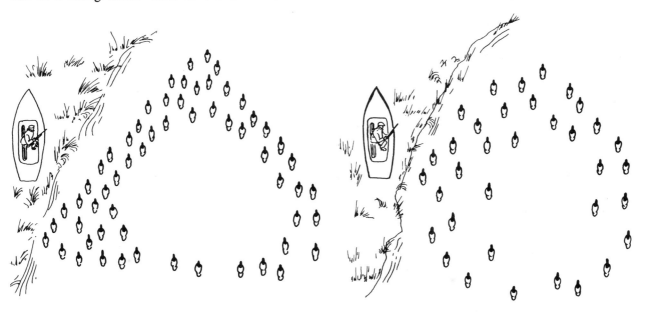

must be operated with skill and taste. Many hunters who have heard of the thrills to be found in duck calling resolve to attempt it without first learning the tonal qualities most desired in an artificial call. They buy a low-pitched call with much the same quality as that of a drake because the sound appeals to them. That is a mistake, as the drake does very little talking (just like the human male). During migration it's the female's high-pitched voice that announces the discovery of a new feeding ground or welcomes new arrivals from the sky. When you buy a duck call, you really should buy a record of duck talk and the manual that goes with it. One such record not only teaches you all of the important calls but also gives you "double calling," the most successful method of calling, which is a secret known only to a few hunters.

Basically, here's how to blow a duck call: grasp the call between the thumb and the base of the index finger at the place where the stopper fits into the barrel. Your hand will be over the end of the call. Place the upper part of the open end firmly against the upper lip. The bottom section of the mouthpiece should merely touch the lower lip. You'll need the loose action of your lower jaw. The sound isn't produced by blowing into the call as you would into a toy horn. It is produced by control from the lips, tongue, throat and diaphragm. Start by grunting into the call, and you will get some indication of the part the stomach muscles play.

After you believe that you have the technique mastered, go out in the fields or woods with a couple of your shooting cronies, get a few hundred yards away from them—upwind—and play your tones. If they report that you sound like a duck, take the caller with you when you go into the blind. If their comments are caustic and perhaps vulgar, you need more practice.

OTHER TIPS

When shooting from blinds, you should arrive at least an hour and a half before sunrise on clear days, and a minimum of an hour on cloudy ones. This gives ample time to set out decoys and get camouflaged and settled in the blind, ready to shoot as the legal hour approaches, and early flyers are not so apt to be aware of your arrival and shooting preparations.

Some hunters take the utmost pains to build and occupy outwardly camouflaged blinds, but advertise their presence to game on wing by smoking, moving about inside blinds and letting light reflect from gun barrels, thermos jugs and their own upturned, expectant faces. Moving even slightly, and talking, when ducks are circling can be equally disastrous,

Fig. 4.10 Calling ducks with a commercial caller (above). (Courtesy of Wisconsin Conservation Department) The guide (below) uses only his mouth and hands to do the calling. (Courtesy of Louisiana Wild Life & Fisheries Commission)

especially when the flyers are black ducks. This cautious species usually circles and inspects spread decoys several times before coming in for a landing.

Strive for perfection in your camouflaging. Kill glare on gun barrels by smearing them with target-shooters' sight-black, and don't forget to smear a little on your own highly reflective facial features, too. Also, take pains to kill shine on new decoys by rubbing their surfaces lightly with fine steel wool, or by swabbing them with a mixture of ordinary beeswax dissolved in a pint of hot turpentine. New, shiny decoys can be warning signals to cautious flyers. In brief, make both your blind and your person blend inconspicuously into the natural scenery.

Whenever possible, try to take a shooting position that puts the wind at your back, for ducks land and take off into the prevailing wind. They use their webbed feet for landings much as a plane does its landing gear, and also use them as rudders for flight maneuvering. When birds are obviously going to settle to your decoys, withhold your fire until they slow down and brake for landings.

How to Shoot Ducks

As described in Chapters 1 and 3, wing shooting is an art, but is fortunately one that can be acquired with patience, practice and experience. The most popular system of shooting at ducks over decoys is the delayed snap or the fast swing. First of all, pick your target. Never shoot blindly at the flock. Pick out one bird. Swing your gun faster than it is flying and at the same angle, pass it by any necessary distance from one to ten feet and squeeze the trigger. Keep swinging that gun as you fire—don't jerk to a halt and shoot. A "follow-through" is as important here as in a golf shot. How far in front of him you aim depends on the bird, the direction of the flight, the velocity and direction of the wind, your reaction time, and how fast you swing. You learn this only by experience. At forty yards, if you're a fast swinger, maybe four feet is enough. If you swing slowly, better use eight or ten feet. Actually, *no* one can tell you how far to lead a duck. But remember that ducks can fly 60 feet in a second. This means they will travel 10 to 15 feet in the fraction of a second required to make up your mind to shoot and pull the trigger. And they will travel several more feet before the shot reaches them. Undoubtedly the biggest cause of misses in duck hunting is shooting behind the target.

The deliberate shot or sustained lead is a popular system with pass-shooters. But it isn't a slow maneuver as the name might imply. It's executed with a smooth rhythmic swing of the gun, starting behind the waterfowl, then past and ahead to the estimated lead, the trigger squeezed with the gun still swinging. This system is a bit more exact, and it will probably kill more birds when the gunner has plenty of time, as in the pass-shooting of waterfowl. However, while less exact, the delayed-snap system is much faster and much more adaptable to various conditions. The fast swinger using the delayed snap will kill a duck while the deliberate leader is still thinking about it, and in certain circumstances the fast swinger will get ducks where the deliberate leader will go home empty handed.

When duck hunting, remember these three important words: *Face the shot!* Because when you face the shot, the spread of your shotgun pattern often will insure clean kills without conscious forward allowance for the movement of your target. Shooting in this manner, you have a clear vision of everything around you. Since you have both eyes open, you aren't watching just one duck but you can keep track of the others. After bringing down your duck, you know where the rest of the flock is and can be ready for the next shot.

TYPES OF SHOTS

Up to this point, we have considered only crossing birds. At least half the time the duck isn't flying exactly parallel to the water. It may be rising a little or dropping a little, therefore it's necessary to know the proper aiming and leading techniques.

QUARTERING SHOT. Right- and left-quartering shots with the target taking on greater elevation are common in wildfowl shooting. One of the best plans for applying the proper swing to shots of this type, as when upland game hunting, is the vertical clock system. Imagine that the exact center of the clock face is the point in space immediately over your gun muzzle as you "face the shot." Then the apparent direction of the duck can be flashed to the brain by the eye as a two-o'clock shot or a five-o'clock shot.

As previously described on page 23, a two-o'clock shot is one in which the target is moving from left to right and rising at an angle of approximately thirty degrees from the horizontal. The five-o'clock shot, on the other hand, is where the target is again moving from left to right, but is descending from the horizontal at an angle of about sixty degrees. A duck taking off from the water on a right-quartering direction is a fine example of the typical two-o'clock shot, while a duck coming in for a landing over decoys often gives a five-o'clock shot. In either case, the zero point will represent the spot at which the duck was first sighted. If you accustom yourself to its use, the clock face will form in your imagination the instant you recognize a duck as a legitimate target.

When using the imaginary vertical clock face method of shotgun pointing, remember that in most instances, the apparent direction and apparent speed are of much greater importance than the duck's actual flight speed. For example, you may get your two-o'clock shot either when the duck is rising in a right-quartering direction or when it moves directly across in front of you. In both cases, however, keep in mind that because the direction of your eye movement is the same, the direction of your gun swing from the center of the clock face (the zero point) toward the two-o'clock position will be exactly the same, too.

When shooting at a duck at either short or medium ranges—from 20 to 40 yards—you can completely forget about the duck's actual flight speed and concentrate solely on its apparent speed. This is simply because at these distances the velocity of the shot charge is rather constant, and the relationship between the actual speed of the bird and the velocity of the shot charge remains fairly fixed.

As has been stated several times previously, your eye rather quickly learns to estimate apparent speed along with the apparent direction, and to combine both factors in its flash to the brain. The muscles of the body, responding to urges of the brain, then go into action with either the fast swing or the sustained-lead system. The speed of the swing is accelerated or retarded as the movement progresses, as a correction of the original estimate of the eye, with the apparent speed of the bird as pacemaker. In general, a quartering shot at thirty-five yards requires only four to six bird lengths.

When the target is over 40 yards, remember that the speed of the bird stays constant but the velocity of the shot charge diminishes rapidly with distance. For this shot, the sustained-lead system is considered best by most experts. Since the bird is moving away from you at a diagonal, he covers more ground than he seems to because your sight line is foreshortened. Lead this bird by plenty. It's better to guess on the long side than the short side, because the short side means a sure miss while the long side still gives you a trailing shot cone that he can fly into.

STRAIGHT-ON SHOT. The most difficult shot for most hunters is the "incomer," where the ducks bore into your blind. Look sharp and decide whether they're skimming in to settle with your decoys or taking elevation to pass over your blind. If they're losing altitude, draw a bead just a few inches below the leader. At a range of twenty-five or thirty yards and an altitude of, say, thirty feet, aim about six inches to a foot below the duck. Don't bring your gun down on the duck, because you'll block your view of it. Come up under it, and when you are just under it, squeeze the trigger. Of course, the higher the duck the longer the lead on this shot, and conversely, the lower the duck the shorter the lead. If the duck is coming in on a direct line with your blind, bring your gun up on its line of flight and pass it and blot him out with your muzzle. Then squeeze the trigger.

It is a temptation to wait too long with the straight-on shot. Don't do it. If you are in a well-concealed blind and the duck is apparently going right over the top of it, shoot before he gets to a distance of approximately twenty yards. If you wait longer than that, your pattern will cover a very small area and you may miss altogether, or if you should hit it, you will retrieve nothing but "duckburger."

OVERHEAD SHOT. Another tough shot, because it's awkward to line your gun straight, is the one taken overhead. If you've twisted the stock against your shoulder you might as well never pull the trigger. Permitting the ducks to get directly overhead before shooting will result in many missed and crippled birds. If they're traveling fast they may be covering one hundred feet a second. Swing on their line of flight and get ahead plenty far—eight bird lengths, maybe ten, at forty yards. Your shot column strings out quite a way, and if you can plant it ahead so they'll fly into it, you'll get hits. Two-eye shooting pays off here (both eyes open), and the sustained-lead system is considered most practical.

JUDGING DISTANCE

The inability of a hunter to judge distance is the greatest single cause of duck cripples. Few hunters go through a season without having cause for self-reproach over unrecovered crippled and dead birds. Even if we were indifferent to the humane aspect, we couldn't ignore the fact that it is idiotic to allow at least one-fourth of the total annual waterfowl kill to be wasted! The hunter who shoots at all out-range birds and occasionally bags one is *not* demonstrating skill but mere ignorance in the proper use of his fowling piece; the sky shooters cripple more ducks than all other hunters put together. A real sportsman waits until the bird is well within range so that if one is crippled a quick second or third shot will help erase the blunder of a partial hit. The extra shot carried in many duck guns should be reserved to rake a cripple the moment it is down.

Many hunters train themselves to estimate the range of waterfowl by the distinctness of feather markings, the eyes, the feet, or other physical features. This system works well under conditions of clear visibility, but in rain and sleet, in fog and mist, or under heavy clouds, distances may be misjudged as much as one-third of the actual range. Strange as it may appear, a light-gray overcast sky is responsible for more misjudged ranges than any other condition. The ducks appear as black silhouettes against a light background, and thus seem to be much closer than they really are.

The best method for a final check on range is to calibrate the width of the muzzle of your shotgun on a 24-inch square of paper at ranges from 30 to

Fig. 4.11 This is the size ducks appear at various distances. Remember to estimate on the long side in calculating lead. (Courtesy of Browning Arms Company)

60 yards. Most large ducks are approximately 24 inches long, and the flesh-and-bone area of their wingspread in normal flight approximates this figure. Thus the gunner who has calibrated his gun muzzle has a final check, in either swinging past or pointing out his target, on the actual range. For example, if the muzzle of a 12-gauge double completely "covers up" a large duck, such as a mallard or a pintail, that duck is too far away to shoot. Similar relationship between the width of any type of gun muzzle and a flying duck can be worked out in a few minutes against the 24-inch paper square.

You will note that this system of final range estimation presupposes that the flying duck may be covered up by the swinging gun muzzle. On a crossing shot at a normal range of 40 yards or less, this would not hold true, as only the front sight of a properly fitted gun would appear against the target. But in shooting at ranges longer than 40 yards, it is necessary to "hold high" to allow for the drop of the shot charge due to the pull of gravity. This drop of shot from gun muzzle out to 40 yards is only about 2 inches for No. 4 shot, but at 60 yards it is 7 or 8 inches. This latter figure closely approximates the depth of body of large ducks. If the range of a crossing shot appears longer than 40 yards, the law of experience is to hold on the top of the duck's body line. Thus covering up automatically becomes a factor in duck shooting at long ranges.

When shooting over decoys, mark off your outermost range with a string of decoys tailing off from the blind if you're working on divers like canvasback, or with a few blocks clumped beyond the main closed-in bunch if you're operating on puddle ducks. Let the outermost decoy be forty yards from the blind. Take forty yards of cord with you and use it to measure off the decoy's placement. Some duck hunters have one or two oversized blocks which they employ as "range" decoys. The decoy marker, however, isn't much help on high-flying ducks, but let's say that a pair comes whistling past low, giving your stool a good looking over. Then you can swing into action with a clear idea as to whether they are inside the range or somewhere out in the wild blue yonder.

Allowance for the drop of shot at long ranges is particularly important to gunners shooting diving ducks on large bodies of water. The divers usually fly low over the water, and thus don't "come in for a landing with their flaps down" as do the puddle ducks. If the wind is from any direction except squarely from the hunter's back, long shots at crossing birds will be the rule, whether the ducks are alighting in the decoys or not.

For high angle or overhead shots, the correction for drop of shot may be disregarded. It's obvious that in a shot directly overhead, the pull of gravity operates as a drag upon the velocity of the shot charge, but doesn't affect the point of impact. Within effective ranges, the pull of gravity on shot velocities is negligible. But be careful of those long shots low over the water—hold high and lead 'em twice as far as for an ordinary 40-yard shot.

Make it a rule to retrieve wounded ducks immediately and to get dead ducks before water currents whisk them from sight. The fact that a duck falls at the hunter's shot doesn't necessarily mean that his sagacity has ended—unless the bird is dead. A wounded duck can dive and disappear mysteriously.

A retrieved cripple can be quickly and humanely killed if you hold it firmly by the shoulders with both hands, its belly up and head pointing away from you, and then bring the bird's head down smartly against some hard object. The method doesn't require much force, nor seldom more than a couple of headraps.

Goose Shooting

The goose is the most lordly of our legal wildfowl and is a wary bird, beautiful in action and a top trophy for gunners. But a successful goose hunter is a specialist. He is as different from a duck shooter as a turkey hunter is from a pheasant gunner.

Many geese are bagged from duck blinds, especially on rivers and in coastal marshes. In such cases, they're shot in the same manner as ducks in a similar situation. As a rule, though, their feeding habits are not identical with those of ducks, and they more frequently are taken in fields of winter wheat or rye, or in cornfields or wheatfields where they seek grain. While the best duck hunting is usually in the early morning hours or late evening, feeding geese often are taken later in the day, and great patience is needed to wait them out.

Skilled goose hunters spend more time in locating fields where geese feed than in actual hunting. A binocular will come in handy here. When a new flock of geese comes out, they are very cautious. They'll probably circle the field several times looking for the best feeding place and for any signs of danger. Geese that have been feeding for several days in one spot will head in as if they owned the field. If you have plenty of time and the field abounds with food, let the geese feed a day or so before you hunt them.

If a field looks good but there aren't geese in sight when you're trying to find a spot to hunt, look for tracks and droppings. If they have been feeding there, they will be back—provided they weren't scared away. In case you discover no indications that geese have fed there, look for another location. Unlike ducks, geese as a rule won't go into a field of standing corn or into corn that has been picked by hand with the stalks left standing. They always feed in the open where they can watch in all directions for enemies.

If a field is not flat, the geese will usually feed in the lowest location. In such spots, there is likely to be a little moisture, which will mean blades of green grass. Furthermore, a low place in a big field is screened from any roads that may be nearby. While the geese can't be seen here, however, they are in an excellent position to watch the horizon in all directions for approaching enemies. The low spot is the first one to inspect for goose signs, and, if any are found, it is the place to make your pit.

Don't hunt geese on a windy day since they don't like to buck a heavy wind. They will more than likely drop into the first field that looks desirable for feed. But you can bet your bottom dollar they won't feed there the next day when the wind has died down.

Now that you have located the geese, ask permission of the farmer to hunt. Promise him that you will fill up the pits after you have used them, and offer him a goose or two if you are successful. Don't disturb the geese, but come back at night to dig the pits. Or, if the geese have left the field in the morning and your time is limited, dig your pits at once and get into them. These same geese may come back before dusk. Don't make a pit where the geese have cleaned out all of the food.

Fig. 4.12 Geese hunters shooting over decoys. (Courtesy of N.Y. State Conservation Department)

When it is impossible to dig a pit, which would be the case if the ground were frozen or if you were shooting from a low river bar, the blind should be as small as possible and made of material that blends into its surroundings. In such locations, a rock blind just big enough to crouch behind is good; or, on a river where high water has left snags and deadheads on the bars, driftwood could be used. Other blinds described for duck hunting can be used on rivers and in coastal marshes for geese.

Many different types of goose decoys may be used. The best decoys are the full-bodied type, with detachable heads and necks which can be turned into any one of several natural positions. Many hunters prefer silhouettes or stuffed decoys. There are some new goose decoys on the market that are also good. In setting silhouettes, be sure you don't have them all facing the same direction, because the geese may not see them when they circle in. They can see stuffed decoys at any angle. In some localities, shooters make decoys for snow and blue geese from newspaper or large white paper napkins. Twist one corner for the head and neck and tuck the two opposite corners under small stones so that it resembles a live goose.

Most goose hunters have their own definite way of setting out decoys. Most guides, however, place their decoys upwind, so that when the geese come in against the wind they won't have to come in over the decoys. They may alight short of the decoys. Geese always feed into the wind or slightly quartering, and there is always a sentinel on guard. Usually he will be some distance from the feeding flock and on a rise of ground. Don't forget to include the sentinel in your decoy set. Place your decoys about thirty to thirty-five yards from the pits—don't bunch them too closely. When possible, the set should be made in an open field, away from roads and fences. Make the set early, before daylight if possible. If you plan to leave your decoys out overnight, it's a good idea to move them around after a day's shooting.

Any gunner who can call geese successfully has a big advantage over one lacking this special skill. Many guides are most adept in doing this by mouth. For most amateurs, however, a goose call is a must. But you can't expect one call to do a perfect job of imitating all the different calls of the various species of geese. You must decide what species of goose you're most likely to hunt, and then choose your call. Goose calls are made with a plastic, metal, or rubber reed vibrating inside a rubber, plastic, metal, or wooden barrel. The tone is changed by varying the effort with which the call is blown.

To be a good goose caller, you must practice. The three best teaching aids are: 1) the wild birds themselves, 2) an experienced caller who will help you, and 3) a phonograph record of an expert calling. Such phonograph recordings are for sale by most of the goose-call manufacturers.

Now, let's get back to the pit and make ready for the first flock. Keep an eye peeled in the direction of the water, but keep down in your pit. Geese have very good eyes and can see any movement for miles around. When you first sight the flock, get out your goose call and start giving out with squawks. If the

geese decide to visit you, they will come in with the wind, circle a time or two, then set their wings. This is the moment that separates men from the boys— what you do in the next few seconds will mean meat on the table or none. Be sure the geese are within range—because of their great size, hunters almost invariably fail to estimate the range properly, and a bird ninety yards away may seem well within killing distance. But keep down. Let one shooter give the word "Fire," then spring up. Keep cool and pick out your bird. Knock over the leader if possible, and the others may become confused and swing back. Never jump out of your pit when you fire the first shots unless the geese have left the field. Geese often circle back to see what has happened.

Guns for goose hunting should be full choked. Sound judgment is necessary, and long shots shouldn't be taken. The standard 12-gauge or the Magnum 12 are recommended for geese. Shot size such as No. 4 is effective for such species as snow and blue geese or for large geese at reasonable ranges. For large Canada geese, No. 2 shot is required, especially for the second or third shot. The 10-gauge has long been recognized as a goose gun, and for shotguns of this boring No. 2 shot is ideal. However, some users of 10-gauge Magnum guns prefer BB's.

Brant Shooting

These birds are found only along salt water. The blue and snow geese are commonly called brant in the Midwest, but this term is erroneous. Only in restricted areas on both the Atlantic and Pacific

Fig. 4.13 (Left) Geese flying over decoys as the hunters wait in their brush blind for a shot. (Courtesy of Wisconsin Conservation Department) (Right) Hunter in a deep pit. He raises up to take a shot at a goose as it comes in. (Courtesy of Saskatchewan Government)

coasts are the true brant found. They usually are taken in conjunction with duck shooting, though in former days when this species was more abundant, offshore blinds and brant decoys were employed. They decoy well to large settings of duck decoys and are prone to fly low over the water. No. 4 shot and full-choked 12-gauge shotguns are recommended for their hunting. They are shot by following the same techniques as for ducks. As a matter of fact, most brants are shot on duck hunting trips. Blinds should furnish good concealment and firm footing. Decoys should be so placed as to bring in the birds before the hunter.

Rail and Jacksnipe Shooting

There are several rails—the sora and the Virginia rail being the most common. Although they provided some sport for the waterfowlers of fifty years ago, they're disregarded by many of the modern shooters because they're small and aren't especially fast birds —they're easy to hit.

The sora, found in a few of the eastern shore states, is the most widely sought. In almost any marshy area in these states with a thick growth of wild rice or wild oats the chances are good that the rail population can be found in mid-September. In the marshes where the water isn't deep enough to float even a shallow push boat, you will have to wade, flushing the birds ahead of you. If you happen to have a retriever that will work ahead of you, the chances are better that you will flush more rails.

Rail shooting usually calls for a guide, or at least a companion, to pole a flat-bottomed boat through the shallow salt-water marshes. In regions where this type of shooting is more popular, a special rail boat is used, and the hunting is limited to a three-hour period at high tide. This boat is a long, narrow craft, built as lightly as possible, having a stool well forward and a poling platform at the stern. The guide or poler must force the boat through the thick tangle of rushes and stalks, and do it as smoothly as possible, for if he thrusts the boat with a lurch just as a bird flushes, the shooter will be too busy trying to stay in the boat to think about shooting. Perched forward on his seat, the shooter must watch the area ahead and on both sides, since the rail flushes without a sound, skims along the top of the stalks for about forty or fifty feet and then settles back. When one of the birds is dropped in this cover, the problem of retrieving is not an easy one. Generally the guide carries along several special markers—usually red- and white-colored billets. When a rail is dropped,

Fig. 4.14 A Virginia rail poses for his portrait. Adult bird grows slightly larger than a quail. (Courtesy of U.S. Fish and Wildlife Service)

the guide throws the marker as close to the fallen bird as his eye and arm will permit. The boat then is poled in that direction, and the marshland close to the marker is searched for the dead rail. The search can be continued after the tide goes out.

Being thinly feathered, rails are easily killed with standard-velocity loads of small shot. Any shotgun will kill rails, and the gauge is a matter of preference for the gunner. However, the 20-gauge, with so-called squib loads (two-thirds of a normal power charge) and No. 10 shot is the most popular with most rail hunters. In doubles, boring of either the improved-cylinder or modified type is very good. In pumps and autoloaders, barrels bored improved-cylinder to modified will suffice. For the real rail shooter, however, the open-bored (cylinder) gun is best, for the range is usually short and a wide pattern is preferred. Such hunters claim that, due to the circumstances of boat movement, thick cover and short flight, rails offer interesting shooting. But, as far as I'm concerned, it is especially good for young shooters or gunners who aren't quite ready for the fast wing-shooting required for other wildfowling.

It has been only recently that the jacksnipe was reinstated to the legal game list by the U. S. Fish and Wildlife Service. (Before shooting either rail or jack-snipe check your state laws.) Their habitat is in marshes and wet meadows, where the hunter must seek them out, usually encountering only one at a time. After being flushed their flight is sudden, rapid and irregular. They're hunted in approximately the same manner as rails.

Chapter Five

LEARNING TO HUNT SMALL GAME ANIMALS

IF ANY SINGLE group of creatures could be said to form the basis of hunting in the United States, the honor would have to go to the small game animals —the rabbits, squirrels, raccoons and opossums. What these small game animals lack in physical dimensions they more than make up for in other ways. It's these common creatures, more than any others, that bring healthful outdoor recreation to so many millions of sportsmen throughout the country, year after year after year. Nothing small about this.

Availability is the number one compensation for small game's size. There are plenty of these little fellers in plenty of places, North, South, East and West—all of them with regional species especially adapted to conditions in the particular locality where they live. But, in addition to excelling in quantity, small game has plenty to offer in the quality department, too. Cunning, elusive and in some instances swift, the small furred animals provide ideal sport for anyone who enjoys tramping afield with gun and dog. Even those fluffy bounding balls known as cottontails are no cinch for hound and hunter where there's plenty of cover. In most wooded regions, wary scampering squirrels are prized game; and in the South, night hunting of raccoons and opossums is a popular, time-honored pastime.

Rabbits

Of all the game that is hunted in the United States, nothing commands the attention of sportsmen year in and year out like the rabbit. It's safe to say that more ammunition is fired at rabbits than at any other American game, including wildfowl. If it weren't for the prolific little rabbit, many thousands of hunters would get a great deal less shooting than they do.

There are some dozen species and over 50 subspecies of rabbits or hares in various sections of the North American continent. Some, such as jack rabbits and brush rabbits, are plain or desert species. Some are strictly northern species, such as the snowshoe and arctic hares. Still others, known as swamp or marsh rabbits, live in wet locations. Overlapping the ranges of all of these, except the arctic hare, is the widespread cottontail, represented by many geographic subspecies from Maine to California and Canada to Mexico.

COTTONTAIL RABBITS

The great abundance of cottontails and the long, open gunning season will always keep them at the top of the list of small game hunting. There are mornings when the ducks don't fly and days the game birds just don't seem to be around. But, on almost any day, rain or shine, snow or slush, the rabbit hunter who has a general knowledge of the cottontail's habits can go into the woods, and return with his game coat sagging in the rear.

The distinctive characteristic of the cottontail is, as the name implies, his short bushy tail. It's elevated when he runs and shows white on the underside. (The swamp rabbit, a close cousin of the cottontail, has a dingy white tail underside.) Both sexes of the cottontail are colored alike in brown coats with white undersides. The size of the animal varies according to the food supply of each locale, but he weighs from 2 to 3 pounds and averages about 13 inches in length. His ears are about 3 inches long.

The cottontail generally prefers the cultivated areas, especially where there are farms and orchards, to the deep woods. As a rule, you'll find him in the fence rows, the borders of woodlots, or the stream bottoms grown up to brush or high grass. In the South, the pine lands where tall, straight southern pines stand rather sparsely, with a heavy growth of high grass and gallberry bushes, are excellent cottontail cover. In the more arid West, bushy areas where plentiful food and hiding places are offered make

Fig. 5.1 The cottontail rabbit. (Courtesy of Florida Game & Fresh Water Fish Commission)

cottontail havens. In other words, Mr. Cottontail is a lover of brush and tangled thickets.

In summer the cottontails' food is primarily herbs, short shrubs and their favorite clover. They're also very fond of dandelion leaves and cabbage, and they sometimes do much damage to farm gardens. Since the rabbits don't hibernate, they must seek winter food, which is usually the bark and twigs of low trees and shrubs such as willows, lespedezas, sumac stands, berry bushes and fruit trees. Whenever rabbits are present, you'll find that these trees and shrubs have been girdled. Cottontails, like all rabbits, usually do their eating in early morning and late afternoon. During the rest of the day they bed down in nearby cover.

Top sport is enjoyed when one or more dogs are employed. (Specific recommendations for the breeds of dogs for various small game hunting can be found in Chapter 8.) The age-old technique of bringing dog-hunted cottontails to bag is to place yourself where the rabbit will be almost sure to circle past you, and then stand there and keep quiet. While a cottontail can cover ground at a good clip, around, over, or down a hill, the animal is in a mental rut all the time, for inevitably he will—if driven by a dog—return to the spot where he was jumped. This homing instinct makes him rather easy for you, since all you have to do is just stand fast and wait until your dog pushes the rabbit back to his starting point. When several dogs are used, the chase can get mighty fast because the dogs usually vie with each other for the "honor" of bringing the rabbit to bag.

If you prefer to hunt cottontails without the help of dogs, you have to "kick" them out yourself. The trick in kicking out rabbits is to work the cover slowly and methodically. If you advance too quickly, you'll succeed only in scaring a lot of rabbits without even seeing them. A cottontail will generally freeze at the approach of a fast-moving hunter, depending on his excellent camouflage coloring to escape detection. Of course, under some conditions a rabbit is hard to kick out, especially when he's deep under a brush pile. He'll usually remain motionless until you're within a few feet of him and many times he is passed by unobserved. But the moment a rabbit loses confidence in concealment, he bolts away at top speed. That's when you have scarcely a fraction of a second to bring your gun to bear on this bobbing and weaving target. Actually, his zigging and zagging doesn't provide an easy shot, and he usually puts the heavy cover to good advantage as he bounces along. A straightaway shot is the easiest, but when he is crossing, lead as you would for ducks. The cottontail can really *move* when he's running from danger.

The key to the amount of cottontails you'll see in any particular day hinges upon the weather. Rabbits don't mind cold, sunny weather, but it's now been established that in real stormy weather they seek hiding either above or below ground and will generally stay put. Therefore hunting them during a driving rain or a blizzard is usually not too productive.

Fig. 5.2 A hound giving chase to a cottontail rabbit. (Courtesy of Wisconsin Conservation Department)

Fig. 5.3 A hunter has just kicked out a cottontail from his hiding place. (Courtesy of Wisconsin Conservation Department)

But just let the storm cease, and the sun come out, and the rabbits will be out, too. An overcast but warm day with not too much wind is also good rabbit hunting weather. After a light snow, it is, of course, fairly easy to track Mr. Cottontail. For this reason, a few states have banned cottontail hunting when there's snow on the ground.

While a few rabbit hunters prefer to use a .22 rifle, rifles may often be dangerous in heavily settled areas, and a running cottontail is usually no target for the average rifle shot, especially for the beginner. The type and gauge of shotgun you employ for rabbit hunting, however, is a matter of personal preference. One is as good as another, from 12-gauge to the .410. But, in the opinion of most experts, the best rabbit gun is one with a full-choke in its barrel. Shot size for rabbits should be No. 5, 6 or 7½. While a cottontail isn't too difficult to kill, the large shot penetrates best through thick cover.

SNOWSHOE AND JACK RABBITS

Of the other North American rabbits, only the snowshoe and the jack rabbit are hunted with any regularity. Actually, both these species are hares, not rabbits. There is a difference between the rabbit and the hare. For example, hares never make burrows but live in nests or "forms" above ground, while rabbits live in burrows which are usually the abandoned dens of other animals. Hares have greatly elongated ears and hind legs; those of the rabbit are much shorter in proportion to the rest of their bodies. Both are equally prolific, bringing forth three litters a summer, but the hare's offspring are born with their eyes open and with a fully developed coat of fur, while young rabbits come into the world naked and blind.

The snowshoe rabbit or hare is distributed in 16 recognized varieties throughout the colder regions of North America from Alaska across Canada and southward in the United States along the Appalachians from Maine to West Virginia, and along the Rockies from Montana and Idaho to the borders of Utah, Arizona and New Mexico. He is called the snowshoe because in winter his large hind feet are covered with thick fur. This enables him to travel easily over soft, deep snow. He is also called a varying hare because he sheds his fur twice a year, becoming white in the fall and brownish-gray in spring.

The snowshoe thrives in thick, fairly low cover and is rarely found in heavy timber. Look for him in cedar and tamarack swamps that aren't too wet and

Fig. 5.4 The varying hare or snowshoe rabbit in his summer dress. (Courtesy of U.S. Fish and Wildlife Service)

in willow, birch and poplar thickets that haven't grown past the sapling stage. In the North the poplar, or aspen, is the snowshoe's staple food. In the Appalachians he is associated with the mountain laurel and the white cedar. In most instances, heavily populated snowshoe range will have scattered small openings adjacent to the densest possible cover. Cut-over or burned-over land that is growing back to forest makes excellent hunting grounds.

To hunt snowshoes, you almost must have a dog or dogs. It's rather difficult to kick them out and get any shots. But with dogs you can have a lot of fun, for the snowshoe won't hole up at all and he'll lead the dogs a merry chase in a circular route that may be several miles in circumference. Upon completing his first circle, the rabbit may begin all over again without pausing for breath. Sometimes your dogs become winded before Mr. Snowshoe finally arrives within gun range, especially if the cover is thick and the snow more than a few inches deep. You should locate yourself in a clearing, or on a knoll, where you can obtain a good view of the surrounding countryside, listen to the dogs, and keep a good watch ahead to try for a shot when the snowshoe makes his appearance. Since many of the shots will be fairly

long, a 12-gauge shotgun with a full-choke is your best gun for this type of rabbit shooting. No. 4 or 5 shot is a good shot size for these big fellows.

The jack rabbit is the largest of the American hares. They're more than two feet long and their ears are from five to six inches long. They weigh four to six pounds. Black-tailed jack rabbits are common on the open plains of the West from Saskatchewan to Mexico. The white-tailed jack rabbits, often called prairie hares, live on the plains with the black-tail, but they range farther North and higher in the mountains. They're larger and weigh six to eight pounds and, like the snowshoe, they change their grayish-brown coat for white pelts in winter.

While the jack rabbit offers some sporty shooting because of his great speed, he doesn't rank high as either a game animal or as food for the gourmet. Most jack rabbits are shot at rather long range with rifles in the small-caliber, high-velocity category. While millions of rabbits are killed annually by hunters, dogs and predators, their greatest enemy is possibly the tick-borne disease called tularemia. While this disease infects other game, it's most prevalent among all species of rabbits and hares, and is transmissible to humans. If you happen to kick out a rabbit that moves very slowly and is inclined to appear sluggish, kill him but don't touch him. Many hunters handle rabbits only with gloved hands as an insurance against possible infection, for the disease can be transmitted if the hands are cut or scratched. (It's been proven that no infection can be contracted when the human skin surface is perfectly intact. But as hunters are likely to have numerous minor scratches from brambles, it's best to take the precaution of using rubber gloves when handling the fresh carcasses, or when cleaning rabbits.) After the meat is properly cooked, the germ is *completely* harmless.

Squirrels

Squirrel shooting ranks right behind rabbit hunting in general popularity with the majority of small game hunters. While there is a great variety of squirrels scattered across the United States, the species most hunted are the gray, red and fox squirrels.

The gray squirrel is the most common and the one bagged by most hunters. He weighs about one to one and a half pounds and measures 18 to 20 inches long, of which about 9 inches is tail. The color of the fur changes with the seasons from a dark, rust-tinged gray in summer to a light silvery gray in winter. In some sections of our country and especially in Canada, a black color phase is known and he is often called a black squirrel. As a rule, gray

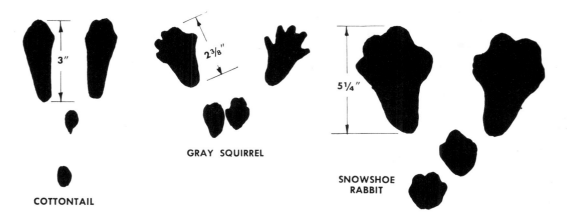

3″

2³⁄₈″

5¼″

GRAY SQUIRREL

COTTONTAIL

SNOWSHOE
RABBIT

Fig. 5.5 The tracks of a cottontail, gray squirrel, and a snowshoe rabbit. (Courtesy of Pennsylvania Game Commission)

squirrels prefer dense woods and heavy oak forest areas. It is the woodman's axe rather than the hunter's gun which has most effectively decreased the squirrel population in the United States.

The red squirrel, often called a chickaree squirrel, is fairly abundant in the forests of North America from coast to coast. He is smaller than the gray, averaging 12 inches in length, including the 4½-inch tail, and weighs about half a pound. He is lively, noisy and quarrelsome, and in the eastern part of his range usually drives away his big rivals. He feeds on pine cones and has the bad habit of robbing birds' nests of eggs and young. The fox squirrel is the largest—20 to 27 inches long, including a 12-inch tail. He weighs about two pounds. He is rusty to blackish in color and ranges throughout the United States. But, no matter which

Fig. 5.6 The gray squirrel. (Courtesy of Florida Game & Fresh Water Fish Commission)

squirrel species you may seek—and in 99 out of 100 cases it will be the gray—your hunting routine will be the same.

The first step is to locate an area where squirrels are known to feed and nest. This isn't usually too difficult since almost every oak or hickory grove in a forest will have its share of squirrels. A farm woodlot, even a fairly small one of just a few acres, if it happens to border a field in which corn is planted year after year, is another favorite location of squirrels. It isn't difficult either to tell if they're abundant in any given area. If they're present, the trees will be full of leaf nests, and holes and hollows will show evidence of use, the bark being smooth and fresh-worn. Tops of stumps will usually have bits of shucks or other cuttings lying on them where squirrels have paused to feed. And below tall trees or feeding trees there will be "cuttings," the refuse left from where squirrels overhead have shucked nuts or cut tender twigs. Also, where squirrels are abundant they are always heard, whether or not they are seen. They can't remain quiet very long, but must always be chattering among themselves, or sounding a warning to all their neighbors that an intruder is present. The best times of day to find squirrels are early morning right after dawn or late in the afternoon. Bright, warm days are also best, for during wet or cold weather they hesitate to leave their nests. Remember that squirrels in the wild aren't at all like their friendly brothers in the city parks. They're cautious and hard to see. When they're frightened—more by the sight of the hunter than the sound of his gun—they can do the disappearing act very quickly.

There are two methods generally employed to

Fig. 5.7 (Above) The results of a good day's squirrel shooting. (Courtesy of Florida Game & Fresh Water Fish Commission) Dogs (below) can be of great value when hunting squirrels. (Courtesy of Pennsylvania Game Commission)

hunt squirrels. In the first, often called the stand-hunting method, you find a grove of trees where the squirrels are working industriously at gathering their winter supplies of food. Move in quietly and find a vantage point where you can sit down and view the surrounding area without too much difficulty. While you'll scare off the squirrels when you first move in, if you remain as motionless and silent as possible, it won't take more than a few minutes for them to forget about you and go back to searching for food. Then you just sit tight until they come within range and pick them off one by one. Calling squirrels with a commercial caller is a good way to bring them closer, once you learn how to use it. For stand-hunting the .22 caliber rifle, equipped with scope sight—2 to 4 power—is the most popular gun. Either short, long, or long-rifle cartridges may be employed.

The second method is to still-hunt or stalk squirrels in their woodland homes. If you walk quietly through the woods, you'll be able to hear the faint rustlings which accompany the squirrel's search for food. You move toward the noise when the game is busy; stop when he stops, then move again, ever closer, until you're within gun range. Usually the squirrel will spot you when you're about 25 or 30 yards away—if you've made a good stalk—and he'll streak for the nearest tree, giving you a tricky shot while he's still on the ground or as he jumps from limb to limb, heading from his own den tree. For this type of shooting, the small-gauge shotgun—.410 being the most popular—is best. Use a fairly heavy shot, such as No. 5 or 6, because a squirrel's hide is tough to penetrate.

A few squirrel enthusiasts use a dog. Such a dog is trained to run through the woods and locate a tree with a squirrel in it, or to chase him up a tree. Some bark, while others just sit and look up a tree, to indicate that a squirrel is up in the tree. But remember that the major protection a squirrel has is his ability to hide. If no other hiding place is available, he'll usually lie close and flat against the trunk or branch of a tree. If you're going to be a successful squirrel hunter, you must teach yourself to look very carefully, realizing that squirrels can hide in places where it would seem impossible for them to be concealed. Luckily for the hunter—not for the squirrel—his tail will usually give him away.

Raccoons

Of all the mammals, the raccoon seems to get the most fun out of life and he can make life most interesting for the hunter. The raccoon, of which there are several subspecies, ranges from Maine to Florida, from Minnesota to the Gulf of Mexico, and even down into the Southwest. He is about the size of a small cocker spaniel; the roly-poly body is covered with thick gray-brown fur and a long, bushy tail ringed with black and white. There's a black mask across the eyes, and his narrow muzzle sprouts saucy whiskers. A full-grown coon may reach ten or twelve pounds, but eight pounds is nearer the average.

Since daytime is bedtime for the raccoon, he must be hunted during the nocturnal hours. The raccoon generally lives with his family in a hollow high in a tree trunk near a pond or stream. (A few will hole up in barns, sheds or abandoned buildings.) They generally eat crayfish, oysters, mussels, frogs and turtles, but are very fond of corn. If you can find a spot that combines a cornfield with a stream, lake or bog, you'll generally find raccoon present. In the North, they seem to prefer a field of standing corn, and this is a good point to start your hunt. In the South, the favorite coon areas are creek bottoms and swamps, where wild fruit, acorns, crawfish and frogs are plentiful. In the prairie country, cornfields and river bottoms are the hot spots.

Coon hunting depends completely on a dog or pack of dogs to track the game and bring him to

Fig. 5.8 The raccoon. (Courtesy of Florida Game & Fresh Water Fish Commission)

bay. That last is never an easy matter. Even though coons are super-abundant nowadays, they're remarkably versatile critters. They're fast afoot, they're excellent swimmers, they can climb trees as well as squirrels and an adult coon is a very formidable fighter. Usually the dogs are allowed to range at will over promising raccoon territory. You then just wait until you hear the melodious sound from your dog that he has treed a coon. You move as quickly as you can to this site and make the kill. Remember that shooting can be tricky in the wavering beam of a flashlight.

In addition to a dog or dogs, a rifle—a .22 caliber one is sufficient for the job—and ammunition, you need for success a three-cell flashlight with fresh batteries, loose, warm clothing, fair night vision, and good hearing. Thorough familiarity with the country you are going to hunt is a real asset, too. You may have hunted a forest for years by daylight, but after entering just the fringe of it at night, you will find you are completely lost.

Opossum

Another small game animal that is hunted at night is the opossum, or as he is better known—possum. He is found from Florida to New York, Texas and the Great Lakes to the Atlantic coast. When full grown, the opossum is about the size of a house cat. The head is small, but has long narrow jaws set with fifty teeth. He has two coats of fur; the inner coat is soft and short, and the outer is coarse, long and a grizzled gray in color. His tail is long and rat-like. The possum is a slow-moving animal and isn't particularly brilliant in his maneuvering when discovered. In other words, he's no raccoon in this sense.

During the day the opossum sleeps in a burrow, brush pile, hollow log or tree. At night it hunts in trees or on the ground for food. He grows fat from eating small birds, frogs, fish, eggs, insects and fruits. He climbs to the tips of branches to get mulberries, cherries and persimmons. Since he feeds on such a variety of fare, possum may be found almost anywhere from the chicken coop to water areas to a wild persimmon grove. The latter is a very good starting point for any possum hunt.

The equipment and requirements needed for a possum hunt are the same as when going cooning. Actually, the hunting technique for the two game animals is very similar, too. That is, you let your dog loose until he picks up the scent of a possum. You just wait until he barks the treed signal and then rush to the spot where he has his quarry up a tree. Once you reach the tree, you have a choice of sev-

Fig. 5.9 The opossum. (Courtesy of Florida Game & Fresh Water Fish Commission)

eral ways to bring him to bag. You either shake him from the tree (the dog or dogs should be tied up before attempting this), climb the tree and pull the possum down, knock him down with a long stick or pole or, of course, pick him off with your small-caliber rifle. But a *word of warning*: Remember that a peculiar trait is the opossum's trick of feigning death when cornered—of "playing possum." The possum falls on his side, often with eyes closed and tongue hanging out. If picked up or shaken from a tree and dropped from not too great a height, he will fall limp, remaining in this condition for many minutes. But the hunter or dog who turns his back, assuming that his prey is dead of heart failure, may turn again to find Mr. Possum gone.

Other small game animals such as muskrat, mink, porcupine, skunk, wolverine, weasel, badger, etc., are hunted in some states and are protected in others. Most of these animals are shot while out hunting for other game such as rabbits, squirrels or upland fowl. In other words, very few hunters go out specifically to hunt, say, skunks. Most skunks, being nocturnal creatures, are shot when hunters are going after raccoons or opossums. Before shooting any of these small game animals, be sure of the state's hunting regulations regarding them.

Field Dressing of Small Game

While more rabbits find their way into more game bags than any group of animals in the United States,
more abuse is heaped upon their little carcasses than all others combined. It's standard practice among a great many rabbit hunters, regardless of the weather, to pick up the freshly killed animal and stuff him into the back pocket of a waterproof hunting coat. Result? The intestinal juices drain into the flesh and the body heat begins rapid decomposition of the whole carcass.

Any rabbit or other small game killed with a shotgun will have the intestines pierced with much shot. Thus, if you want good fried rabbit it's smart to get those insides right out, aside from the fact that this reduces the carrying load. It's a simple matter. Just make a single cut from the brisket to the vent, pull loose the diaphragm walls, pull out the windpipe and gullet and the whole works will fall free. To complete the job it's best to split open the straddle by cutting through the pelvis, removing any droppings which may have lodged within.

In order to permit some dissipation of the body heat, stuff the cavity loosely with dry leaves or grass. When there's snow on the ground pack the cavity with it, allowing it to chill the flesh for a few minutes. Then shake it free and wipe out the cavity with a rag carried for this purpose. Some hunters remove the head and feet at this stage, saving weight.

Squirrels are also good subjects for this same treatment, and all game birds, with the possible exception of woodcock, quail and snipe, should be drawn as soon as they're taken and the cavities packed loosely with leaves, moss or grass.

After field dressing rabbits and birds, the game may be placed in a plastic translucent bag and, when wrapped thus, the meat will be kept clean and sweet, and the hunting coat will be free of soil marks. Plastic bags are common household articles. Daily, housewives purchase groceries packaged in plastic bags. Fresh vegetables and fruit are packaged in this manner to prevent dehydration and loss of vitamins and for ease in handling. Fortunately for hunters, an ample supply of clean plastic carriers are readily available. Three or four bags take up less room in the coat than a pack of cigarettes. Then in the field, separate pieces of game can be stored in each bag and later, at home, the containers can be discarded, or washed and dried for the next occasion. At the close of the season, the coat remains clean and free of bloodstains. The need to scrub the rubberlined pocket of your hunting coat with hot water, soap and detergent is eliminated.

Chapter Six

LEARNING TO HUNT BIG GAME ANIMALS

THE HUNTING OF big game animals is a sport completely in a class by itself. It is the most exciting of all gunning sport simply because of the sheer size of the trophy. But to obtain your prize, rugged stalking, physical discomfort, expense, time, heartbreak and even personal danger are involved. The trophy that represents the sum total of items, however, is well worth it all for any *real* hunter.

To hunt big game, unless you're *completely* and *thoroughly* familiar with the countryside in which they reside, the services of a professional guide or outfitter is a *must* prerequisite. To obtain a list of guides and outfitters in a given area, write to the agency (listed in the Appendix) of the state or province in which you intend to hunt. From this list, select and write to several outfitters, requesting such data as cost of a hunt, type of hunting trips conducted, description of the region they hunt, type of accommodations they have, what equipment you must bring, things you can do and see in addition to hunting the game you're after and dates available for hunts. After receiving their answers, you can then select the outfitter or guide who meets your requirements best and request a firm booking, sending the deposit required. Average cost for hunting pack trips ranges from $25 to $50 a day per person, which includes everything. But remember that no reliable guide will ever guarantee you a kill. Most will show you the game; from there, you take over. In the normal course of events, your chances of taking game on one of these hunting trips are about fifty-fifty.

Of all the big game mentioned in this chapter, the exception to the rule about hiring a guide is when going after deer. The reason for this is that deer are available almost anywhere on the North American continent. Therefore, to teach yourself how to hunt big game animals, it's best to start with deer. Then, once you have learned the principles of this phase of the sport of big game hunting, you

can, if you wish, go after such big fellows as moose, elk, caribou, mountain sheep, bear, mountain goat, etc.

Deer

The deer family includes about sixty species, ranging in size from the huge Canadian moose down to the Chilean pudu, which is almost as small as a rabbit. The best known of the hunted larger species—the moose, the elk and the caribou—are fully discussed later in this chapter. Here, we concern ourselves with how to hunt the three common species of the whitetail deer, the mule deer and the blacktail deer.

WHITETAIL DEER

Greatest of all the big game species, from the standpoint of nationwide distribution and the number of hunters to whom they offer sport, is the whitetail deer. They are found almost everywhere in the United States, excepting the Pacific seaboard and the arid wastelands of Utah and Nevada. They are also abundant across southern Canada to the Rockies.

The whitetail normally is a shy, timid animal, given to hiding in thick, brushy woods and swamps to avoid his enemies. Although often bold during the "rutting" or mating season, the buck is usually more wary than the doe. When startled, he "blows." This is a whistling sound which, in many instances, seems to be an involuntary warning to other deer in the area. He then takes off in a spurt of speed, which has been estimated to be as much as 40 miles per hour. The first rush seems to be a combination of four or five leaps followed by a great, high jump, often covering from 15 to 20 feet. The natural gait is a smooth-paced trot, at a speed ranging from 10 to 20 miles per hour. The whitetail is an excellent swimmer and, like other members of the deer family, the winter coat has air-filled hairs which enable it to

Fig. 6.1 Pack hunting trip on the move to the big game hunting grounds (above) and the return back to the main base with success (below). Note the antlers on the back of the second horse. (Both photos courtesy of Bill Browning, Montana Chamber of Commerce)

ride fairly high in the water. The summer coat isn't so buoyant. A deer can swim a steady four miles per hour and has confidence in its ability in the water. Although the whitetail's vision is far from good, he can pick up a movement at considerable distance. Nature, to atone for the poor vision, has given the deer an excellent and keen sense of smell and hearing.

The whitetail isn't migratory, and most of his traveling is done over a half-mile radius, except that bucks, during the rutting season, often travel more extensively in their search for does. The whitetail is even-hoofed, with a narrow heel and a typical white band above each hoof. The color of both male and female is similar, and normally there are two seasonal variations. The summer coat is a reddish brown and the winter coat is a dull brown with a blue or gray tinge. The buck sheds his antlers each year, usually by late December. The new antlers begin showing in early May, when food is once more abundant, and the excess vitality from eager eating goes into this new bony growth, which in early development is soft and filled with blood. The growing antlers are covered by a soft velvety coat and when fully formed the velvet is rubbed off by scraping on shrubs and small tree trunks. This usually also rubs the bark off these small trees, and these "antler scrapes" are used by hunters as "buck signs." The famous trademark of this deer is his white tail-flag.

Fig. 6.2 Typical hunting camp on a big game hunting trip (above) and the food looks mighty good, too (below). (Both photos courtesy of Bill Browning, Montana Chamber of Commerce)

Fig. 6.3 The whitetail deer.

There are about nine subspecies of whitetail deer, from the large northern whitetail to the diminutive key deer in Florida. The mature male northern or Virginia whitetail will weigh between 150 to 300 pounds on the hoof. Those on the heavy end of the scale are few and far between. It would be better to say that the average is closer to the lower limit of 150 pounds. There are, of course, exceptions. For example, some tremendous whitetails have been shot in Maine—deer that have weighed over 400 pounds.

Except for the winter season, and the limitations fixed by a specific range, food is seldom a problem to the whitetail, for it has a goat-like appetite and will eat almost anything that is green. In the summer food includes grasses, leaves of shrubs and trees, roots, twigs and aquatic plants. In the fall he particularly favors apples and acorns, and in winter seeks out evergreens, with honeysuckle and rhododendron ranking high in choice. The highest rate of mortality occurs in the early spring, when the deer is weakened from the hard winter. When crowded, deer will eat the available food supply and then starve rather than move on to a new area. Since a deer is nocturnal, and does much of his feeding and traveling at night, it's apparent that two of the best periods for hunting are at daylight and dusk. You can then often catch your deer in the open "edge" country, at the beginning or end of such periods of movement. In daytime hunting, the whitetail is ordinarily brushed-up.

There are three basic techniques employed in hunting whitetails: 1) still-hunting, 2) driving and 3) shooting from a stand. Each has advantages and each has a place in the deer hunting picture. While still-hunting and shooting from a stand can be accomplished by a lone hunter, the driving method requires several hunters.

When shooting from a stand, you let, in effect, the deer hunt himself. In short, you plan to put yourself at some particular spot where at some time during the day your deer will either be found or will pass by. This method requires a thorough knowledge of the terrain. You must know where they are during the hours you'll be hunting, the trails they use, the areas on which they feed and the possibilities of other hunters moving game toward yourself. On the basis of such familiarity, you then post yourself at a likely spot and wait for Mr. Whitetail to make his appearance.

Shooting from a stand, often called runway watching, is most likely to produce right after daylight and just before dusk, when deer are going back to cover or moving out to feed. They love to travel the same old wood or logging roads and trails. There's hardly a well-used trail in good whitetail country which deer don't travel of their own accord at least once every two or three days, and usually more often than that. This is especially true in areas where there are enough hunters afield to keep them moving whether they want to or not. Usually under such conditions, a deer rarely can hole up in thick brush all day without somebody disturbing him and as soon as he runs, in spite of his care, chances are good that he may blunder into a hunter or a stand.

spooked a deer that would have walked up to him in a few more minutes. Remember that when the opportunity for a shot does come, move slowly. Many a whitetail has lived to tantalize another hunter, another day, just because the hunter, after an all-day wait, swung his rifle up too quickly and the deer spotted him.

Driving of whitetails is a form of hunting popular in the South and East. A drive can be staged by as few as three or as many as 50, though a dozen-man party is typical. The leader of the drive stations some hunters "on stand." The locations for the stands should be determined well in advance from a knowledge of the country, the areas where deer are apt to go, or runways that have proven good on previous drives. Spots such as canyon apexes, low saddles between drainages, ridges and logging roads or trails are good for deer stands. The number of hunters put on stands is dependent upon the over-all number of hunters, the amount of country to be covered and upon the deer population of the area. If you're

BUCK RUBS

Fig. 6.4 Signs of growing antlers. (Both drawings courtesy of Pennsylvania Game Commission)

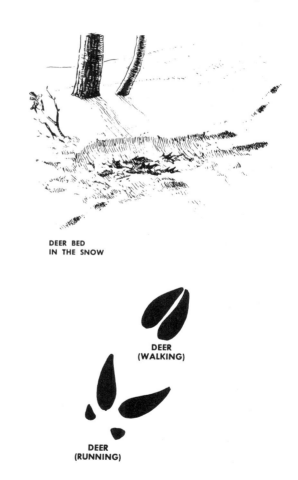

DEER BED
IN THE SNOW

DEER
(WALKING)

DEER
(RUNNING)

Good spots to watch are runways along the edge of a swamp or thick cover. In some southern states, many hunters take their stands in a tree and watch for deer. This is extremely effective. It gets one's scent off the ground, and besides, animals traveling along seldom, if ever, look up. In many states, however, this kind of hunting is illegal. Once you have chosen your location, conceal yourself as best you can and be sure to remain still. If the cold becomes unbearable, light a small fire. Deer pay little attention to smoke unless they smell it, and if they do that, they'll smell you too and the fire will make no difference. Many successful hunters do all their runway watching in cold weather beside a cozy little fire. But you must be patient and resist the temptation to wander. Many a hunter has left his stand and

Fig. 6.5 Deer signs you should look for. (Both drawings courtesy of Pennsylvania Game Commission)

placed on a stand for a drive, select an inconspicuous place to stand or sit down where you have good observation, and remain absolutely still. Don't quit your stand until you know your hunting partners have finished the drive.

All hunters not placed on stands become beaters or drivers. Their purpose is, of course, to drive any deer out of the cover and toward the gunners on the stand. Though most deer taken on drives are killed by the standers, if you're a beater don't overlook the likelihood that you may have some shooting. Gun-wise old bucks often skulk quietly around a beater or slip through a gap in the line, circle back and hole up in the same area from which they were just driven. Successful standers on one drive become beaters on the next if the hunting party is well organized.

One of the major drawbacks of this method of deer hunting is its inherent danger. Despite the conscientious regard of every hunter for the safety of himself and others, the necessary quick shooting by a number of hunters in a small area is an ever-present hazard. The beaters sometimes come across the countryside in an uproar of noise and calls. This is partly to scare up the deer, and partly to let the men on stand know that the hunters are drawing near, and to hold their fire.

Still-hunting is really a misnomer because in it you move about, moseying through the woods, following a track at times, pausing now and then. The first fundamental of still-hunting is to watch the wind. Hunt into it, across it, or on any angle the terrain and cover make necessary. But never hunt with it. If there's too little wind to determine its direction, toss up a handful of crumbled dry leaves or grass, or light a cigarette and watch its smoke. Also remember that wind can change direction rather quickly, especially in mountain country. Almost any game animal, especially deer, will scent you a quarter of a mile away if the wind is right.

The second fundamental is to move slowly and carefully, being careful not to break any limbs underfoot or allow swinging branches to pop against your clothing. Weather has much to do with still-hunting success. There's little use trying it on dry, still, crisp days when dead leaves crackle underfoot. Rain or wet snow, plus a light wind, are ideal. As you move along, make frequent stops. If there's wind to cover your movements, take a step or two when it sighs in the trees. When it dies away, stand still. Halt at the tops of ridges, rims of ravines, edges of thickets and borders of clearings. Look over every foot ahead before you move on; wait long enough to give a deer a chance to show himself. Remember

Fig. 6.6 A hunter stalking a deer (above) and the reward that all deer hunters want (below). (Both photos courtesy of Bill Browning, Montana Chamber of Commerce)

that it's not the amount of country you cover that brings success, but the care and skill you use in getting over the terrain.

Get into the deer country at daybreak. The game is up then in search of food. If you find fresh tracks in the snow, a little study of the trail will determine if the deer are feeding or traveling. Note the direction of the tracks and what the game is feeding on, then make a short circle. Feeding whitetails make some noise, but much less than you would expect. You'll seldom see them in the clear. Look for the flick of an ear, the twitch of a tail, or the movement of a leg. Sit still when in good country or look for a movement or pattern of color that doesn't seem natural. You may spot the nose of a buck thrusting at you around a tree or see a bush twitch as the deer browses. During and just before the rut, you also will find the bucks rubbing their horns on the trees and small brush. If you're above them, as you should be when possible, you can easily locate their whereabouts by the flick of a brushtop on which they're rubbing their antlers.

The deer won't become frightened until it sees you move. For that reason, you should try to act like a deer, moving from cover to cover, never hastily. You should try at all times, however, to be in the clear for a quick shot, and not to get entangled in brush or anything else that restricts your arms and vision. Your rifle should be carried in the ready position, muzzle to the front, left hand grasping the forearm, right hand ready to turn off the safety or cock the hammer. If you're startled by a slight movement, or a noise such as that of a deer getting up from his bed or jumping, you must look first to be absolutely sure that the object is a legal deer and not a man or domestic animal. Then push the rifle straight forward, muzzle pointing towards the deer, butt close under the shoulder, at the same time throwing the safety off. Follow the deer with the front sight, and when he passes or jumps through a fairly open place between trees, in almost one motion raise the butt to the shoulder, drop the head into the line of aim, put the front sight on the lower front portion of its chest, and squeeze the trigger, much like shooting a shotgun at a bird going straight away. Generally speaking you'll have about twice the time you would have in bird shooting. But don't be discouraged if you are unable to get your sights on the deer, or don't have time to shoot. A shot at a deer jumping through thick woods is very difficult. Probably your successful shot will be at a deer that is just sneaking off at a walk, or at one that is moving and not aware of your presence. These are easy shots. Above all be absolutely certain that you're shooting at a legal deer, and not at a human being. You may only have five or six seconds to make this identification, but you must be certain, or don't shoot.

In whitetail hunting where short-range shooting in heavy cover is the rule, the carbine is usually the weapon of choice. Short-barreled and light, it's easy to handle in dense woodland. While any caliber between .30 and 8-mm. is suitable, the widest preference is concentrated around the .30/30, .30/06, .32, .300, .35, .308, or .348. For whitetail shooting, many prefer open or peep sights. Also, in use in certain areas, shotguns, loaded with buckshot or rifled slugs, are employed. While many states impose the shotgun on deer hunters by law, it's doubtful if it weren't for this whether it would be used too much. A 12-gauge gun is most efficient, loaded with 00 buckshot or rifled slug. Buckshot is a reasonably good killer up to 50 or 60 yards, while 100 yards is considered maximum effective range of the rifled slug.

MULE DEER

Muleys are western deer. They range from the Dakotas and northwest Texas west throughout the Rockies, south well down into Mexico, and north well up into the central Canadian provinces. These deer, however, aren't very plentiful far from the eastern foothills of the Rockies, although you'll find them clear to the West Coast, where they mingle with their cousins, the blacktail and, occasionally, the whitetail. Unlike the latter, which prefer heavily wooded and brushy country, the mule deer's domain is sparsely timbered, rugged mountain terrain, cut with ravines and gullies.

The muley is darker in general color than the whitetail, and the buck's antlers are unlike his eastern cousin's in that they don't branch from a main beam. Instead, they're bifurcated, separating into tines, or points, often "every which way." Often twenty or more points will be found on a monstrous old buck. Two other distinguishing marks are the muley's tail and ears. A mule deer's ears are unusually large, giving rise to his name of mule deer. His tail, instead of being a sizeable flag, is an insignificant little rope, ending in a tassel of black hairs. The metatarsal, or musk glands, on a mule deer's legs are much larger than those of a whitetail. The muley on the average stands a little higher and, on the average, runs heavier than the whitetail. There are also about nine subspecies of mule deer, and like the whitetail they vary in weight.

Mule deer hunting may be either stalking or still-hunting. If the big deer are unmolested and not wild, very often they bed in some tiny patch of redbrush

Fig. 6.7 The mule deer. (Courtesy of U.S. Fish and Wildlife Service)

out on open sidehills in the sun. Sometimes they even bed in some tall clump of sagebrush. If hunted hard, they take to the dense lodgepole on the north slopes for their bed grounds. After the fall rains, if the weather is warm, the big deer will simply stay on the north slopes eating mushrooms. As a rule, mule deer are more easily hunted than whitetails, owing to their love of the open sidehills of the mountains, and their peculiar habit of bouncing straight up and down when they have been scared but haven't yet seen you. They bound high, look for you, and snort or whistle like a whitetail. When jumped from their beds or feed grounds, they usually go off in very high bouncing jumps, and come down with each jump with the front legs stiff, then bound high again over the tops of small brush or logs.

Mule deer are nocturnal, but continue their feeding and moving about well into the day. At sunup mule deer like to be on the sunny slopes, just under a ridge, possibly for the mild warmth. Within two or three hours, they mosey on over the ridge to shade up for the day in the timber of north slopes. Canyon apexes are fine places to hunt, especially if two partners hunt together. Each takes a side, slowly working out the hillsides, and converging at the apex or saddle. Any muley in the gulley is apt to be not at the very bottom but on one slope or the other. If the animals are approached with skill, they often are within shooting range before being spooked. If alerted, they may be depended on to move to higher ground, either up one of the canyon sides or towards the apex, where the hunter may get his shot in the open, just as they top out. Dusk is another good time to hunt mule deer. At this period, they again move out from shade to begin feeding. The big drawback to hunting at this later period is that mule deer country is ordinarily big country and, this late in the day, you're apt to be far from your camp and won't get in if you hunt too late.

Stalking and still-hunting are very similar and, actually, the major difference is that in stalking you're on the actual trail of an animal, while still-hunting is more or less a trial-and-error method. But the basic technique is very much the same.

The most favorable time for stalking deer is right after a light snowfall. Not only will you be able to track your quarry in the snow, but you'll experience less difficulty in doing so with a minimum of noise. If you teach yourself to walk slowly and quietly, listening carefully and looking several times at everything you suspect might be a deer, you'll see most of the deer before they discover you. It gives you a chance to size up a buck before you shoot: his weight, pace, physical condition and sex can be determined, if you use the old Indian prescription for hunting deer. The more deer you see, the more skilled you'll become at hunting and the more particular you can afford to be about what muley's head hangs in your trophy room.

In mountain stalking it's often possible to have the rays of the rising sun at your back. This is a great help; deer, apparently, see no more easily than man into the direct rays of the sun. Likewise, a sunset at your back will make it hard for the game to see you. Since man is most conspicuous when his figure stands out against the sky, the stalker should cautiously avoid exposing himself on a sky line. In looking over a ridge into a high basin, crawl up to the top, remove your hat, and if possible, peer through scrub bush or a crack in the rocks, inspecting everything carefully before exposing another inch of your head. Repeat this process until either you spot your muley or know that it's not there. A small bush or other growth often will afford something to look through, and may even be carried in the hand and held before the face as you peep over. Remember that the face reflects light like a mirror, and the deer will see it instantly if the sun is on you.

If a mule deer is jumped, like most other species of deer, he often runs a wide circle, only to wind up in cover a few hundred yards or so from his original point of departure. In such a case, you may use almost the same technique employed when hunting rabbits, except on a more grandiose scale. That is, if you fail to get off a shot after jumping a muley, you may still be able to get him by advancing a few hundred yards past the jumping point, find a slight rise and wait for him to return. Even if the deer doesn't circle back before nightfall, chances are very good that he'll be feeding in the same general locale on the next day.

Some hunters call deer with deer calls. The Alaskan natives and sourdoughs call them with a blade of coarse marsh grass held between their palms and blow on it to form a bleat that can't be heard very far, yet is effective. Others call deer at times just before the rut by rattling a pair of horns together, when a curious young buck may come close to investigate. Commercial deer callers are now on the market.

Experienced mule deer hunters are choosy when they select their equipment. Included will be a rifle which fires a high-speed bullet that has a flat trajectory over long range. The most popular calibers are .30/06, .270, .300 and .250/3,000 Savage. A majority of these rifles will be scope-sighted, usually with 2½- or 4-power scopes. A rifle of this kind in the hands of a good hunter will consistently kill deer at ranges up to 300 yards—sometimes farther. The mountain hunter needs a good binocular. Many a small buck and some big ones, too, have gone their way unmolested because their antlers couldn't be seen with the naked eye. This is particularly true in the dim light of morning and evening. Compact 6-power binoculars are adequate and easiest to carry. More powerful glasses, up to 9 x 35, do a fine job but are bigger and heavier as the power increases. Glasses larger than 9 x 35 are impractical.

BLACKTAIL DEER

This deer is often called the Columbian blacktail or coast deer, and inhabits a well-defined, limited range along the Pacific coast from midway in California to Sitka, Alaska. He has bifurcated antlers, and his tail is wide, black on top throughout its length, with a white border, white beneath, and held straight up like that of the whitetail, when running. The blacktail is approximately the same size and color (he's sometimes darker and has a black swath along the back) as the whitetail, and his preference of habitat is similar to his eastern cousin. That is, the black-

Fig. 6.8 The results of a good shot—a big buck. (Courtesy of Bill Browning, Montana Chamber of Commerce)

tail usually sticks to the brushy and thickly forested sections which have clearings and openings in which he may feed. Because of this, the same hunting techniques and armaments employed for whitetails may be used for the blacktails.

Moose

The lordly moose is the world's largest member of the deer family. An average bull moose will weigh from 1,000 to 1,110 pounds and a *really* big one may exceed 1,800. Actually, among the herbivorous animals of the world, only the elephant, rhinoceros, hippopotamus, American bison, gaur and the Cape buffalo of Africa weigh more. Not only is the moose a heavy animal, but he's also a tall and seemingly ungainly one. From the ground to the tips of his antlers he usually measures about ten feet. He has a formidable appearance no matter how or when you meet him. A moose can also often be dangerous, because of his inclination to charge a hunter. As a matter of record, several hunters have been killed by moose.

Unlike the smaller species of deer, the moose doesn't accept civilization. With settlement of the east, his numbers were sharply reduced, and with the push westward, he retreated farther north. Today moose range over most of Canada and Alaska, as far north as timber grows. A thin arm of moose population also extends southward into Wyoming, Idaho and Montana.

The typical habitat of the moose is rolling, timbered country that is wildly punctuated with swampy meadows, or muskeg, and unnamed lakes and meandering creeks. His food is comprised chiefly of lilypads, and the buds and twigs of maple, willow, alder, poplar and other trees that afford convenient browse. Moose beds are to be found on grassy knolls and in tangled windfall country.

There are two common ways of hunting moose: stalking them on foot or still-shooting them from a canoe. The early part of the hunting season often finds the bulls still frequenting the shores of wilderness waters, and the noiseless glide of a canoe can be a definite advantage in effecting a quiet approach. But when the rutting or mating season comes, the bulls, in a belligerent mood, roam the forests into higher country in search of their mates. Here they are best hunted by stalking on foot, and the great problem is to move without undue noise through what may be a dry Indian summer woods, for, while the moose's sight is comparatively dull, his hearing and sense of smell are supremely acute.

A mighty bull, in spite of his great weight, can

Fig. 6.9 The biggest of all deer—the moose. (Both photos courtesy of U.S. Fish and Wildlife Service)

move without sound through the forest, but generally he's careless with his massive headgear, and one may hear for more than a half mile the clack of antlers against dry branches. In soft earth or snow the track of a bull, often six inches in length, is easy to follow; a persistent stalker is frequently rewarded with a shot, for sooner or later a moose will wander across a muskeg or down to a lake shore. By the track alone you can't always be certain of the moose's sex, but broken lower branches and scraped bark may mark the passage of antlers. Except in the matter of size, the moose track may well be compared to that of a deer.

When bulls are frequenting an area, you may observe young trees with scarred and shredded bark where antlers have been rubbed to remove the velvet. Too, there is the wallow which the bull digs with his hoofs and in which he divests himself during the mating period. Thus it is possible for the normally acute human nose to pick up a bull's scent when he's upwind or has passed through a thicket where the air is still. Some woodsmen compare this scent to the odor of stale tobacco. Like deer, moose sometimes will circle back to check up on a stalker.

Experienced moose hunters and guides often employ a birch-bark call, which simulates the call of a cow, to call bulls fairly late in the season, after they are fully in rut. While young bulls may rush to the call, the wiser, older males will approach carefully, if at all.

In mountainous country, moose are often spotted with binoculars at great distances, then stalked on foot or horseback. The hunter will post himself on top of a ridge, or basin-rim, and thoroughly glass every inch of country below. Moose in such country, especially as they move about at daylight and dusk, are easily spotted for they are the blackest objects in the woods. Binoculars are good, too, for determining the size and quality of the trophy's antlers. When you're shooting for an outstanding trophy, many beasts may have to be studied before the desired one is found.

Considering his great bulk and strength, a moose isn't an especially hard animal to kill, but just the same there are as many varied opinions on the correct caliber of rifle for moose as there are moose hunters. Actually most hunters wind up using a .30/06 in one model or another because it certainly does the job. But the .270 is also more than adequate and so is the .280. Add also the .300 Savage, .308, .348 Winchester, .35 Remington, .300 Magnum and even the Army surplus .30/40. The con-

Fig. 6.10 The elk. (Courtesy of U.S. Fish and Wildlife Service)

trolled expansion bullet weighing from 170 to 220 grains will be satisfactory. Those employing .270 for big game, such as the moose, consider that the 150-grain bullet does the best job. Regardless of the rifle you use, be sure it's equipped with a good 2½- or 4-power scope sight.

Elk

The second largest member of the deer family is the elk, more accurately known as the wapiti. The bull elk is about five feet in height at the shoulders and may weigh from 600 to 800 pounds. His head, neck and chest are dark brown; the rest of the body is pale brown except for a large gray-white patch on the rump. His backward-sweeping antlers have a spread of three to five feet, with five to seven points on each branch.

Elk once wandered over most of the United States and southern Canada. After the continent was settled they disappeared in the East, but they're still plentiful in the Rocky Mountains. Actually, they are becoming more numerous through the years and recently have reached the point where their increase is limited only by the carrying capacity of available winter range. Wyoming has the largest herd, closely followed by Montana, Idaho, Colorado, Oregon, New Mexico, Washington, Arizona and California. Actually, eleven states and two Canadian provinces now permit elk hunting within their boundaries. Since most of the herds are rather carefully controlled, you must watch the various state game laws for open seasons from year to year.

Generally speaking, elk are timber animals. They feed, move about and are found in the openings adjacent to heavy timber at the daylight and dusk periods of the day. For the daytime hours they seek out the most impenetrable tangles of blow-down, thick alder and cool shade imaginable. But this species of deer is migratory in that it follows a changing food supply and will shift with seasonal temperature changes. In summer, elk range high into the mountain crags and upper timberline to escape the heat. As the late fall snows begin, they move from the higher lands to the valley for their winter range.

Elk are the most polygamous of deer and the bulls will have harems of up to a dozen or more cows, depending upon their ability to hold them against the invasion of other bulls. During the rutting season in the fall, fights between the bulls are common. They challenge one another with a far-reaching "bugle call"—a high-pitched trumpeting that slides down the scale into a deep roar. The two animals face each other about 20 feet apart, paw the ground and then crash together. Bellowing with rage, they repeat this again and again, until the weaker one goes down. Rarely is the loser killed, but occasionally the antlers of the fighters lock together and both die of starvation.

There are two basic ways in which elk are brought to gun: still-hunting and stalking. The latter is the most popular and many experienced stalkers can catch their prey unaware, take deliberate aim and fire at medium range of 150 to 200 yards. To locate where the elk are, check for tracks, droppings, bed forms and, above all, the bulls' bugling. Once your objective is sighted, make your approach downwind —the elk's sense of smell is extremely keen—and with the least possible noise. Elk seem to be able to spot you even more readily than do deer. What's more, if they get spooked, they leave, and do it in a hurry. This is one of the greater differences between their behavior and that of deer. While deer may circle, and even when they do pull out not go far from their familiar neighborhood, elk high-tail it, and keep going, not hundreds of yards but miles. You can pick up tracks and trail, if you want to tramp five, eight, maybe ten miles, but if you're in "elk territory" it's a better bet to work it, trying to find another band. In stalking elk, as with any other game, go slow, stop often, stand still with some timber screening you if convenient, and look and look for the slightest movement.

The characteristic of elk to spook very easily and to keep on traveling almost completely eliminates the possibility of driving them, as you may with deer. The one way in which an elk may be brought to you in a stand is by calling him. Most elk "bugles" are made of seasoned bamboo and, after a great deal of practice, you can teach yourself the thrilling, pealing call of the bull elk. To have your bugling efforts successful, you must be in elk territory at daybreak. (The bull usually bugles from daybreak till about nine o'clock in the morning, then remains quiet for the rest of the day.) Once you have concealed yourself on a ridge overlooking a canyon, basin, or drainage apex, give out with the bugle call. If after a wait of at least ten minutes there's no answer, give another call. If you've made the shrill call authentic, and if there's a bull in the canyon below you, or within a half-mile or more, he'll usually answer—a challenging, angered battle-cry, which at a great distance is quite like a pealing whistle. That's all you need. You mark down the location, then slowly and skillfully stalk to within shooting range. In some instances, it's possible the bull will come to you.

Elk are tough, big beasts and the bulls are espe-

Fig. 6.11 Four different poses that any elk hunter would like to see. (All photos courtesy of Bill Browning, Montana Chamber of Commerce)

Fig. 6.12 Caribou. (Courtesy of U.S. Fish and Wildlife Service)

cially hard to put down for keeps. The three most effective spots for placing your bullet are in this order: the neck—and you hope you break it—the front shoulder and the spine. Any other shot, even a fatal one, may entail a man-killing session of tracking in roughest country, for an elk can take plenty of lead and carry it miles before he drops.

When going elk hunting, never go under-gunned. Each year the .30/06 kills more elk than any other caliber—with either the 180- or 220-grain bullet. The .348 packs wallop enough for elk but, although it's fine for timber shooting, it's not a long-range weapon. The .270, with 150-grain bullet, still has enough penetration for quick kills, and the .300 Magnum is probably the best long-range rifle you can possibly employ. Always check with state regulations to see if there are any firearms restrictions for elk hunting. Your rifle should be equipped with a 2½- or 4-power telescopic sight.

Caribou

There are three important species of caribou, all more or less alike except in general coloring and in size: the small, light-gray barren-ground caribou of the Far North; the woodland caribou of the more easterly regions of Canada, including Newfoundland; and the mountain, or giant, caribou which ranges along the Rockies and neighboring highlands from Alaska through Canada and has been observed as far south as Montana. The mountain caribou bulls sometimes approach 700 pounds in live weight, and their heads are the most desirable trophies of all the mentioned species of caribou. The mountain caribou prefers the park-like plateaus just below the timberline. His food consists, primarily, of ground moss and the moss which festoons the lower branches of trees. In color he is a dark gray, sometimes almost black, except for the throat and rump. The older bulls can frequently be identified at a considerable distance by the predominance of white on their necks. The woodland caribou is smaller in size, ranging from 300 to 400 pounds, and lighter in coloration. As its name implies, it is found in forest regions at much lower altitudes than the mountain species.

The track of the caribou can't be confused with that of any other member of the deer family, for it's extremely large and spreading, sometimes appearing almost like twin half moons an inch or two apart. By virtue of these "web feet" the animal is able to tread with safety on spongy ground where a man wouldn't dare venture. Unlike other members of the deer family, both males and females have large irregularly branching antlers, but these are smaller and more slender in the females. During the rut, which begins shortly before the first of October, each herd of cows and calves is dominated by a single bull, although many of the finest specimens may be seen traveling alone. Caribou are, of course, distinctly migratory animals, but the giant species may spend the entire year within limits of certain plateaus no greater than 30 or 40 miles in extent.

A characteristic which should be emphasized to the hunter is the super vitality of the giant caribou. He'll keep his feet and travel a long way after receiving a shock that would have put a moose to earth. In addition, a wounded or frightened caribou differs from his cousins in that he generally seeks fancied security in the heights, after the manner of a mountain goat. Consequently, you need a caliber in the neighborhood of the .30/06, .358, or .300 with a load perhaps of a 150- to 180-grain bullet. Remember that the rifle you employ should be capable of firing a high-velocity load with flat trajectory and it should be equipped with telescopic sights.

Caribou are sometimes called stupid, although the old-time hunters prefer to call it curiosity, which prompts these creatures to stand and watch a human being as he approaches in plain sight. But once let them catch man scent, and they may travel for miles without stopping and not return to the scene of their fright for perhaps a year. Therefore, you must plan your stalking route very carefully to keep you downwind and out of the intended victim's sight. To select your victim, inspect the herd from a downwind vantage point with binoculars and, once you pick him out, move in on him. When stalking your prize, keep a watchful eye on the older cows that may be wandering about and feeding several feet away from him, for it generally is a cow that gives the danger signal and starts the herd moving. Once your prize caribou is within range, shoot, if possible, when he is faced two-thirds broadside. Aim high and at a point just behind the shoulder. A bullet well-placed through the shoulder, heart and lungs generally brings the caribou to earth quickly. Head shots should be avoided, not only because they sometimes fail to put him down, but also because you might damage your trophy pair of antlers.

Bear

The bears of North America constitute four distinct

Fig. 6.13 A caribou migration. (Courtesy of National Film Board)

and easily recognized species: black bear, grizzly bear, Alaska brown bear and polar bear. This family includes the largest of all flesh-eating land animals in the world. Lions rarely weigh as much as 500 pounds and the biggest tigers stop short of 600 pounds, but the polar bear and the grizzly may weigh as much as 900 or 1,000 pounds. The great Alaskan brown bear has been known to scale 1,500 or 1,600 pounds. Though they're classed as flesh-eaters, their teeth are suitable for either tearing flesh or grinding vegetable food, and their diet is likely to include grass, grain, nuts, roots, fruit, grubs, insects, snails, crabs, frogs, snakes, eggs, fish—almost anything, in fact, that is eaten by any animal. Most bears are especially fond of ants and of honey.

Bears seem clumsy creatures. This is due to their peculiar gait. In the first place, bears are "plantigrade" or flat-footed; the heel of the foot rests on the ground like a man's. In the second place, they move both legs on one side of the body forward at the same time. This gives them a rolling motion. In spite of the apparent clumsiness, the black bear can be extremely fleetfooted when occasion demands, and it takes a special breed of hound dog to keep up the chase long enough to run him down. Even so, a bear race usually lasts from several hours to two days, and when the bear is finally cornered it may kill several of the hounds that venture too close. It can stand on its hind legs and strike out like a cat with its powerful front paws.

All species of bear are more or less individualists, and therefore are potentially dangerous. As a rule, the black bear generally detours at the scent of man, but this is not necessarily true of the Alaskan brown or the grizzly. Both of these animals are accustomed to being king of all they survey, and quite often resent the arrival of anything that threatens their rule. In most instances, if they receive a whiff of man scent, they'll circle around, look the situation over carefully and decide to avoid the intruder if he'll keep out of their way. But, should they confront a hunter at close range, anything can happen and usually does. If the first shot fired by the hunter be a hurried one, he may find himself in a rather dangerous situation.

Any bear wounded or brought to bay is a dangerous antagonist. While few sportsmen would consider going off and leaving wounded game, the hunter with a wounded bear in thick cover is foolhardy if he goes in that cover after the animal. The best bet is to locate a vantage point that will permit you to overlook the exit points, and if the day is well on, wait until the following morning before taking up the trail again. Even the black bear can be a mean

Fig. 6.14 The black bear. (Top photo, courtesy of Florida Game & Fresh Water Fish Commission; bottom photo, courtesy of Montana Fish and Game Commission)

customer in thick cover, if wounded. As for the Alaskan brown or the grizzly, a hunter who pushes through a thicket after wounding one of these bears wants to commit suicide.

Most wild bears hibernate from two to six months, even in warm climates where food is plentiful the year round. The winter quarters may be a cave, the base of a hollow tree, or a den that the bear scoops out for itself. Some states and provinces have both a fall and a spring (before and after hibernation) bear season, a few don't protect bears at all and in some localities, where bears have multiplied to the point of becoming pests, hunters are encouraged to shoot them at any time of year. The majority of bears are killed, however, by moose, caribou, or deer hunters when one happens to stumble over a watcher on his stand or when a stalker is on his move.

BLACK BEAR

The black bear range includes almost the entire North American continent, except in the extreme north, and they exist wherever there's extensive forest land sufficient to shelter them. They aren't gregarious but are solitary animals, and except for a female with her cubs, it's unusual to see more than one black bear at a time. In the fall when the coat of the bear is at its best, the fur is entirely black except for a brown patch on the muzzle and an occasional white spot on the breast. Its senses of hearing and smell are very keen and enable it to avoid enemies. The least suspicious sound or odor is sufficient to start him from his lair, and it requires a skillful hunter to run him down or approach within rifle range. A large black bear may weigh 500 pounds or more, but the average weight is much less. The average adult black bear is about 60 inches in length and stands 30 inches high at the shoulder.

There are several characteristics of a bear which, if interpreted in conjunction with the country he inhabits, will give the hunter a clue as to how to hunt for him. For one thing, a bear likes berries—service berries, elderberries, huckleberries, wild raspberries and the berries of mountain ash. Similarly, bears will work whole hillsides, once they find grubs or numerous rotten logs filled with ants. And though bruin is a great traveler, he will often return to such areas for days, until the morsels of food are used up. In like manner, old, abandoned orchards in wild country will be raided until the fruit is gone. Other good places to watch for a black bear are around old, abandoned cabins, creek beds and any spots where

Fig. 6.15 Many black bear are killed by deer hunters. (Courtesy of Pennsylvania Game Commission)

Fig. 6.16 The grizzly bear. (Courtesy of National Film Board)

a camper's garbage has been thrown. No matter how old, such man-made dumps continue to be investigated by wandering bruins. As with other species of big game, the two best times to hunt a bear are from daylight till mid-morning, and dusk till dark. Bears are on the move these times of the day.

Still-hunting or stalking is universally practiced in the North, but in the mountains and swamps of the South, where the heavy underbrush makes still-hunting impracticable and often impossible, dogs are employed to drive the game toward standers posted at strategic spots around the swamp or the ridges where the hunt is taking place. (In a few northern states, bear hunting with dogs is illegal.) Actually, in real black-bear country, the same kind of sport can be enjoyed without using dogs. A properly planned and executed drive by hunters on foot or horseback will often get a bear out where the standers can get a shot.

Still-hunting black bear is much like still-hunting whitetail deer. Patience, thoroughness and quiet movement are necessary. First you must find the area where bear signs are in evidence—tracks, droppings and indications of feeding. From there, if in flat, brushy country, you hunt quietly, always downwind,

hoping to surprise the bruin and get a shot. When hunting in mountainous country, you can often employ binoculars to keep watch for feeding game, after which the stalk is begun.

The average black bear isn't hard to kill with a well-placed bullet in the chest cavity. Any good deer rifle in the .30 or .35 caliber class will do the job. Bullet weight should be between 150- and 180-grain. While telescopic sights aren't essential, the 2½- to 4-power scope is widely used by northern and western hunters.

GRIZZLY BEAR

These bears are really rare in the United States, few being found outside the limits of the national parks in the northern Rockies. There are still plenty in northern British Columbia, western Alberta, and southeastern Alaska. In size some are about equal to that of the black bear, but the largest reach a length of eight feet and a weight of about half a ton. They vary in color from a light yellow to almost black. The tips of the hairs are lighter, giving them the grizzled appearance from which come their two common names, grizzly and silver-tip.

Despite differences, the track of the black bear can be confused with that of the grizzly. If, however, the imprint of the claws is distinct and shows five points instead of four, the animal in question probably was a grizzly. In hard or vegetated country a good place to look for tracks is on felled trees from which the bark has burned or weathered away. Other indications of the presence of bears are claw marks on aspens or poplars, although these may be very old. Both black bears and grizzlies travel in well-defined trails, so a hunter who takes time to familiarize himself with a certain area may be successful in making a kill from a point of vantage. In the higher country of Canada bears normally den up sometime in November. Sportsmen specializing in grizzly hunting choose to invade the Rockies, Selkirks, or other westerly ranges after the spring thaws which, naturally, vary somewhat with the latitude and elevation. At that time grizzlies are to be found on the snow slides where they break their long fast on green vegetation.

You need plenty of patience to hunt grizzly bears. From a vantage in grizzly territory, you scan the countryside with binoculars until your target is sighted, and then you begin your stalk. It's very important to knock down the grizzly with your first shot if it's at all possible. On a broadside shot try to place it through the shoulders, which will generally put the

Fig. 6.17 The antelope or pronghorn. (Courtesy of U.S. Fish and Wildlife Service)

bear down and keep him down. If the bullet doesn't break the spine you'll need another shot to finish him off, but the important thing is that you have immobilized the grizzly with your first shot. The killing or downing shot from the rear is one that hits just above the tail, breaking the spine at the hindquarters. If this doesn't kill the bear, it will break him down and give you time for a well-aimed follow-up shot. A shot at the front of a grizzly when he's facing you isn't advisable, because it's not easy to put a bullet in a vital spot. His skull is plated with a hard, thick bone that can deflect even a heavy bullet with a lot of punch, and a throat shot that will hit the spine is preferable to a chest shot since one of these big bears can do a lot of damage, even with a couple of bullets through the chest. The only safe shot is one which immobilizes the bear, for this at least gives you a chance to try your own footwork and get in a less hurried shot under much less pressure.

To stop a grizzly, you need a heavy caliber rifle such as a .300, a .30/06, a .348, or you may wish to go as heavy as a .375 Magnum. The need for extremes in bullet weight—220-grain is about right—can't be overemphasized. The use of a telescopic sight, of at least 2½-power, can be a valuable asset to the grizzly hunter.

ALASKAN BROWN BEAR

These bears are found in Alaska and neighboring islands on down into British Columbia. They attain the enormous weight of 1,500 pounds or more, and when they rise up on their hind legs may reach a height of nine feet. As the name implies, the coat is a uniform dark brown. The techniques and armaments suggested in grizzly hunting hold good for the big trophy brown bears.

Antelope

The pronghorn antelope of our West are not true antelope. They can be distinguished from the true antelope by the fact that they shed their horns annually, but the bony core from which the horns grow remains in place throughout life. Pronghorns once were abundant from the Missouri River to the Pacific Ocean and from southern Alberta to Mexico. Not many years ago, the pronghorn antelope seemed finished as a game animal in the United States. Mexico was the only place on the North American continent where the animals could be hunted legally, and only a handful of American sportsmen ever had shot one. But the picture has changed for the better. The comeback of the antelope herds has been one of the most spectacular in modern conservation. In many Western states the antelope once more is on the list of legal game.

Antelope probably are the most deceptive-looking animals in North America. For one thing, they are very small. Even the largest bucks seldom dress out at more than 100 pounds, and the average is nearer to 80. Yet, in spite of their small size, they are so conspicuously marked that they look large. Seen on bright days with the sun glittering on their white bellies and rumps, they always seem nearer than they are. But at dawn and dusk and on cloudy days, they fade and shrink and at such times look farther away than they are. Estimating the range is decidedly difficult. In addition, the white of the belly which makes them so easily seen also makes them easy to miss, as the hunter has a tendency to shoot at the most conspicuous part. The coloration is also important when obtaining a good trophy, which certainly is a major objective in taking this animal, and this will be the head of an older buck. A buck has a black "mask" that extends from his nose to his eyes. The doe has only a shadow of this black streak. The buck has a definite black mark under his neck, across the white patch there; the doe does not. A buck holds his head stuck out nearly level as he runs and a doe doesn't.

The basic method of hunting these colorful prairie ghosts is to drive by jeep or ride on horseback to the edge of known antelope country and study the surroundings through high-powered binoculars. With the low sun of early morning or late afternoon—the times the pronghorn should be hunted—at your back, you'll be surprised at how far you can spot an old buck on the plains. A little practice will enable you to develop so-called antelope eyes—that is, you can look out across the prairie and detect the reddish-brown and white animals against a background of similarly colored browse, weeds and dry grass.

After the animals are spotted, and you have picked out the prize pronghorn you want for your den wall, the entire hunt may be reduced to one fundamental procedure: take full advantage of every available change in elevation and possible cover so that you can come within range from an unsuspected direction and be unseen by the animals. In other words, you must look for ridges, small gullies, washes, or draws that will afford cover and then use them to best advantage during the stalk. As you move toward your target—generally crawling on your stomach—be on the alert for other antelopes you might not have seen. If these are spooked they probably will scare the animal you are after. When you get to the place from which you want to shoot, very slowly raise your head, preferably alongside a bush so you don't change the horizon line. If possible get into a prone position and

make the first shot count if you can do it. But if your first shot misses, stay down and shoot again. If the animals haven't seen you, you'll probably get a second standing shot, and possibly even a third, as antelope have a tendency to mill about when they're surprised, instead of running off as deer do.

If you have to take a running shot, be sure to allow plenty of lead. (Running antelope have been clocked at better than sixty miles per hour.) The best method to do this is to swing with them, pass them a good long way and to pull the trigger while the rifle is still moving. That way, you can kill a crossing antelope by holding about three lengths ahead at 300 yards. Even at 100 yards, you have to hold ahead of a running antelope even though you may be shooting the fastest-swinging rifle that has ever been manufactured. Vital spots are those of other game and pretty much the same as deer. They are smaller than on a mule deer and about like those on a whitetail. Head, neck, heart, forward spine—you drop your game mercifully—if you hit these targets.

As a rule, antelope have to be shot from 250 yards up to as far away as you can hit them. The rifle employed, therefore, must have sufficient initial velocity to carry its shocking power well out to the maximum range. The most popular calibers in antelope armament are the flat trajectory loads in the .257, .270, .30/06 and .250/3000. Telescopic sights are essential to a successful pronghorn hunt. One of 4-power is satisfactory, and if you're a real long-range expert, you might well take one of the 8-power target scopes with you.

Mountain Sheep

Roughly speaking, North America's wild sheep range is coincidental with the Rocky Mountains, extending as far south as the northern part of Old Mexico and northward throughout most of Alaska. In this range there are two main species: the bighorn sheep and thin-horned sheep. Of the two, the bighorn is the best known and is generally distributed over the Rocky Mountains in the western portion of the United States and into Canada. This sheep has big, curling horns which measure at the base from 15 to 18 inches for a mature ram. They are light gray-tan and their builds are rather blocky. There are several subspecies of the bighorn, varying slightly in hair (wild sheep have hair, not wool as the name might imply), horn shape and color. However, they're all much alike and the major difference is that they're larger in the northern part of their range and smaller in the south. For example, a Canadian bighorn may reach up to 350 pounds, whereas the Mexican bighorn seldom reaches 200 pounds.

The thin-horned wild sheep are the white Dall

Fig. 6.18 The steps of an antelope hunt: (Above, left to right) Find the tracks and spot the herd; (Below, left to right) Fire the shot and, if necessary, finish off the antelope with a hand gun. (All photos courtesy of Bill Browning, Montana Chamber of Commerce)

Fig. 6.19 A herd of bighorn sheep. (Courtesy of U.S. Fish and Wildlife Service)

Fig. 6.20 A herd of thin-horned mountain sheep. (Courtesy of National Film Board)

sheep of Alaska and Yukon Territory and the very dark gray (appearing sometimes black from a distance) Stone sheep which are found in British Columbia and Yukon Territory. The so-called Fannin sheep, which is gray and white, is an intergrade between the Dall and the Stone sheep and is hunted in northern British Columbia and southern Yukon Territory. The thin-horned sheep aren't so large as the bighorns, and few rams will ever weigh more than 200 pounds.

Sheep have wonderful vision, probably the best of any animal on our continent. Experienced wild sheep hunters agree that a ram's eyesight is equivalent to that of a man equipped with 8-power binoculars. This keenness of vision, plus the fact that sheep inhabit the high cliffs and peaks above timberline, combine to make a real challenge to the hunter. In any sheep herd, one individual acts as guard. Perched upon a spire of rocks, he looks downward for any sign of danger or enemy. Once anything of a suspicious nature is spotted, the band is warned and they take off.

Once you get into sheep territory—a reliable guide is almost a must to get you there—you can scout the entire countryside with binoculars of at least 8-power for signs of sheep. Certain known sheep traits will help you to concentrate on the most likely spots. For example, feeding sheep can usually be seen in tiny openings and top-most saddles between the peaks of crest country. The high line of a pass between drainages is another good location to watch. When rams move about they travel, as a rule, single-file, which makes their trails fairly easy to spot with binoculars. Also this "spreads out" any movement, thus making it easier to locate the sheep themselves.

When the sheep are located, care must be taken not to disturb them. Undoubtedly they have seen you, so if there's a good ram in the herd, the thing to do is not to make them suspicious. Get out of sight and choose a stalk route by which you can come upon the ram from a totally unsuspected direction. This often entails circling away and around an entire mountain, coming up from behind him. Stalking a spotted ram may take an entire day or even more. Remember that care must be employed to keep him from seeing, hearing, or smelling you. Also, you must keep from spooking other sheep, which will alarm the one you want. A thoroughly scared ram will go clear to another mountain, and one of the most futile things you can do is to try, on the same day, to find a ram you have shot at and missed.

When the sheep aren't feeding, they may be found bedded down in high, open points where they can jump, unimpeded, in two or three directions. In the rocks just under the top-most rim of a basin-edge is a good location to look for bedded sheep. In such a case, it's best to go high and to look down on them when they are bedded down. Sheep don't often look up, and often you can stalk quite close from above. However, stay away from the skyline or the sheep will surely see you.

Sheep aren't particularly hard to kill with a well-placed shot in the chest cavity and, since your shooting will be in open country, usually from a prone position, it shouldn't be too difficult to put the bullet almost where you wish. But to do this, your rifle must be an accurate precision instrument, capable of shooting reasonably flat for distances of three hundred yards and often more. Three good calibers for sheep hunting are the .270 Winchester using 130- and 150-grain bullets, .30/06 using 150- or 180-grain ammunition and .300 Magnum, using 180-grain bullets. Such rifles should be equipped with telescopic sights of 2½- to 5-power, and with gunslings, both for shooting and for carrying in rough country.

Mountain Goat

The mountain goat is one of the few big game animals of North America that has experienced little change in numbers or reduction in range since primitive times. Much of its territory lies north of the international border in the Cassiar Mountains and the Cariboo Range of British Columbia and in the Alaska Range and Chugach Mountains of Alaska. In the United States, its range is confined largely to the more rugged terrain of Washington, Idaho and Montana.

These big white animals aren't true goats at all, but really antelope—members of the same family as the pronghorn. Both sexes have small, black, smooth and sharp-pointed horns, and it is rather difficult, at a distance, to distinguish between a billy and nannie. A big billy may reach weights up to 300 pounds; adult nannies may weigh up to 250.

Both in summer and in winter mountain goats frequent the rugged country close to the timberline. For food they depend chiefly upon the browse of low vegetation. The goats bed down on high ledges where they are safe from almost every danger except snow and rock slides. Morning and late afternoon are the best periods to catch them feeding; goats in their midday beds aren't easily discerned from any distance. For hours at a time a band may move but little, while feeding on some ragged slope. On such terrain scent is quickly dissipated into space, and the problem in goat hunting isn't so much locating the game as ascending the steep mountainsides where they reside. Yet old chin-whiskers doesn't alarm easily, and a hunter is often permitted the several hours necessary for a successful stalk. It's an advantage, but certainly not essential, to work above the game before approaching within reasonable shooting distance. Actually, goats pay but little attention to movement and subdued noise across space, although they may be within 200 yards. They depend almost entirely upon their climbing ability and their rugged terrain for safety. When approached from below, they simply start climbing upward when their enemy is sighted, and keep on going at no great speed until they force the hunter to call it quits. When approached from above, however, they usually become very much alarmed. But even when spooked, they will generally run—which is really an awkward trot—around the point of the mountain and be found at about the same elevation on the other side.

While few big game animals are harder to knock off their feet than the big mountain goat, the same equipment, in general, is required as for wild sheep —good binoculars, telescopic sights and a rifle in the .270 or .300 category class.

Boar

European wild boar are found in western North Carolina counties and eastern Tennessee. They like deep-forest country and a minimum of interference from man. In the early part of this century, an Englishman named George Moore leased a large tract of mountain wilderness on Hooper's Bald, a wild and practically impenetrable area, just southwest of the Great Smokies. He had long dreamed of establishing a huge game preserve and enclosed a large, timbered tract with a great fence. One day in the year 1910, a group of curious mountaineers from the surrounding country gathered on the mountain top. The sight of heavily bolted crates being transferred to the Bald had stimulated an inquisitive and speculative interest among these natives. Included in the Englishman's menagerie were several wild boar which attracted more attention than any of the other animals released. The spectators stood awed by the beasts as they scrambled into the forest. Thus the opening of the big crates on the mountain top was the beginning of the American history of the wild boar. They seemed to find the climate and terrain suitable and they multiplied, spreading out over thousands of acres in the vicinity of the Nantahala and Cherokee National Forests with some in the Great Smoky Mountains National Park and the Chattahoochee National Forest. A limited number are also hunted

Fig. 6.21 The mountain goat. (Courtesy of U.S. Fish and Wildlife Service)

in Corbin's Park, New Hampshire. It's wise, when planning a hunt for wild boar in any of these areas, to write to a conservation or game commission of the state involved for full information on local conditions and laws. A guide is always a requisite unless you're familiar with the sport and the country.

The wild boar is ferocious and is considered the most vicious of all mammals that roam the American forest. It has great speed and endurance. The wild boar takes the greatest toll of dogs of any American big game, and the hounds surviving battle carry scars made by the boar's razor-sharp tusks. The wild boar differs from a feral or wild pig in several respects. The legs are longer and shoulders higher. In addition to the coarse, long, guard hairs which are split at the tips, he has a curly underfur. When alarmed, he runs with his tail straight up. These animals sometimes will charge a man on sight, even though not wounded. The average boar weighs from 150 to 300 pounds, but many have been reported scaling as much as 600 pounds.

The country in which the boar is hunted favors the animal rather than the hunter. The cover is heavy and a shot at 50 yards is considered to be extremely long range. The heavy thicket is the boar's protection and he knows it, so if you're going to hunt him

you have to do it on his terms. Owing to the country they inhabit, it's impossible to hunt boar without dogs.

On a boar hunt, the shooters take their position on stands where it is hoped the chased animal will pass, waiting for the dogs to chase him near enough for a shot. Stand-hunting is the most popular manner in the wild boar quest, though some hardy adventurers will try to follow the dogs. Of course, if the dogs hold the boar, the hunters should rush to the spot for the kill. But the hunters have to be extremely careful when they shoot, for the wounded animal is more dangerous than before. Sometimes when the hunters arrive at the fight scene, the dogs have the boar beaten. The dogs are then pulled off so that an accurate killing shot can be fired. The shoulder shot is usually considered best since the chance of hitting the lungs or heart is better. When shooting from a stand, most guides advise shooting the boar any place you can, just to get him down so that the killing shot can be dispatched.

While any deer rifle is usually suitable for boar hunting, be sure to select the heaviest possible load in the caliber preferred because of the ruggedness of the terrain. The sights should be adjusted for 50 yards and you must know how to zero your rifle at

Fig. 6.22 The steps of a mountain goat hunt: (Above) Spot the goat by binoculars; (below left) stalk the goat (below right) and the final reward. (All photos courtesy of Bill Browning, Montana Chamber of Commerce)

Fig. 6.23 The Russian or European wild boar is cornered by dogs (above); the hunter, after the kill, gets the reward. (Both photos courtesy of North Carolina News Bureau)

any range from 10 to 50 yards. Open iron sights are usually preferable since you'll need sights that can be aligned very quickly. Some boar hunters employ shotguns and rifled slugs. This is possible because the range is short and the shocking power of one of these slugs is great.

The only native wild hog of the United States is the peccary, or javelina (pronounced *hahveleenah*), of the Southwest. He is built along the lines of a runted domestic pig and weighs between 50 and 70 pounds. While he is smaller than the European wild boar, he is just as ornery, but isn't considered as dangerous to hunt because he packs less muscle and has shorter tusks. The peccaries herd together in groups of 10 to 40 head and travel the dry brush and desert country of the states of Arizona, New Mexico and Texas.

The peccary is hunted either by still-shooting with dogs or by stalking. With still-shooting, the odds are against the peccary, unlike the wild boar, because he is short-winded and the dogs can usually corner him fairly easily. The hunter can then move in for the kill.

When stalking these wild swine, you ride out into the country known to harbor them and once signs of their presence are found—tracks and rootings— you get as close to the herd as possible to get off your shot. Stalking peccaries requires a knowledge of terrain, constant attention to the wind, quick thinking and accurate impromptu marksmanship. Any good deer rifle can be used for these animals, but be sure that the load has plenty of wallop to kill quickly.

The wild razorback hog of Georgia and Florida swamp areas isn't a boar, but is hunted in the same manner as the peccary. While it offers a great deal of sport, it is not dangerous to either the dogs or hunters.

Field Dressing of Big Game

Once downed, a deer (or any game) should be dressed as quickly as possible. There is no need to "stick" a deer. It can be dangerous if the deer is not yet dead and it does almost nothing to bleed the

Fig. 6.24 The wild razorback hog. (Courtesy of Florida Game & Fresh Water Fish Commission)

Fig. 6.25 Field dressing operation on a fine antelope trophy. (Courtesy of Bill Browning, Montana Chamber of Commerce)

carcass once heart action has stopped. Prompt cleaning of the body cavity does the job.

There's no need to hang an animal for dressing. Simply turn the carcass over on its back, insert the point of the knife at the end of the rib cage (sternum) and make a single cut the full length of the body cavity, almost to the vent. Be careful not to cut deep enough to get the intestines. Now prop open the cavity with a short stick and reach in with the knife to sever the diaphragm, a wall of muscle which grows along the inside edge of the last ribs, separating the chest cavity from the abdominal cavity. Cut this free all around the inside, then turn the carcass on its side and pull all entrails free from the cavity, cut-ting a bit where necessary along the backbone. Now cut completely around the vent, freeing the rectal tube until it can be pulled out for a few inches. Tie this firmly with string, then, from the inside, pull the tube back into the body cavity. Roll the animal over on its belly and shake out the insides by lifting it first on the head and forelegs, next on the hind-legs, until the entrails are free. Once again reach up into the chest cavity and cut loose the windpipe and gullet. Now you can pull the whole mess of insides away from the carcass and your buck is ready to cool out. Once again turn him belly down and shake out loose blood clots, allowing the cavity to drain for a few minutes.

Chapter Seven

LEARNING VARMINT HUNTING

YOU DON'T HAVE to put your rifle or shotgun away at the end of the hunting season. That is, if you turn to varmint shooting. You'll have worlds of fun, you'll benefit wildlife and when the next hunting season rolls around the practice you'll have had will probably enable you to hit your desired targets instead of missing them. In other words, varmint hunting fills the big gap between seasons and keeps your hunting eye sharp, your coordination keen. Fortunately, the animals classed as varmints—fox, coyote, bobcat, mountain lion, woodchuck, prairie dog—are, almost without exception, not protected by closed seasons, so that you can enjoy field shooting the year around. In a few states you don't even need a hunting license to take varmints or predators.

There are two types of varmints: the kind you shoot primarily for fun and practice and the kind you shoot primarily because they prey on farm stock, poultry, or wildlife game. Some states even pay bounties for the latter class of varmints or predators. For example, California pays the following bounties: male mountain lions, $50, females, $60; crows, 15¢; magpies, 10¢. In Pennsylvania, bounty payments of $5 are paid for the great horned owl and $4 for red or gray fox. Over thirty states have some type of bounty system and you can check if yours is one of them by writing to the state conservation or game commission.

Foxes

There are two major species of foxes—the red and the gray. Color is the obvious difference, but it goes a lot deeper than that. The red is an animal of the open woods and fields, built for speed, like a miniature greyhound in a fur coat, while the gray is an animal of the brush and rocks, heavier built, and often fat. A red's paws are large and heavily furred on the soles, and his tracks are like a dog's. The gray

has small feet, almost hairless on the bottom, and his tracks resemble those of a cat.

In most sections of the country the fox has no enemy but man. The very low prices paid for red fox and gray fox pelts in recent years have resulted in a great number of these animals almost everywhere. Keeping foxes under control doesn't mean wiping them out entirely, but today most people don't realize the number of foxes present in their area. This is true, most particularly, of the gray fox, which is the most destructive to small game. When the gray fox takes over an area, the red fox for the most part simply moves out. The gray will lie close sometimes, just like a rabbit, and let you almost step on him before breaking cover. This trait, more than anything else, has led many people to believe that there are no foxes around because they seldom see them.

Almost any rifle of medium or high velocity will do but the most popular calibers are the .30/06, .270, .257, .220 Swift, etc., and, of course, a host of the bobcat calibers. While a few fox hunters prefer iron sights, the majority like the scope sight best. Scopes of 4-power seem to give the best results. The 12-gauge scattergun, loaded with short Magnum shells, also does a fine job on fox. The 16- and 20-gauges can be used too, but shots longer than 35 yards shouldn't be taken with these lighter gauges. Best size shot to use is No. 5 or, if you use a 20-gauge, No. 6.

The most important item for hunting the fox with any degree of success is a good "strike" dog. This is true particularly if most of your hunting is in areas where the gray fox outnumbers his red cousin. As mentioned above, the gray fox lies very close and on most occasions has to be routed right out of bed. Unlike the red, the gray fox doesn't range very far and is therefore harder on the local game, as his hunting is confined to a smaller area.

The method that is generally found most productive is to use two hunters and two dogs. One man keeps the dogs on leash until his partner gets to his stand, which for best results and so that no one is in danger of being shot accidentally is on the corner of the cover diagonally across from his shooting partner. In this manner each man can watch a side and an end. No signal is given when the man reaches his position. Then the dogs are turned loose, no word being spoken to them so that the fox thinks that just a couple of dogs are about. This is a common procedure with farm dogs.

If a strike is made by either dog, the other immediately goes to him and helps to work the line. The fox usually makes a short circle if the cover is of sufficient extent. Then when the dogs get closer, he sneaks out to leave that cover in favor of another. If all is well, the hunters secure a shot. The range of shots for this kind of hunting is not long. Two hundred yards is a long shot; most are taken at 100 yards and under. Sometimes a trail isn't struck for quite a little spell as the fox is curled up, fast asleep under some evergreen tree or in a patch of greenbriars.

It's obvious that a fox running in a circle will be traveling upwind part of the time, downwind part of the time and crosswind the rest. You'll get few shots with the wind carrying your scent to the fox, so try to stand where the wind will be blowing from the fox to you. Never cross the fox's circle to get to the other side. Go around and be sure to keep downwind. Some foxes may pay no attention to your scent, but the majority will leave the vicinity. Once you've chosen a location, stick to it unless you think the fox has seen or scented you. If you're continually moving about you'll scare more foxes than you'll kill. Should you choose a good location, and the fox doesn't leave the area, you're pretty sure of eventually getting a shot, although it may take several hours.

When hunted, red foxes like to keep to high ground. Ridges, benches along a hillside and the edges of flat-topped hills are your best bets. Young foxes sometimes run in thick brush and slashings, but an adult prefers open woods, pasture and bare fields. Gray fox, on the other hand, prefer very thick overgrown brier patches, fencerows, dense cover, rocky areas and evergreen forests. But choosing a good spot at which to wait is simplified by a fox's habit of keeping to trails and paths whenever possible.

Another increasingly popular method of shooting fox, without dogs, is to call them to you by using a

Fig. 7.1 (Left) the red fox. (Courtesy of National Film Board) (Right) the gray fox. (Courtesy of Florida Game & Fresh Water Fish Commission)

Fig. 7.2 A fox call (at the left) and a crow call will both bring foxes on the run. Crow calls are best to use in early May when young crows are constantly falling out of the nest and into the mouths of the hungry foxes. (Courtesy of Pennsylvania Game Commission)

fox call. There are several good calls on the market and one can usually be purchased at your local sporting goods dealer. But, in order to call foxes, one factor must be present at all times. There must be foxes in the vicinity. It's surprising how many hunters go in a woods and blow on a call. They expect a fox to trot in—yet they never checked to see if any were in the neighborhood.

There are several methods of locating foxes. For example, body hairs from the animals can usually be seen clinging to their dens or their favorite hideouts. Another method of determining whether foxes live in the area is to check for kills. Chicken and bird feathers, pieces of rabbit hide and parts of their favorite summer food, the groundhog, are often lying around the den entrance. Also, if a fox stays on a farmer's land he'll usually know about it and where it stays. He will usually be glad to tell you where the dens are and the fox's habits.

Always try to get on a spot of ground fairly clear in all directions to aid you in shooting. If possible, select a place higher than the surrounding area. A fox can be spotted better and the sound not pinpointed by the animal as quickly, if the caller is slightly above it. Call from a shaded spot.

Wait a few minutes after arriving in position before you start calling. It gives the wildlife in the area time to settle down and increases your chances for a shot. Call softly at first. Many times a fox will be close by. Soft calling will bring him trotting in but a blasting call would drive him away. Call fairly continuously, stopping every two or three minutes for a short duration, then begin calling again. If nothing appears in a short time—say two or three minutes— try raising the volume of the call. After eight or ten minutes it's best to leave if no fox has moved in. Only on rare occasions will foxes come to you after a stay longer than ten minutes. Watch carefully as you leave the area. Sometimes a fox who was slow coming to the call will be seen sneaking away.

If you shoot a rifle, or even a shotgun, here's a good idea to insure excellent shots: in an area where you feel the fox will travel to the call—such as an old game trail, log road, etc.—place a piece of old meat, chicken head, or other fox dessert. The fox, as he moves toward the caller, will stop to investigate the food and give the shooter an excellent standing shot.

Without question the best times to call foxes are very late in the evening or just after light in the early morning. The fox is a night roamer and he begins to prowl when dark approaches and is usually still about at daylight. If he's had poor hunting luck all night, he's especially likely to come sailing in. The worst times of course are the hours just before and after midday. Hunting all night, the fox usually rests and sleeps during this portion of the day and is hard to call. Also young foxes are easier to call than their elders. The best time of the year to bring in these youngsters is late May. Big enough to get into trouble and still not so sharp as the older and more experienced animals, they answer a call readily.

Often you'll get chances at foxes or other predators while you're in search of other game so it pays to always keep your eyes peeled and searching the open hillsides, the edges of the brush-covered areas and the tops of small knolls. The real hunter watches the surrounding terrain more or less instinctively, without thinking about it. And this practice should be followed by the beginner, also. Watch for anything which appears to be out of place, or anything which moves. Any animal or bird will move eventually. All you have to do is to watch it carefully and intently until it does move. Then you can more readily identify it, because each species has characteristic colors or actions which you will recognize as soon as it does move.

The most important thing to bear in mind is that while hunting foxes, with or without dogs, you must move about with a minimum of noise, stopping often to look and listen.

Coyotes

Coyotes are among the most destructive enemies of wildlife game. These little prairie wolves slaughter thousands of fawns annually, and when conditions are in their favor, they think nothing of killing full-grown deer and antelopes. While the Southwest is still the best area for shooting these wild canines, almost the entire tier of northern states contains enough of them to make hunting worth the effort.

The coyote is wild, wary and one of the most intelligent creatures in the wildlife kingdom. His so-called cowardliness could be more aptly described as a sound judgment of what constitutes mortal danger. Remember that these gray-coated terrors don't present too big a target—about 6 to 10 inches vertically by 18 to 20 inches horizontally. As

a rule, you hunt them, though under slightly different conditions, in much the same ways you do foxes. That is 1) by running them, 2) by shooting at them from concealed locations along their known trails and 3) by calling them. The latter method is fairly new and is increasing in popularity among coyote hunters in densely wooded sections. A calling device, which sounds like the wail of a rabbit in distress, is employed to bring the curious coyote within the range of the concealed caller's rifle.

When running coyotes on wide, flat expanses of land, such as prairie or desert, hunters use jeeps, horses or light trucks. In areas where hounds are employed to chase these varmints, the hunters follow on foot, horses, or jeeps. Once the beast is cornered by the dogs, the hunters move in for the kill.

Actually, any rifle in caliber range of .257 to .300 is suitable for coyote shooting. The cartridges must have long-range accuracy, flat trajectory and high muzzle velocity since most shots are taken at a dis-

Fig. 7.3 A coyote howling after just killing a rabbit. (Courtesy of U.S. Fish and Wildlife Service)

tance of 200 yards or more. Telescopic sights of 4-
to 8-power range and gunslings are very important
in this type of shooting.

Bobcats

These notorious predators will take young pigs,
lambs and newborn calves, as well as prey on fawns
and even full-grown deer during a shortage of other
prey. Perhaps the most common diet is the rabbit.
Although there are several species of bobcat, they all
may be described as oversized housecats with
stubby tails and tufted ears. They are brownish-tan
with dark spots. The head looks large because the
hair on the cheeks and chin is somewhat tufted.
Bobcats range in weight from as little as 20 pounds
up to as large as 50 pounds.

In New England and throughout the Great Lakes
region, the bobcat inhabits thick evergreen swamps
full of blow-downs, making occasional forage trips
out into the wooded hills. In the South, he goes for
the tangled swamps and bramble thickets. In the
Northwest he pads silently through the thick pine
forests of the mountains. And in the Southwest he's
a creature of the cut-up desert canyons and rock
piles. To hunt in such habitats requires a well-trained
dog or dogs of stamina, determination, speed, size
and courage. While most dogs employed in bobcat
hunting are hounds, purity of breed isn't essential
just as long as they have these prime requisites.

In the northern and western states the bobcat
usually trees rather quickly, but in the South the
chase may last for hours. The usual method of hunting bobcats in northern areas is to scout tracks—
since a great deal of this hunting is done with snow
on the ground, it's not hard to identify their cat-like
tracks—in cat country, and once one is spotted, the
dogs are let go. The hunters hide themselves at advantageous points in the area where the bobcat is
being run and wait until he comes within gun range
or is treed. Another procedure, often followed by a
lone hunter, is to walk with the dog on leash until
a track is struck in the snow. The dog is then released and the direction of the chase can be ascer-
tained. Be sure to keep ahead of your dog, watch
for the cat to circle, and shoot him when you get
the chance. In southern regions, a pack of dogs is
generally employed to run the cat and they continue
after him until he is cornered or treed. Then the
hunters move in for the kill. A few hunters in recent
years have had success in calling bobcats in the same
way as foxes, by using an injured-rabbit caller so
popular for coyotes. *Early* morning when trails are
still fresh is the best time to start any bobcat hunt.

In bobcat hunting, either a light rifle in the .25-

Fig. 7.4 On the ground (above) the bobcat looks just like
a house cat. (Courtesy of U.S. Fish and Wildlife Service)
When treed (below) he becomes a dangerous, snarling
beast. (Courtesy of Florida Game & Fresh Water Fish
Commission)

to .32-caliber class or a shotgun loaded with No. 2 shot or BB's can be employed to bring a cat down when he trees, or to fire at him as he crosses thicket openings with the dogs barking behind. Bobcats are not too difficult to kill. Being thin-skinned and fragile-boned, they belie the old tale that cats have nine lives. If crippled, however, they live up to their press clippings as vicious, stubborn antagonists.

Mountain Lions

The mountain lion, also known as the cougar, puma and mountain panther, ranks as the world's fourth largest cat. In the Western Hemisphere, only the jaguar is larger in size. The body of the male mountain lion—which is a uniform reddish-brown color—may be from four to five and one-half feet long, and its tail from two to three feet more. The female is considerably smaller. A mature lion might weigh as much as 200 pounds but will average closer to the 130 to 150 pound range.

There's no question that the mountain lion is a vicious killer, but for some reason he isn't inclined to attack humans; at least, if he does feel the inclination he usually thinks better of it. Instances of even the hungriest and most ornery of mountain lions attacking humans are exceedingly rare. Of course, when one is wounded or cornered it behooves the hunter to be cautious.

Once common almost everywhere in the United States, the mountain lion is all but extinct east of the Rockies. Well-trained dogs are a prerequisite for good lion hunting. But even with dogs, hunting this big cat is sometimes a rather rugged sport, and this is part of what makes a lion a prized trophy for the hunter who takes part in the chase and is present for the climax. In the first place it is necessary to keep within hearing distance of the dogs and arrive on the scene as soon as possible when the lion trees or makes his final stand. The chase may lead five miles, ten miles, or more. You can just about bet that the lion is going to head for the roughest terrain available. If he gains rough rimrock country he has a pretty good chance of losing the dogs. For example, he can climb a tree and jump to a rock ledge. Even if the dogs can follow this, a series of maneuvers such as climbing and jumping leaves a broken trail requiring a renewed search each time. The chase of the dogs and the lions is usually accomplished on horseback.

The most popular rifles with lion hunters of the Southwest are the .32 Special, the .35 and the .300. The .30/30 also packs ample punch to knock a mountain lion off his perch. The load used in these

Fig. 7.5 A cornered and treed mountain lion. (Courtesy of U.S. Fish and Wildlife Service)

calibers is either 150 or 170 grain. Due to the short range of mountain lion shooting, iron sights are all that are needed.

Mountain lions are not the easiest varmint to find. There are many hunters who have hunted in lion country all their lives and have never seen one in the wild. Therefore, unless you are very familiar with their habits and where they live, it's usually wise to hire the services of a good guide—and his dogs. The guide who is continuously scouting the countryside will usually have a good idea as to where a mountain lion can be found. The conservation or game departments (see Appendix for addresses) of the states where lions are to be found can generally furnish the names of guides who have dogs.

Woodchucks

Of the various varmint targets, the woodchuck (the ground hog) is probably the most popular. This well-known burrow digger of fields and wood lots ranges over most of the United States, but is most abundant in the East and Midwest. Woodchucks are actually large ground squirrels and average about two feet in length, with a short hairy tail about six inches long. They are rodents with sharp chisel-like

Fig. 7.6 A woodchuck looking for food on the ground (left) and in the hunter's favorite position (right). (Both photos courtesy of U.S. Fish and Wildlife Service)

teeth and possess skill in gnawing. Usually we think of the squirrel as a creature that chirps. The woodchuck is gifted with the ability to whistle. The male and female are colored alike, being a brownish-gray with black feet. Den digging is a specialty with them. Since they're extremely clean in all their habits, they seldom use their den the second year, thus it makes a home for other den-lovers.

There are two successful methods of hunting woodchucks. The first is to locate a network of burrows, conceal yourself nearby, and sit quietly to wait for the chucks to appear. The other is to roam through promising territory, spotting a target and then trying to get within firing distance before the chuck disappears into his den. This stalking often entails crawling along on the stomach for several hundred yards. A good pair of binoculars is a great help in locating woodchucks.

Actually, finding a chuck isn't too difficult. Any gently rolling country is a good bet if it is not of shale or clay—and does not have milkweed growing in the fields. A good spot is where you find rabbit or chuck dens along post-fence rows, stone fences and also rock ledges or old chestnut tree snags. Look around the foundations of abandoned barns or houses—and be sure that no human is occupying them. In clover fields, hunt along ravines running down hillsides. In dense woods, a good area is within 25 to 100 yards of the edge of the woods. Look for any spot that might appeal to a chuck for a den. The late spring and summer are best hunting times for this wary little beast. In winter, he hibernates.

The woodchuck may feed on the succulent grass as much as 25 or 45 yards from his burrow, but you can depend upon it that he has selected a feeding area that gives him a view of the adjacent terrain. At regular intervals he will sit up and survey the area, and it takes little to send him scurrying for the mouth of his burrow. Once a chuck is located, the smart shooter will look over the terrain and decide the route he must follow to reach a point within reasonable range, and still keep below the line of the woodchuck's vision. Once arrived at his shooting location, the hunter must make a slow and careful check to insure that his quarry is still there. Then he must make an estimation of the range in order to know just where to hold. At this point, it's important that the shooter knows everything possible about the trajectory of his rifle. Normally, the chuck shooter will have his rifle zeroed at 200 yards, which means he must know how much lower to hold if the chuck is at 150 yards and how much higher if he is at 200. Then the rifle must be lined up on the quarry with a minimum of movement on the part of the shooter. It's almost impossible to overestimate the importance of very carefully selecting the exact point of aim before firing at a woodchuck. The chuck hibernates annually, has a low sense of feeling, isn't too easily affected by shock and can sometimes take an almost incredible amount of pounding and still get underground.

There are a number of almost instantly fatal shots on chucks: the brain shot at the butt of the ear, from the back of the skull, or in the front or side of the skull. The brain area is very small, usually one to one and one-half inches in diameter, and at 100 to 300 yards or more is difficult to hit. Try it if you can hold that close. Another fatal spot is the throat, from in front. The bullet cuts the spine, breaks the neck, or gashes the jugular vein. It may also cut the windpipe. A shot lower in the neck, which breaks the neck, is fatal. A bullet through both shoulders from one side, and placed rather high up, is instantly paralyzing and fatal. One through both lungs, or a lung and the upper part of the heart, especially if it is a very high-speed bullet, is fatal. All other shots on woodchucks should be avoided, with any rifle. If you lose chuck after chuck, many of which are visibly hit, you haven't picked your shots with sufficient care.

There are many special varmint rifles available to the chuck hunter today. These weapons all propel high-velocity bullets along a flat trajectory and are notable for their long-range accuracy. Among the most popular are the .22 Hornet, the .220 Swift, the .222, the .257 Roberts, the .250/3000, and the .270. The 87-, 100- and 117-grain bullets are excellent varmint cartridges. A woodchuck is a rather small mark at the necessary ranges when you're using iron sights, so the modern varmint shooter equips his rifle with telescopic sights ranging in strength from 2½ to 8 power.

The status of the woodchuck has changed in recent years. While most farmers still consider the chuck a pest, many states have given him the status of a game animal, and he is protected by a closed season during a portion of the year. Therefore, before any indiscriminate shooting of woodchuck, check your state laws.

Prairie Dogs

Prairie dogs are often considered small editions of the woodchuck, and throughout the plains of the West they live in "cities" which in the old days were often miles in extent and contained unnumbered millions. The United States Fish and Wildlife Service, through a poisoning program, has now thinned them out pretty well, as one colony will consume enough feed to support many heads of cattle. But they're still common, and their decrease in number has heightened the sport of picking them off, because it has made them harder to find and more wary. Also remember that a prairie dog is a small target. Standing full up on his haunches, he does well to reach 12 inches. But he's not a bit over 3 inches of sound target broad. Sticking his head out of a hole, the dog is no more than four square inches of target, if that.

Prairie dogs are extremely keen-eyed, and in a city there are hundreds of pairs of eyes on a constant lookout for possible danger since they live in

Fig. 7.7 A pair of prairie dogs. (Courtesy of U.S. Fish and Wildlife Service)

Fig. 7.8 The Ducks Unlimited cameraman actually caught this crow in the act of destroying a waterfowl nest and its eggs.

wide open spaces where all sorts of predators can catch them. Thus, with each member of their colony at constant vigil, it's almost impossible for you to approach unseen. Once danger is sighted, regardless of how far away, the first dog to discover it lets out a shrill whistle. At this alarm, every dog races for its burrow, but doesn't dive in. Instead, each sits up on the mound and joins in sounding the alarm. Often there will be scores all whistling at once. This, of course, is the time for you to get your shot off. Or, if your shot set off the alarm, you may get a second. The closest dogs now all dive for cover. This sometimes makes possible a longer shot or two before the rest follow the example.

But once all your targets have taken cover, it doesn't mean your shooting is necessarily over. These animals have great curiosity. In a few minutes a head will poke out, then another, and another. By waiting until some of the dogs have ventured away from their dens, you will get several more shots. But this trick will work only a couple of times. Then they will go down and stay down for extended periods of time until you tire of waiting. For this reason, it's a good idea to have two or more cities located within a short distance of each other. Then, after you have several shots at one, you can move to the next, and keep going back and forth between them.

Popular among prairie-dog hunters are the .22 Hornet, the .243, the .244, the .257, and the .270,

though some use a rifle as heavy as the .36/06. Telescopic sights ranging in strength from 4 to 8 power are almost a must.

Before leaving the subject of varmint animals it may be wise to mention that such small animals as cotton rats—which love to destroy the nest of Western quail—pocket gophers, chipmunks, ground squirrels, rock chucks and rock squirrels produce good shooting in certain parts of our country. These all are small target and are exceedingly wary because of their natural enemies, so pinpoint accuracy in small-caliber varmint rifles is essential to consistent scoring. But, before hunting any of these species, check with your state's hunting regulations to be sure that they are not protected.

Crows

To American farmers, the crow ranks first in destructiveness. Flocks hit corn, peanut and pecan crops hard; destroy wild quail, turkey, duck, songbird and domestic chicken eggs and young; ruin watermelon patches, and raid orchards. Authorities say that in some localities crows destroy 11 per cent of the potential annual wild duck crop.

Unlike some wildlife species, the crow has shown a steady increase in national population since 1900, instead of a decline. In many localities, feeding flocks startled into flight number hundreds of birds and momentarily blacken the sky as they take wing. Studies seem to indicate that you can control the common crow only by locating and destroying nests and by shooting. Crows are practically impossible to trap in numbers and evidently know the story of Lucrezia Borgia, for they avoid poisoned bait entirely once a poisoning case is a cornfield breakfast topic of crow conversation.

As a rule, resident crows limit their daily activities within an eight-to-ten-mile radius of their nighttime roosting spot although on occasion they may fly double the distance to attend a special gathering of the clan, or in seeking newly sown fields to raid. Resident flocks are not hard to find and three or four days of morning and late afternoon field observation will surely pinpoint preferred flyways. In areas where crows are conspicuously plentiful, your shooting activity will be limited only by your time and pocketbook. There are no closed seasons nor bag limits on crows, and most landowners are happy to have outside assistance in fighting the destructive pests.

Crow hunting, however, isn't easy. Crows are exceptionally smart birds, with as high an IQ as you can find in the bird kingdom. Let a lone sentinel spot you entering a field or patch of brush and it opens up on its loud-speaker to blare out a warning to every bird dipped in black paint in that area. Smart crows won't come near that spot for hours. Or just try pussyfootin' toward a flock feeding in a freshly manured field or on dead game near a highway. Before you get within gun range, the cagey crows flap toward some faraway spot and wait until you have cleared the coast before swooping back.

Unlike a duck, the average crow isn't a durable bird and large size shot aren't necessary for kills. Only a few pellets of fine shot from a modified or full-choke bored shotgun will kill crows regularly up to 50 yard ranges—if you can catch the tricky targets in the shot pattern. Also, the smaller the size of lead shot contained in a shotgun shell load, the more pellets per ounce and the denser the shot pattern. Similarly, the smaller the gauge of the shotgun the crow shooter uses, the smaller should be his shot size selection. Stick to sizes 7½, 8 and 9 shot, preferably, and even in the big 12-gauge, don't go below No. 6 shot, averaging about 223 pellets to the ounce. You want the densest killing shot pattern you can get, and only in shot sizes 7½, 8 and 9 will you find 345, 409 and 505 small shot per ounce, to give you that pattern.

A 20-gauge gun, usually of lighter weight than a 12, is faster to shoulder and swing and more comfortable to shoot. A 20-gauge is excellent for really close shooting from a blind. It isn't so good when the hunter isn't well concealed, his presence known and wary birds circling a good distance from the gun; then, a 12-gauge, giving ten yards more effective killing range, will be the better performer. A really good shot who will limit his shooting to fairly close ranges can even kill crows consistently with a .410 and No. 9 shot loads. Try Skeet and trap loads, in all gauges, rather than the maximum energy shell loadings. They'll kill just as many crows, and at less money per shot.

Using a flat-shooting .22 Hornet or .257 Roberts caliber centerfire varmint rifle with scope sight, a rifleman can get excellent shooting over baited spots by building a blind 10 yards away, zeroing-in his rifle for the exact range and then patiently calling and waiting—with the emphasis on waiting and continued concealment. The user of a rimfire .22 rifle and long rifle hollow-point cartridges should sight-in his equipment so that bullets will hit one inch high at 50 yards, on the nose at 75 yards and not too low over 100 yards of flight with the same determined sight setting. Due to its trajectory curve as related to sight settings, the rimfire .22 cartridge isn't a reliable crow hitter when the range exceeds 100 yards. For long range shooting, the centerfire varmint shooting calibers—the .22 Hornet, .244 Remington, .257

Fig. 7.9 Lots of wing spread (over forty inches) makes the crow a highly maneuverable target for the gunner. (Courtesy of Pennsylvania Game Commission)

Fig. 7.10 Peering out of the blind, decoys in place, these gunners are ready to tackle the morning flight of crows. (Courtesy of Pennsylvania Game Commission)

Roberts, .220 Swift and the .218 Bee, to name several—are definitely superior.

If you locate a crow roosting grove, don't plan any shooting at its location, as the birds will quickly forsake it altogether. Instead, select a shooting stand somewhere along a flyway leading to the roost. Generally there are three or four such flyways and it is a good idea to locate all and shoot each in turn rather than locate a single flyway and hunt it repeatedly.

The shotgunner, whose shooting must necessarily be done at fairly close range, particularly needs the helpful camouflage of thick cover or an erected latticework of brush common to the area's vegetation. Branches, cornstalks, hay, or dead grass common to the area being hunted can be woven into rusty chicken wire and used in the rapid construction of shooting blinds. Take care to build blinds small in size and of a height that matches other objects in their immediate neighborhoods. Anything bulky or foreign to the terrain will not escape a crow's discerning vision and he will quickly put added distance between himself and the suspicious spot. He'll also pass the news to other crows in the area, and your time and efforts will go for naught. Perhaps you can find and occupy an old abandoned automobile body,

long rusted and long accepted by crows as a natural, innocuous part of the landscape. Once in a while, use of it as a shooting blind may provide good sport.

Place decoys in back of your blind or to one side, but in plain view of the incoming birds. These papiermâché crow decoys may be placed on the top of small trees or fence posts, near a big horned owl decoy. The big owl is the crow's natural enemy and whenever one is found, crows dive, peck and worry it out of the area. Some hunters trap a live owl by setting a baited trap on top of a high pole. A weak spring trap seldom inflicts injury to the bird. The owl is then penned, later leg roped and tied to a pole during the hunt. The factory-made papiermâché owls also serve the purpose.

The purpose of decoys is to get and hold the attention of members of a flock while at the same time diverting attention and interest from your shooting stand. The latter should be within easy killing range of decoyed fliers, but not so close that attracted crows will spot both decoys and waiting gun.

Crows prefer to approach decoys upwind—so the shooter should plan to take most of his shots downwind. The birds also tend to fly low when facing a north wind and high against a south wind. Such facts and existing conditions should be considered when selecting a shooting stand and setting up nearby decoys, preparatory to efforts to imitate animated crow talk.

Diversified hunting methods definitely will get you more shots. For example, if after several days of good shotgun shooting you find that the black marauders have learned to keep just out of effective shotgun range, then carry a scope-sight-equipped rifle on your next trip. The change of tactics will *probably* fool them!

On other occasions, a slow stalk can be made through thickly wooded, low-height tree areas, the hunter sounding his crow call as he moves forward. When an answer is heard, he quickly takes cover and then really puts persuasiveness into his calling until the black target is enticed into shotgun or rifle range. However, this method has a limited potential, for sooner or later circling crows will spot the hunter and leave the area. When that happens, the shooter must either move to a new and distant sector or call it a day.

Decoys, good blinds, wearing of camouflage clothing and skillful calling go together—with calling and concealment being considered top-ranking by expert crow hunters. While it's practically impossible to approach a crow closely while carrying a gun, it isn't too difficult to entice him to move in closer if you talk persuasively in language he understands, all the time remaining concealed. Like his eyesight, a crow's hearing is exceptionally acute. It isn't uncommon for a crow to pick up the sound of the hunter's calling and wing half a mile for an investigation. Expert calling can mean the difference between scoring big kills or downing only a few of the worthless predators.

Commercial crow calls aren't expensive and with a little practice will give good results. Concentrate on learning to properly sound the urgent, high-pitched distress cry of a young crow in dire circumstances and needing help. Also master the "high ball" call, which can sometimes bring back birds that escape first salvos, and the "wake for the dead" mourning call used by relatives and friends of crows that have just experienced unexpected demise. Other imitated calls are relatively unimportant in relation to total results obtained.

Don't take chance shots at first incomers that fly high and out of range as they answer your calling, yet approach with suspicion and caution. Instead, withhold your fire until most of the circling flock are in certain gun range, then get into action fast. Having your gun in ready shooting position helps. Also, if you leave your blind to set up killed crows as additional decoys, be careful not to leave any empty shotgun shells or rifle cases in their neighborhood. Crows have what seemingly amounts to binocular vision or perspicuity for shiny objects—including a hunter's upturned, expectant and uncamouflaged face. When called crows prove especially wary, you have to exercise every precaution and even resort to theatrical grease paint or a head net to better camouflage your person.

In hunting crows you'll be matching wits with the smart rascals every trip afield, but each time you kill one you'll be doing wild-game conservation and the farmers a good turn. Besides, the sport is an excellent way to perfect your shooting coordination for next fall's hunting.

Other Predator Birds

There are a few other predator birds that are usually open season to varmint hunters. They include the great horned owl, the magpie, the starling and, in some states, the raven. In a few states, some species even have bounty value.

GREAT HORNED OWLS

These are the "black sheep" of the otherwise good owl family. They are very destructive to upland

Fig. 7.11 The winter camouflage dress of a crow hunter. Note how the gun barrel is covered with white tape. (Courtesy of Pennsylvania Game Commission)

Fig. 7.12 The great horned owl. (Courtesy of Pennsylvania Game Commission)

game—they usually kill the equivalent of a hen pheasant or a rabbit each day to feed themselves and their young. These aggressive, powerful birds are fairly fast in flight, and they are so heavy of body and rather dense in plumage that it generally takes a load of No. 6 shot in a close-bored shotgun (anything between 12- and 20-gauge is good) or a rifle of the .222 class as the absolute minimum. The .243 and .244 twins are substantially better, both in killing power and wind-bucking ability, and the .270 is still better. *A word of caution*: treat a crippled great horned owl with respect. He has a pair of talons and beak that are second only to those of the eagle and he'll use them to give a vicious wound if care isn't exercised.

MAGPIES

These attractive-appearing black-and-white birds with long tails are members of the crow family but confine their range to the West. The magpies, like other members of their clan, are very destructive— they not only raid the eggs and young of beneficial song and game birds, but on occasion they will gang up on any sick or crippled domestic or big game animal for a kill. They are crow-like in intelligence, gregariousness and suspiciousness, and thus are hunted in the same manner as crows and with the same type of weapons.

STARLINGS

These aliens brought to the United States from Europe have become a national pest in recent years. In at least one state starlings are on the bounty list (5 cents for each killed). You may use the same guns and ammunitions as recommended for crows.

Many states have various birds that they consider predatory species. Two of these—golden eagles and ravens—are protected at all times in some states, and in others can be hunted at any time. (These birds can be bagged with the guns and ammunitions recommended for the great horned owl.) Some predatory birds have a dual status with the law. A typical example is the statute in Minnesota which permits a bounty of ten cents per dozen to be paid on blackbirds, which are in the *protected* class by the Federal Migratory Bird Treaty Act. Because of the contradictions in state laws, be sure to check with them carefully before doing any varmint hunting.

Chapter Eight

LEARNING TO HUNT WITH DOGS

THE OLD ADAGE that a dog is man's best friend is never truer than when that animal is of a sporting breed and the man a hunter. It isn't absolutely necessary, of course, to have a hunting dog, but it is, purely from a practical standpoint alone, highly advantageous. A good hunting dog can cover a great deal more ground than a hunter, and can do it much more efficiently. The dog can locate much more game than the hunter; he uses both his eyes and nose to do this job. Man hunts only with his eyes and, compared to the keen senses of the sporting dog, his eyesight is quite inferior. A dog can often maneuver game into a position where a shot will be afforded, while a hunter working alone cannot.

From a conservation standpoint, dogs are highly valuable in finding downed game, locating cripples which the hunter would surely lose and retrieving fallen game from spots the gunner can't reach. When you consider that the average hunter scores clean kills on only approximately one-half of his shots, plus the difficulties often involved in locating wounded game, the dog that has been trained to retrieve is a very definite asset. In addition to the conservation factor, there is the game that otherwise would never go into your bag.

Besides these two major advantages, there is the thrill you get out of hunting with your dog. If you are fortunate enough to own a good dog and have learned to employ his capable assistance on the hunt, you will seldom venture afield without him. Remember this very important point about a hunter and his dog. You can call a hunter a bum, blaspheme his wife, scorn his car—but *never* criticize his hunting dog. You're apt to be murdered, and any "hunting" judge will let your murderer go free, claiming justifiable homicide.

Hunting Dog Breeds

Many blends, breeds and strains of hunting dogs have been developed to meet local needs and personal tastes. Most, however, are specialists that can be fitted into one of three functional categories: 1) retrievers, 2) bird dogs and 3) hounds.

RETRIEVERS

Retrievers are generally used only by those hunters whose main activity is waterfowling. What sort of animals are these retrievers? Usually they are larger-sized dogs, ranging from a weight of 60 pounds up to 90 for the heavy specimens. Their heads are broad, with well-set ears; the eyes are expressive and their general behavior is characterized by good manners. Since the retriever breeds are products of careful breeding, much emphasis has been placed on coat development. The coats are double; they have a soft undercoat of furry hair and an overcoat of longer guard hairs. The coat is oily and serves the dual purpose of repelling water and, because of the countless billions of entrapped air cells, it forms a buoyant life jacket which is a swimming aid. The retrievers' powerful build is further aided in water work by the well-webbed feet and heavy tail which is used as a steering device. A well-developed scenting ability and retrieving instinct are next in line of retriever qualifications. Tractability and an even, cheerful disposition are definite "musts."

It must be remembered that the primary function of a retriever is to wait patiently at heel, or in or near the blind, until a bird is down. Some folk require the dog to fetch on command, others want him to get into action as soon as the bird is hit. In either case, his work in waterfowling consists of periods of well-behaved waiting and periods of extreme activity. It's then easy to understand why tractability and disposition are basic requirements.

We don't want to omit the fact that some retrievers can be taught to find game, such as quail, pheasant and other birds, for the gun in addition to retrieving, but ordinarily they are the specialists who depend on nose, brains and memory to solve problems that stop many other dogs. Nothing in the way of weather, temperature conditions or terrain over which he must work should deter or slow a retriever. He should show a happy, eager willingness to do his job even though it means biting a path for fifty yards through thin ice to get to a bird.

So far we have talked about these fine dogs and, in general, about their uses on a few days each year. Practical folks want to know about the problems of keeping them the balance of the year. Again we point to the trait of good manners inherent in most retrievers. These dogs rapidly assume their place in the family circle. When the puppy grows up and has learned his lessons, he becomes a citizen of responsibilities. He adopts the family and all its worldly possessions. The retriever is no lap dog, yet there is no dog more fond of affection. In fact, he will demand attention—he will butt you with his nose until you place your hand on his head, and he will want to rest his chin on your lap. Furthermore, prolonged stays indoors will do more to ruin a retriever than any one other thing.

When one of these dogs becomes well established with a family, he quickly learns all the folks who regularly visit the place as well as those who, through fear or ignorance, have been unfriendly to him. In other words, the dog makes the decision as to whom he should challenge. Once he tells you to stop, don't try to "sweet talk" him or to bully your way past him. When a mother leaves the place with junior in his carriage, only a chain will hold the dog from

Fig. 8.1 (Above) A retriever at work. (Courtesy of North Carolina News Bureau) (Below) All he asks is a pat on the head for a job well done.

Fig. 8.2 A pointer (Courtesy of Suffolk Lodge Game Preserve)

policing every inch of their route just as effectively as a squadron of motorcycle police clears the route for a public dignitary. His clear honey-colored or brown eyes look at you in a level, unfaltering manner and the expressive wrinkles in the brows are able to convey many of the basic human feelings.

The preceding comments apply to the popular retrieving breeds now recognized by the American registering groups. These breeds are: the Chesapeake Bay, American water spaniel, Labrador, golden, flat-coated and curly-coated retrievers. The order in which they are listed is not indicative of their popularity, but a recognition of the Chesapeake and the American water spaniel as the two breeds originating in this country.

BIRD DOGS

Birds dogs—usually either pointers or setters—are usually employed for upland game hunting. These dogs locate their prey by air, or body scent, not by keeping their noses to the ground for foot scent. When a bird is located, they point, and then retrieve it after the gunner has made a killing shot.

POINTERS. For those of you concerned with the pointer-setter question, here is a brief sketch of the respective backgrounds of these dogs. As a race, pointers have existed for a long time. Dogs of the same general type have been used for the purpose of finding game for several hundreds of years in Spain, France, Germany and Belgium, and it is believed by many writers that the earliest English pointers were imports from these countries. However, it is safe to say that four great English dogs—Bounce, Major, Hamlet and Drake—were the first good pointers, from whom all later good pointers were bred.

As a dog, the pointer is responsive to gentle treatment, but one doesn't ordinarily associate the pointer with the lavish show of affection found in the setter. Of course, there are exceptions in both cases. Perhaps what we mean can be explained better by the fact that in training a pointer will stand rougher treatment or more force than will the average setter; there is no danger of breaking that spark of spontaneity and dash which might be called spirit. No one wants to own or hunt with a dog that works like a puppet or trained seal. Pointers may be started in serious training at an earlier age than setters.

The characteristic short, smooth coat of the pointer adapts him to the warmer days afield in the southern states and lessens the problems of freeing the coat and feet of cockleburs which are so numerous in upland game country. This apparent advantage is dimmed sometimes when a particularly game dog has been beating the briars all day and becomes a mass of scratches and small cuts from muzzle to tip of tail. Some hunters believe that this punishment eventually deters a dog from getting in and combing the tight cover. But on the whole, pointers are hard-hunting, keen-nosed, rugged dogs, possessing the speed, gameness and class which is the delight of the bird hunter's day afield.

A relative newcomer to the field is the German short-haired pointer. Bred in Germany by painstaking breeders who were always aiming for a goal, the short-hair is an entirely different bird dog. His background includes outcrosses with bloodhound, fox hound, and English pointer, and carefully selected animals have perpetuated the better qualities in the dogs we have today. The goal mentioned before was the achievement of an all-purpose dog. As a result, short-hairs are good pointing bird dogs, night-trailers on cold-scent trails, good for hunting rabbits, and proven retrievers from land or water. These alert, powerful dogs also make intelligent companions and watchdogs. As hunters, their range is less than those of setters and English pointers and their speed is restricted. While these last two characteristics might appear to be black marks, they are nonetheless excellent traits for the hunter on foot who is neither inclined nor able to race through the cover after faster dogs. Of one thing we may be sure —the refining process of public favor will either establish the breed or relegate it to the discard.

All too often a great deal of the literature pertaining to bird dogs commits a serious omission. This trait of retrieving is either barely mentioned or omitted altogether. We recognize the fact that it isn't practicable for birds to be shot in every trial in order to determine whether or not the dogs have the retrieving instinct, yet it appears that various trial sponsors should hold retrieving up as a goal for sportsmen and breeders to aim for. Certainly the saving in lost game is more desirable than excessive class or range. Perhaps the retrieving ability of the German short-haired pointer will have an appeal to the ever increasing numbers of conservation-minded sportsmen and in turn help to establish the breed more firmly.

The Weimaraner, the really late addition to the hunting scene in the United States, is just beginning to show his worth in pointing and retrieving. It has the same general hunting characteristics as the German short-hair, but is a much bigger dog.

SETTERS. Like pointers, setters as we know them had

their original development in England. As most of our American dogs trace their ancestry back to English stock, which gave us the Llewellin strain, many folks call any black and white with brown or blue ticks a "Llewellin" which isn't necessarily so. It could more properly be called an English setter.

Somehow the sight of a fine setter working out a piece of cover gives the observer much the same sort of thrill as the playing of the National Anthem at retreat on an army post. The physical grace in motion, guided by an active intelligence, the alert, intense manner and very joy in his work, evidence a sort of visual poetry that beggars description.

Devotion is a passion with a setter, and must be met with gentleness and affection on the part of his owner. He loves to be with his master and once there is a bond of mutual understanding between man and dog, the dog's every act is dedicated to a determination to serve and please. Perhaps because of his gentle nature, the setter usually develops more slowly than the pointer. Many puppies don't get serious training until after their second year. The long, silky coat of the setter, with the feathered legs and tail, give the impression that Mother Nature tried to carry the bodily grace out to the very tips of the hairs. This coat provides more warmth in

Fig. 8.3 A German short-haired pointer brings back a ringneck pheasant. (Courtesy of Wisconsin Conservation Department)

Fig. 8.4 A setter. (Courtesy of Suffolk Lodge Game Preserve)

winter but it has a fatal attraction for cockleburs.

The Irish setter, as his name implies, claims "the auld sod" as his home. His rich chestnut or mahogany color, with perhaps a white spot on the throat, chest or toes, marks him as an aristocrat. A good hunter with a fine nose and intelligence, he has his own devoted following. However, his range and speed are more restricted and the larger, faster English setters and pointers have almost eliminated him, as well as the Gordons, from most field trial competition. This does not mean that he is any the less a good gun dog. To many, in fact, the closer hunting trait makes him more useful as a gun dog, particularly where the going is rough and the cover must be searched thoroughly.

The little known Gordons are Scotland's contribution to the bird dog breeds. While the Duke of Gordon fancied the big black and tan dogs that today bear his name, many other Scottish breeders were partial to the same type. Again, the same comments as to range and speed that were made about the Irish setter apply to the Gordon. In addition, it may be said of both dogs that their dark colors make them difficult to see in heavy cover. Both are staunch, methodical workers of great endurance and tractability. Both have been used with great satisfaction

as turkey dogs whose principal job is to trail, find and flush a gang of turkeys and then bark when the birds are in the air in order to guide the hunter to the spot. After the blind is built, dog and man hide until the calling has been successful or unsuccessful in bringing a bird to the blind.

SPANIELS. These dogs, including the American cocker spaniel, the English cocker spaniel, the Brittany spaniel, the English springer spaniel, and the Clumber spaniel, are body-scent seekers that flush game within shotgun range. In other words, their task is to stay within killing gunshot of the hunter, find birds by body scent, flush them out and retrieve them. (They don't point as a rule.) Generally, the Clumber, Brittany and English springer spaniels do these jobs very well. They are also good all-round dogs, hunting squirrels and rabbits as enthusiastically as upland birds, retrieving ducks readily when the water and weather aren't too cold. The cocker spaniel seems to have lost its former ability as a result of so many generations having been bred more for home and show bench than for hunting purposes. It has gained in beauty, but lost much of its hunting instinct. When a field-worthy cocker is found, however, the lucky owner will have himself a first-rate bird dog that can be trained to find, flush and retrieve. Cocker and springer spaniels are excellent—there are none better —for mourning dove hunting.

HOUNDS

All hounds trail by spoor, or from the scent left by the feet of game—hence are often called foot-scenters. Their job is to find, flush and pursue their

Fig. 8.5 A pair of bird dogs on a woodcock hunt.

quarry, baying as they go. The excitement in their bay or bark increases as the trail grows "hotter"— that is, as they get closer to the game. Some hounds, like the Basset and beagles, follow slowly. These are particularly preferred by rabbit hunters because of this very characteristic. Rabbits are likely to go underground when pushed hard by a fast-trailing dog. Fox, 'coon and cat hunters, on the other hand, prefer larger, stronger and bolder dogs that push game fast and relentlessly. Some of these dogs even tree the game and all but climb the tree to call the hunter's attention to where their quarry is hiding.

While the Basset and beagle hounds are employed primarily as rabbit dogs—and there are none finer —they are useful in hunting every species of upland game as well as squirrels. Their affectionate nature and loyal disposition make them excellent household pets as well as very fine gunning dogs.

The bigger hounds such as Plott hound, coonhound, blue-tick hound, and foxhound can be trained to run almost anything that walks and gives off a scent. They can also be taught to tree many species of big and small game including raccoon, opossum, wildcat, mountain lions, etc. They are also good on game which runs and fights such as wolf, fox, coyote, bear, deer and boar.

Small terrier breeds are sometimes used on vermin and burrowing animals. But as a rule, the small breeds of hounds do a better job.

Which Breed Should I Buy?

You should choose the breed, or type of dog, that will best suit the needs you expect to put it to. Thanks to the breeders who have worked so meticulously to provide a wide choice of breeds, you can find one suited for every hunting job. However, when you expect to do several types of hunting, yet still can afford only one dog, you should select a breed which will give you amiable companionship afield as well as being adaptable to varied hunting situations. For example, the beagle and Basset hounds both make fine pets, and excellent rabbit dogs, yet will usually hunt upland game birds fairly well. Again, the springer and Brittany spaniels will hunt upland birds well, yet can double as waterfowl retrievers if properly trained and used in water that is not too cold. The German short-haired pointer and Weimaraner are also good dual purpose or all-round dogs.

There are two good sources of information about the qualifications of a hunting dog. One is what you see with your own eyes and the other is records of field trial performances. Actually, field trials are the

Fig. 8.6 Some species of dogs work well for both waterfowl (above) and upland game birds (below).

Fig. 8.7 (Above) A hound has just treed a raccoon. (Courtesy of Pennsylvania Game Commission)

Fig. 8.8 (Below) These hounds were successful in bringing this black bear to bay. (Courtesy of North Carolina Department of Conservation & Development)

best place to see good hunting dogs in action. In the last few years, they have become very popular in the United States and there are few places where you can't travel a short distance to see dogs at work on game native to your area. Before purchasing any hunting dog, attend as many of these trials as you can, study the dogs and talk with their owners. While field-trial performers are seldom available, except at high prices, closely related dogs often are. Decide which of the dogs you see in competition comes closest to what you want, then investigate the availability of similarly bred stock. If you wish, take someone with you who knows dogs, but remember that there is the chance that he won't be able to resist trying to steer you to what pleases him and not necessarily you.

Be sure to get the best possible dog you can afford. It costs just as much to raise, keep, house and feed the poorest-bred puppy as it does the best-bred one, and it would probably take longer and cost more to train the inferior one with less satisfactory results. If there's an occasion when you should bend yourself a bit on price, it's when buying a quality hunting dog.

How much you should pay to get the dog that you wish depends on you, the seller, and supply and demand. Avoid a puppy priced so low that he couldn't have been raised properly for the amount involved. A grown and trained dog's price should be related to his quality, worth of his training and his age. If you don't feel you are qualified to select a dog or if it's impossible for you personally to inspect the dog you're interested in, it might be worthwhile to ask one of the recognized professional trainers in the area to look him over for you and give you his opinion of him. There are many such trainers all over the country who aren't interested in selling dogs but, for a reasonable fee, are willing to appraise them fairly for potential buyers.

WHY REGISTRATION

Today more than ever before we are becoming conscious of the importance of blood lines. Our cattle, hogs, chickens, roses, corn and practically everything we raise comes from known stock. Since so little is involved in the registration of dogs, yet in some cases so much to be gained, it is only consistent that a certified record of the dog's ancestry be kept. Failure to register a dog that is otherwise eligible is more often due to indolence. Records of this sort are invaluable in selective breeding. Should a puppy develop outstanding ability when mature, his worth to his owner in stud fees is material—but it depends on whether or not the dog is registered. Surely a litter of puppies can be given away with a clean slate when the formalities of registration cover the litter. Puppy shots, worm treatment and registration go hand in hand. The new owners feel that they have a little more when they know that the new pup can go as far as he can in dogdom's Hall of Fame when there can be no question as to his breeding.

About Field Trials

Basically, field trials are nothing more than competitive tests of dogs' abilities on their special game. A bird dog field trial serves its fundamental purpose best when it is a test of a dog's ability as a hunting dog. Sometimes one witnesses a trial which gives the impression that it is more of a dog race than a bird finding test. Many authorities hold to the first definition given above. Open all-age stakes usually find the big-going or wide-ranging dogs entered, and this type dog does not often conform to the average quail hunter's idea of a good gun dog. Yet all quail hunters do not hunt the same way. Some walk, many ride horses, mules, carriages, or cars, depending on the country hunted. Consequently, the wide-ranging dog can cover the territory thoroughly and at the same time keep ahead of the hunter.

This is meant to point at the evident confusion in the minds of some hunters between the types of trials being held. Compared with the open events, the amateur shooting stake is the one more nearly appealing to the average hunter. Most events are over a half-hour course. This usually allows about twenty-two minutes on the course and eight minutes in the bird field.

In this type of trial, the judges look for bird searching ability, range, speed, ease of movement, general appearance or class and the way in which the dog handles. In the bird field the dog is judged on the way he handles planted birds, his style on point and his steadiness to shot and wing.

As was stated before, trials are the test of the ability of the dogs, yet the spirit of rivalry, camaraderie, the formation of new acquaintances and the renewal of old bring out the best in sportsmanship. Field trials are public spectacles that catch the eye of folks in a community and become extremely popular events when properly conducted. For the participants, it is particularly true that conservation of our wildlife wins a new supporter whenever a new field trial enthusiast is born. Many people today spend the time and money following trials that formerly was spent on meat-getting expeditions.

No hunting dog of any type, breed, or ancestry

is any better than his environment and the patient intelligence with which he is broken to the gun teach him to be. Whether you train your dog or have it done by a professional, he needs help from you if he's to become a good, steady worker. No attempt will be made in this book to tell you how to train a hunting dog. There are many good books already available on this subject. However, it's well worth repeating that a well-trained dog is the greatest single contribution that the average sportsman can make to the conservation of game. But regardless of this, there's nothing more gratifying in the whole category of hunting than to see a hard-working, determined dog accomplish his mission.

Chapter Nine

LEARNING HUNTING SAFETY

A GUN IS an instrument for killing. It is neither a toy nor a plaything. It is a *deadly* weapon. Records compiled by the National Safety Council and other interested organizations indicate that approximately 2500 people lose their lives in gun accidents each year, with about one-third of the total coming as a result of hunting mishaps.

Most hunting accidents occur from one of these three principal causes: mistaking humans for game, failure to keep the gun safety catch on when not shooting and humans stepping into line of fire. Other major causes include accidental discharges resulting from dropping or bumping the gun, improper crossing of fences or other trail obstructions, failure to properly unload and dismantle the weapon when stowing it in cars, dirt or other foreign objects blocking barrels, thereby causing them to shatter when fired, and ricocheting bullets.

Almost every hunting accident could be avoided if every hunter kept in mind, whenever he is afield with his gun, the few common-sense rules of safety in gun handling. These rules have been aptly listed by the Sporting Arms and Ammunition Manufacturers' Institute under the appropriate title, *The Ten Commandments of Safety.* Thus, the following section of this chapter should be thoroughly studied and all but memorized, not alone by the beginner but by the old hand as well—the old hand who has become so familiar with his guns that he has forgotten caution. Remember that when it is considered that the life saved may be your own, taking the time to practice these few simple rules seems well worth the small amount of effort required.

The Ten Commandments of Safety

1. You should know your gun and how to operate it safely. Treat every gun with the respect due to a loaded gun.

The modern hunting gun—either shotgun or rifle— is designed and built with every essential safeguard, so that in the hands of a competent and discriminating hunter it's absolutely safe. To take full benefit of these safeguards, you must know your gun thoroughly, inside and out. You must know what actions on your part produce what reactions on the gun, and when, and why. Once you have taught yourself all about your gun, and have a certain amount of actual practice in firing a number of shots or rounds with it, then and only then are you ready to venture into the field to hunt.

The second sentence of this rule is cardinal in all gun safety. Don't assume that other hunters are obeying the *Ten Commandments of Safety.* Rather, assume that every gun is loaded, no matter who is using it or where it is, until it has been *definitely* proved otherwise. Make it a practice to leave the breech open when handling your own or other guns. Be *absolutely* certain that there are *no* shells in the chamber and magazine. Be more than just sure. It's foolhardy to assume that a gun is unloaded simply because it should be unloaded. Look twice, three times and always be suspicious that any gun might be loaded. If the above procedure is followed by all gun owners, those deplorable "I didn't know it was loaded" accidents would never happen.

2. Guns carried into camp, home or automobile, or when otherwise not in use, must always be unloaded and taken down or have their actions open; guns always should be carried in cases to the shooting area.

No gun should ever be loaded except during the time in the field when actual hunting is taking place. This means no loaded guns in houses, camps or automobiles. (In many states it's unlawful to carry a loaded gun in a car.) Even when you pause to rest, unload your gun. Your gun should never be loaded when it's out of your hands. Never lean a loaded gun against a flat surface, such as a wall, the side of blind, fence, tree, or against an automobile. In any of these locations, a gust of wind or a slight jar a distance from the gun can knock it over and cause it to go off. Remember that if a gun has been left loaded, intentionally or inadvertently, tragedy is stalking at the careless offender's heels.

3. *Always be sure barrel and action are clear of obstructions, and that you have only ammunition of the proper size for the gun you are carrying.*

Never attempt to shoot an obstruction from the bore of any gun. To do so is to invite disaster. Almost invariably the gun is completely damaged, and very frequently the shooter and those nearby are injured. The effect of shooting an obstruction from a gun barrel may be likened to that of a high-speed express train hurtling into a freight train stalled on the same track. The stalled train isn't pushed ahead by the impact of the moving train; instead everything telescopes and literally explodes.

Unless care is exercised, snow and mud can plug a gun's muzzle and can be dangerous since the hunter may not know about it. The only sure way of guarding against this is to not get into the bad habit of placing the muzzle on the ground. Also, never form the habit of resting the muzzle on your foot when stopping to catch your breath or for a talk with your gunning companions. In addition to running the risk of blowing off your foot, there is often the chance of plugging the muzzle. If you stumble on snow or in a marsh and aren't sure as to whether or not the muzzle touched the ground, always investigate. When checking the barrel of a gun, always look through the breech end, never through the muzzle end.

Always be sure your firearm is in top condition and needs no repair. If your gun does need repair, take it to a good gunsmith—attempting to repair a gun is *not* for the average do-it-yourselfer. A faulty or worn mechanism can cause a gun to misfire or go off when it isn't desirable. You can, however, take good care of your weapon by following the tips given in Chapters 1 and 2. But be sure to remove any oil or grease from the chamber before firing. If present to any appreciable degree when the gun is fired, it may well result in damage to the weapon.

Be sure to check your shells very carefully before loading. A 20-gauge shotgun shell in a 12-gauge barrel can spell disaster for the careless hunter. Many serious accidents occur each year from this cause, and it can't be stressed too strongly that it's absolutely necessary to always check your shells and shell chamber when loading. If you change guns while out on a hunting trip, remove *all* the shells used for that gun from your hunting clothing and replace with shells of the right caliber. If different calibers or gauges are used at virtually the same time, inspect each shell before putting it in the gun. Also, in the case of shotguns, don't use present-day smokeless-powder loads in guns having twist steel or Damascus barrels. Such guns were made for black-powder loads developing only about half the breech pressure of modern smokeless-powder loads. Play it safe. Don't take a chance.

4. *Always carry your gun so that you can control the direction of the muzzle even if you stumble; keep the safety on until you are ready to shoot.*

The safest method of carrying a gun while walking in the field is either in the bend of your elbow, or in one or both hands, with the muzzle pointed at the ground and slightly ahead of you. Have one hand always holding or ready to grab the gun in the case of a stumble, to control the muzzle. To relax your arms, it is often desirable to carry the gun over your shoulder. In doing this, be sure that the trigger side is up. Never slip off the safety with which all guns are equipped until you're actually raising the gun to make the shot.

When a group of hunters are working up a side hill or when in any situation where a slip or fall is possible, it's safe practice not to have a shell in the chamber of your gun. It requires very little time to jack a shell into the chamber, should the chance of a shot present itself. Another safe way of handling a shotgun in such situations is to open the lock and carry it disengaged. Carrying a loaded shotgun this way doesn't delay or interfere with your shooting efficiency. In bringing the gun to aim, it will automatically and instantaneously engage for performance. No motion is lost in the swing.

5. *Be sure of your target before you squeeze the trigger; know the identifying features of the game you intend to hunt.*

Possibly the most tragic and unforgivable of all hunting "accidents" is the case of one hunter mistaking another hunter for wildlife game. Think of it! A man aims his gun at another man and deliberately pulls the trigger! Calling it carelessness doesn't come even close to the reason for it. No one could possibly mistake a man for any type of game —game and men do *not* look alike—because of indifference or lack of care. To commit such an enormous blunder, a man must become so emotionally charged with the overpowering desire to *kill* that his mind plays tricks on him, as if in the grip of a raging fever—as indeed it may be at the moment. Don't be trigger happy. Never shoot at vaguely seen or imagined targets, at a sound, or a movement. See your target plainly and know definitely what is in the line of fire and behind your target. Remember that a good hunter takes his time, picks the game which is within range, and makes his shots count. He knows what he is shooting at, and makes sure that no one is in range. Be certain that you're a *good hunter*.

6. Never point a gun at anything you do not want to shoot; avoid all horseplay while handling a gun.

During the course of a hunt, all too often hunters become careless and permit their gun barrels to waver in the direction of fellow hunters. This is especially noticeable in the close confines of a blind or duck boat. Don't leave loaded guns leaning in precarious positions against a blind. It's a good practice not to load any guns until after the stool is set and all the gunners are in the blind. The best way to hold a gun, when seated in a blind, is across the thighs, pointed down toward the front of the blind and slightly inclined to the left. Never balance your gun, trigger guard off or down, with the barrel on the front wall of a blind and the toe of the stock on the seat. It's unstable in such a position and could fall off.

It is common courtesy not to shoot across your companions in a blind unless they tell you to and thus expect you to do it. As a rule, the right hand takes the right hand shots, and vice versa. If you miss or cause a cripple, you should get out of the way and ask the other fellow to take over. If two ducks come in, each man should shoot at the bird on his side. If more than two come in, the same general rule should apply. However, suppose eight or ten ducks are flying across the blind from right to left. The left-hand man takes the lead one; but the right-hand man shouldn't shoot at the last duck. He should, instead, shoot at the fourth or fifth from the right; because, if he underleads, he has a chance of knocking down the bird immediately following the one he shot at with the tail end of his shot string.

Two gunners in the same duck boat needn't create a problem of safe shooting. While shooting simultaneously, it's true, the hunter's shot may hit his partner. The safe solution, therefore, is to sit back-to-back or side-by-side. Standing up in a boat is, of course, risky, as the shooter is apt to lose his balance and upset the craft. It is advisable to stand up and shoot, therefore, only when the craft is resting on shore, marshes, or bogs. Partially grounding the boat steadies it. At the same time, it provides the hunter with solid footing, removing the necessity of stepping and sinking into marshland if the water becomes too choppy for a well-aimed shot. If your boat overturns in deep water, stay with the boat. Don't try to swim ashore.

Remember that the rule, "Never point your gun at anything you do not wish to shoot," applies to yourself, too. Actually, even though you're convinced that the gun is unloaded, pointing it at random is a foolishly hazardous procedure. And a shocking number of accidents are still attributed to the fact that someone didn't know a gun was loaded.

7. Never climb a tree or fence or jump a ditch with a loaded gun; never pull a gun toward you by the muzzle.

While afield, where climbing fences is necessary, the gun shouldn't be used to boost the hunter. This is a bad practice from which not a few fatal accidents have resulted. A sure sign of a "green" hunter is climbing fences with gun in hand. More seasoned shooters know this is dangerous as well as foolhardy. The gun can easily become fouled in the fence wires and accidentally fired while the hunter is engrossed in clearing the obstacle. The gun carrier himself or his companions may be the target of a stray shot as well as not. Be gun wise. Break open a shotgun or unload a pump or automatic before attempting the climbing operation. While this may appear to be a great deal of trouble, it isn't once the habit has been acquired. Also take the sensible precaution of placing the firearm on the ground on the *other* side of the fence. Then climb over yourself with both hands free. Don't lean the gun against the wires, though on the other side—because in climbing over you might disturb its perch and upset it. The jar in dropping may cause the gun to fire wild. When climbing a stone wall, place your weapon to one side, with the muzzle facing forward, and climb the wall some safe distance away.

When climbing a tree, unload or break open your gun and use both hands to go up the tree. Then have someone hand you the gun. A hunter who does this with a loaded gun is inviting a twig or a branch to set it off.

It is also a mistake to use your weapon as a cane, wedge, or lever, from the standpoint not only of damaging the stock but also of inviting an unwanted discharge.

8. Never shoot at a flat, hard surface or the surface of water.

The force of the shot on such a surface isn't absorbed, it's deflected. Therefore, never shoot at water, flat rocks, etc., from which shot may ricochet.

9. Store guns and ammunition separately, beyond the reach of children.

Guns that are carelessly stored between hunting trips and at the end of the hunting season cause many unnecessary accidents. If there are children in your home, special precautions must be taken. Not only must you make sure that the weapon is unloaded at all times, but the gun and ammunition must be kept out of their reach. It's a good idea to keep your firearms and ammunition under lock and key. Also be certain to teach your children about the dangers of playing with a gun.

10. Avoid alcoholic drinks before or during shooting.

This rule shouldn't need any great elaboration. If you must drink, don't go hunting. If you wish to go hunting, don't drink. This means even *one* drink.

If these *Ten Commandments of Safety* were strictly followed there would be no gun accidents. It's obvious that they are not strictly observed, for each year the newspapers report numerous shooting accidents that occur in the field, or in the home or camp after a day of hunting. As was stated in Chapter 1, hunting is a wonderful, thrilling sport. Basically it isn't a dangerous one. But only careless, thoughtless people make it so. Don't you be one of them.

Other Safety Precautions

Too many hunters enter the woods every year without the necessary respect for them. Falls of all sorts can be experienced, if the hunter isn't aware of the conditions that cause them to occur. The results can be minor in personal injury, but can also be very serious.

Travel side hills with extreme caution, watch your footing and keep your hands free to use any available brush or tree to stop sliding. A carrying sling for your rifle is invaluable for this purpose. This enables you to have both hands free for this checking of your slide.

Travel slowly, watch your footing, place your foot down firmly. Shift your weight smoothly from one foot to the other, and above all, stop when looking around, so your attention can be concentrated on one thing at a time. When you start moving again, keep your thoughts on your footing, and be prepared at all times for that slip or that small stone to turn under the leaves. Don't walk to the very edge of a ledge, no matter how solid it may look. Too many dangers are hidden under the leaves or brush, or under the snow. Large and solid looking rocks can shift under very little weight, and cause falls of dangerous results.

Travel in terrain suitable to your age and physical condition. Don't try climbing up the steep side of a ridge in one continuous scramble. Stop and rest, get your breath and take it in stages. Pause just before you put your head over the top. If you should find a shot awaiting you when you look over the top, that pause may mean the steadiness you will need to make a good hit. But of most importance is that the stops on the way up can avoid a heart attack! No one can assure himself of possessing a heart immune to this possibility due to the strenuous exertion of climbing the side of a mountain, regardless of age or his physical condition!

Choose your footwear with care. Make sure your shoes fit properly—not too tight, but with the proper support for your ankles. Wear woolen socks, but avoid putting too many pairs on your feet so that your shoes fit too tightly; this will stop circulation. Loose shoes cause blisters from rubbing, which can become very painful and in some cases become infected from the dye in your stockings.

Use a shoe with the type of sole which insures footing suitable for travel on rocks, loose dry leaves, or snow. Avoid smooth leather soles; they are no good for any type of terrain, and become extremely slippery in dry forest conditions. Ripple soles, crepe rubber treads, or cleat rubber treads seem to be the best type to use.

If you intend to hunt in strange country invest in a topographic map, and get some idea of the terrain and surrounding area into which you intend to go. Avoid the embarrassment of being lost, buy a compass and learn to use it. It can prove to be your very best friend at the proper time. Always carry plenty of matches and a few chocolate bars. The comfort of a fire and a bar of candy to munch on is a great help to your morale, should you have to spend the night in the woods. If you should have to spend the night in the forest, do not roam around in the dark; that is utter foolishness! Instead, spend the last hour of daylight gathering a supply of firewood, so you can keep your fire going. Remember that fire can be seen for miles, to say nothing of the comfort you will get from it on a cold night. Do this, and wait for daylight to resume finding your way out! Carrying a small flare-type fire starter in your pocket at all times will insure your getting a fire started regardless of how wet it may be.

Frostbite is something you must guard against while hunting in cold weather. It can be detected by white spots on the face or if the ears turn white. When this happens, cover with your hand or with some warm clothing. Rub gently. Elevate the nipped extremity and drink warm coffee, cocoa, or tea. If you're out in the cold and your feet become numb and heavy, remove the boots at once and wrap the feet in something warm, such as blankets. Massage them gently until they become warm agan. Of course, the best bet is to dress properly so you won't get cold.

So that other hunters—the careless variety—can't

possibly mistake you for wild game, wear plenty of yellow or red. Also be careful not to stop in a clump of brush or to shake out a white handkerchief before blowing your nose with it. If you shoot an animal such as deer be sure to drag it out rather than carrying it over your shoulders.

Use a little common sense, and proceed with caution, bearing in mind the safety of others and yourself at all times. This will result in many years of enjoyable hunting without the inconvenience of personal injury to yourself or your companions. Bear in mind that the forest isn't man's natural habitat; he is not endowed with the natural instincts and ability to roam this terrain. He must adapt himself to conditions that prevail and make use of the proper judgment and apparel to travel safely and comfortably. Together with good hunting manners, consideration for others and the common courtesy due all fellowmen, this indeed can be the "sport of kings" enjoyed by all, with only a pleasant memory to remind one of days gone past in this greatest of all privileges we engage in.

Prevent Forest and Grass Fires

Forest and grass fires destroy lives, homes, timber and crops. Fires also destroy wildlife and reduce or limit hunting pleasures. Ordinary precautions can eliminate most grass or forest fires. But precautions cannot be left to "the other fellow." You must do your part! Observe these simple common-sense rules:

1. Select a suitable place for your campfire, preferably beside a stream or lake. Remove all combustible material down to the mineral soil. Extinguish your fire with water.

2. Limit smoking to the campsite or while resting in a safe place near a stream or lake. Don't smoke while on the trail. Never discard lighted matches, burning cigarettes or cigar stubs, hot pipe ashes, or any burning substance which has not been completely extinguished.

3. Observe all fire-prevention rules applying to particular hunting areas—especially rules posted as a result of unusual dry spells.

Game Laws

For most hunting, licenses are required. These are granted by individual state governments and are usually available at county courthouses, town halls and quite often at hunting gear dealers. The fees range anywhere from $1 to $5 for residents; $2 to $25 for non-residents. (Some states require a special license for big game—deer, bear, elk, etc.) With the license you also receive a copy of the state's hunting laws and, of course, they must be followed to the letter.

When hunting waterfowl, in addition to the state license, and if you're sixteen years of age or older, you must obtain a federal duck stamp. It's illegal to hunt waterfowl without these licenses, and the dollars you spend for them help to maintain your sport. The federal duck stamp (cost, $3) must have your signature written across the face thereof and can be purchased from your local post office. Persons under sixteen years of age don't have to possess such a stamp.

In all states there are open and closed seasons on most game (except the so-called varmint species); before you hunt any area be sure the season is open for the species you plan to shoot. This is especially true when you plan a hunting trip to out-of-state fields and woods. To obtain this information, write to the proper department of the state—listed in the Appendix—where you're planning to hunt.

The Conservation Law

All of you have heard the saying "innocent until proved guilty." This is true in Civil Law (town or city laws) but it isn't so in the Conservation Law. Since all wild animals—four footed, fish or any other—belong to the state, a person caught with illegal game or protected animal is *guilty until he can prove his innocence*. The possession of an illegal animal is proof of the puddin'. All that a game warden has to do when he catches a man doing something illegally is to bring him to court, produce the animal and the man is guilty unless he can prove otherwise. If he can't, he is fined according to law.

A lot of people hesitate to "do something about it" when they see a violation of the Conservation Law simply because they aren't sure of their "rights." Some are afraid to make enemies or don't want to be tattletales or stool pigeons. This shouldn't be. If someone were stealing chickens from your chicken coop or broke into your house, you'd do your darndest to catch him. You should also try to stop a man from breaking the Conservation Law because he is taking something that is equally yours. He's stealing it. Not only that but he is spoiling your hunting and making it hard for other people to stay honest, too.

Everybody has the right to arrest a violator of the Conservation Law because the man has committed a misdemeanor. So you see, people can "do something about it" if they want to; they have the right and the power to do so. Just be sure that a crime has been committed or is being tried. *Don't guess— know!* Be sure the person you arrest knows why he's arrested. And, if he shoots anything illegally, be sure to bring the animal to court with you. You can't convict the person unless you have witnesses to prove you're right.

Your Game Protector is your friend. If you aren't sure of your Conservation Laws, call him up and ask. He's just as anxious to tell you the law as you are to find out. It makes his job easier. (He also may be able to give you a few tips on where to hunt.) Help him do a good job by following the law and being courteous in the field when you are hunting. His job is to enforce your laws, and he figures if he can explain the law to someone, there'll be fewer violators. By all means get to know him.

That brings us to field conduct. There are a couple of things to keep in mind while you're out there having fun hunting. When you come to posted lands or waters, better stay out unless you have permission from the person controlling the land or water rights. If you trespass, you commit a misdemeanor and are liable to a fine of from $10 to $100 for the first offense, and you lose your hunting license for that year. You also are liable to a fine of $10 to $50 for any damages you caused plus the court expenses. It's foolish to trespass or tear down posters. You're breaking the law and can be penalized if caught. Besides, you are making it hard for other hunters to follow the sport.

Rumors get around if you trespass. The first thing you know, all the landowners are starting to put up posting notices. Then you wonder why you are not able to hunt. Be wise. Ask the landowner if you can hunt or fish on his property. It doesn't take much effort and creates a lot of good will. Ninety-nine out of a 100 landowners will be tickled pink to give you permission. You'll be a friend for life if you bring back a rabbit for his supper. Think it over. Behave yourself and don't be a game hog. You're hurting your friends and you're hurting yourself.

Chapter Ten

LEARNING ABOUT SHOOTING PRESERVES

THOUSANDS OF HUNTERS each year are finding shooting preserves to be the answer to their prayers. Limited by posting or crowded by too many other hunters, a great many sportsmen have turned to preserve put-and-take or pay-as-you-go hunting. There are still many open areas in all states where there is good bird hunting, but on many of them the pressure of the number of hunters is mounting and public stocking programs seldom provide sustained hunting.

Shooting preserves are operated by private ownership for a profit. Since the operators do not depend on native birds, an extended season of six months is allowed on pen-raised birds and there is no bag limit. The raising-pens take the place of natural reproduction in the wild. Shooting preserves, open to the public, are now operated in all but eight of the fifty states.

The shooting preserve offers many advantages to the average hunter. For instance, convenience is no minor attraction. You know where to hunt to bag game, and you can go directly to the area with expectation and assurance of opportunities for shots. You can't but gamble when making the rounds of free open-to-hunting land tracts during a short hunting season; only on a paid shooting preserve, or a privately-owned, heavily fenced-in and guarded tract, can you rate your hunting chances better than an even 50-50. Since many of the shooting preserves are located close to big cities it makes hunting possible where no wild game or shooting privileges now exist.

Furthermore, with steady, annual increases in the number of hunters afield each regular hunting season, more and more hunters are finding it difficult to get permission to hunt on wild-game-inhabited private property. "No Hunting"—"No Trespassing" —signs, unfortunately, mean just that, and seemingly are to be found on every tree and fence post when one starts looking for a nearby place to bird hunt. Many such posted areas have become paid shooting preserves, appreciated by patron hunters and profitable acreage to their owners.

A shooting preserve is an ideal location for a father to introduce a maturing son to field shooting. Uncrowded and assured of a number of reasonably good shots at game, the two can establish lasting principles of good teamwork and safe, efficient gun handling afield. Visiting sportsmen-friends and business men with known hunting preferences, but limited time, can be given a good time afield by their hosts, at nominal expense.

Congested living and highway traffic have made the keeping of a bird dog in the city a problem, and city-kept bird dogs are declining in numbers. It is discouraging to invest up to $300 in a good, trained hunting dog and then run the increasing risks of his urban maintenance. But most shooting preserve operators own and work trained hunting dogs to retrieve cripples and reduce stock losses. In some cases, use of a dog is part of the charged hunting fee; in others, there is an extra charge for the trained canine and his handler.

Where the paying hunter has his own dog, the preserves offer perfect field settings for their training and working. Dog men are enthusiastic about the convenience of available training acreage and birds to be found.

Your hunting safety factor is increased when you hunt within the boundaries of a paid preserve. Most operators take care to assign and restrict each small party to a designated hunting area, and to see that fundamental safety precautions are understood and observed. The intoxicated patron isn't allowed to hunt, and persons who imbibe after they start hunting are courteously but resolutely denied preserve use privileges.

The preserve operator, being a business man, fully realizes that his continued success and income depend on making his shooting preserve attractive and safe to patrons. You, as a paying guest, agree to reasonable conduct rules when you enter the preserve to do your hunting; otherwise, you don't hunt! Where patrons are inexperienced in the safe handling of firearms, most preserve operators take time to give brief demonstrations or arrange for an experienced shooter to accompany the party afield.

There are two main reasons why hunters are reluctant to try shooting preserves. They have the idea that pen-raised birds are like "shooting fish in a barrel." The preserve operators know this and raise their birds in long exercising pens where they have room to fly. Where conditions permit, the birds are released several days before the area is hunted to allow them to get conditioned to the wild. Ring-necked pheasants never tame down and can be released 10 minutes before the hunt begins and 99 per cent of the flights will be satisfactory. Special care must be taken with quail and chukars or they will not make suitable targets. The secret of sporty preserve shooting is raising game birds conditioned to flying.

The second reason hunters won't try shooting preserves is the cost. The average hunter doesn't consider what a hunting trip costs. At a preserve, it's paid out in one lump sum; but in the wild the cost is stretched out over a day of driving, meals and often lodging, plus other factors. A day's hunting in the wild may produce few shots but hunting on a preserve assures a certain amount of shooting and game to take home.

There are two systems generally employed to charge for the use of the shooting preserve. The first, and the most used system, is to charge a minimum daily hunting fee, for which a designated number of birds are allowed. Extra kills are paid for on a per capita basis known to the hunter before he walks afield. Should he fail to connect with any of the provided targets—due to his own poor marksmanship—he doesn't get a refund, however.

The second, preferred by many patrons of the poor shot class, is the pay-only-for-what-you-kill fee system. Under this system, the kill cost per bird usually figures a little higher than the minimum daily fee system.

While most shooting preserves charge a straight per bird fee (generally from $4 to $8) regardless of the species hunted, a few have variable price ranges. For example, each pen-raised pheasant released and killed will cost a hunter $4 to $8; each quail, $2 to $4; and chukar partridge, $3 to $6. Charges vary, of course, according to the facilities and services offered by the shooting preserve.

The usual minimum size of a preserve is 500 acres, which provides plenty of hunting area. The paying customers are the ones who determine how much sport a shooting preserve must provide. If the customers demand tough wing shooting, and are willing to pay for the best, the operator will give it to them. If the hunters want easy field walking, birds stocked close to trails, and all open shooting, the operator will cooperate. Most shooting preserve operators go in business to make a living, rather than as a sideline operation; they are willing to supply the type of hunting sportsmen demand. For example, the wild-bird die-hard can have it as wild as he wants it. His birds can be set out the night before if he so wishes. The operator, in this case, nets the birds in their pen, then places them into a crate, sets the crate in the bushy cover of the portion of the preserve to be hunted by his customer, opens its door and lets them go free to their own desires. Quail will usually sit tight in a covey in some nearby field until the customer and his dog arrive the next morning, but chukar partridge and pheasants may well spread out over several acres or more. Quite often some may even wander off into an out-of-bounds section of the preserve where another party will be hunting or may even leave the preserve altogether. In either case these birds would be "lost" to the hunter.

Since the customer usually has to pay for his birds whether or not he succeeds in bagging all of them, the most preferred method of releasing them is the so-called flighting one. This gives him a much surer guarantee that he'll get his quota and still have as much fun as hunting them in the wild. In this method, the birds are carried to the field in a crate and are allowed to fly away singly while he watches them and notes the distant spot at which each apparently lands. Then, when all have been set free, he and his dog have a full day's hunt ahead of them. While he still might not find all his birds, he has a very good chance of getting shots at some extras that might have survived previous hunts.

If the hunter doesn't wish to take the time or doesn't have the stamina to climb hills and fight thickets all day, there's another method of release often employed. Here, each bird is placed in cover so dense that it can't fly but must run. When it eventually reaches a place where it feels it will be safe, it squats. The operator, meanwhile, ties a strip of white cloth to bush cover where the bird was liberated. When the customer, making his rounds, spots the white flag, he directs his dog to the location and it easily picks up the scent. Should the bird decide to move cross-country in the interim, as frequently occurs, the hunter gets some extra sport he didn't bargain for.

Regardless of the method of release employed—

there are many others used in addition to those mentioned here—any birds the customer takes in excess of his quota, of course, he must pay for. At the end of the day before he takes his birds home they are tagged or marked in some manner to prove they are not wild ones shot illegally out of season.

The ringneck pheasant is by far the undisputed king of the preserve birds. Mallards are second and quail are third. The chukar partridge ranks fourth. All, however, offer the hunter the same amount of sport as when in their natural habitat. Actually, it is often just as difficult, but a great deal more fun, to bag pen-raised birds as it is "wild" ones. For instance, on some shooting preserves the duck blinds are so arranged that only overhead shots are possible, and the average score, believe it or not, is one mallard downed for every twelve shots fired. But, in any case, you "shoot till you win." You generally agree beforehand on how many ducks you want to take, and you simply keep shooting until you get your quota. Dead birds and cripples are promptly recovered by your retriever, so you don't even have to wet your hands.

Hunting licenses are required on shooting preserves in most states. In many instances preserves issue special low-cost licenses for non-resident hunters, good only within the shooting preserve boundaries during specified periods, and often of short duration. Sunday hunting is permitted in some but not all states. Hunters are advised to bring their own ammunition after learning recommended shot sizes from preserve operators.

Each state conservation department sets the regulations for preserves within its borders. In most states having licensed shooting preserves it is customary to impose a recovery percentage of pen-raised birds released. New York State, for example, allows only 80 per cent of the total number of pheasants released to be recoverd. This means that for every five ringnecks stocked, one must go free to surrounding farms as wild game. Most operators are happy to recover 70 per cent of released birds, especially if their preserves are open to the average hunter. New operators often recover less than 60 per cent the first year. Birds flying outside the boundaries of licensed shooting preserves become wild game, subject to regular hunting season dates and state game laws.

Most conservation departments—see the Appendix for addresses—will furnish lists of licensed preserves within their state. Many rod and gun editors, outdoor columnists and sports broadcasters will have useful information about shooting preserves in their areas. State listings are also available from the Sportsmen's Service Bureau, 250 East Forty-third Street, New York 17, New York.

If you haven't tried this modern managed hunting, there's a pleasant surprise in store for you. This is especially true for persons who have undertaken to teach themselves how to hunt.

SOURCES OF STATE HUNTING INFORMATION

PLANNING TO GO HUNTING in a strange state or in Canada or Mexico? Here are the addresses of departments that will send you the correct seasons, limits and license fees (laws), and excellent *Where-to-Go* material.

UNITED STATES

ALABAMA *Laws*—Dept. of Conservation, Game & Fish Division, Montgomery 4.
Where-to-Go—Information & Education Section, Dept. of Conservation, Montgomery 4.

ALASKA *Laws*—Dept. of Fish & Game, Subport Bldg., Juneau.
Where-to-Go—Division of Tourist & Economic Development, Klein Bldg., Juneau.

ARIZONA *Laws*—Game & Fish Dept., 105 Arizona State Bldg., Phoenix.
Where-to-Go—Development Board, 1521 West Jefferson St., Phoenix.

ARKANSAS *Laws*—Game & Fish Commission, Game & Fish Bldg., State Capitol Grounds, Little Rock.
Where-to-Go—Publicity & Parks Commission, State Capitol, Little Rock.

CALIFORNIA *Laws & Where-to-Go*—Conservation Education Section, Dept. of Fish & Game, 722 Capitol Ave., Sacramento 14.

COLORADO *Laws & Where-to-Go*—Dept. of Game & Fish, 1530 Sherman St., Denver 1.

CONNECTICUT *Laws*—State Board of Fisheries & Game, Hartford 15.
Where-to-Go—State Development Commission, State Office Bldg., Hartford 15.

DELAWARE *Laws*—Chief, Information & Education, Game & Fish Commission, Dover.
Where-to-Go—State Development Dept., 45 The Green, Dover.

FLORIDA *Laws*—Game & Fresh Water Fish Commission, Tallahassee.
Where-to-Go—Development Commission, Carlton Bldg., Tallahassee.

GEORGIA *Laws & Where-to-Go*—State Game & Fish Commission, 401 State Capitol, Atlanta 3.

HAWAII *Laws & Where-to-Go*—Hawaii Visitors' Bureau, 2051 Kalakona Ave., Honolulu 15.

IDAHO *Laws & Where-to-Go*—Dept. of Fish & Game, 518 Front St., Boise.

ILLINOIS *Laws*—Dept. of Conservation, Div. of Law Enforcement, 102 State Office Bldg., Springfield.
Where-to-Go—Dept. of Conservation, Div. of Education, State Office Bldg., Springfield.

INDIANA *Laws & Where-to-Go*—Dept. of Conservation, Division of Publicity, 311 West Washington St., Indianapolis 9.

IOWA *Laws & Where-to-Go*—State Conservation Commission, East Seventh St. & Court Ave., Des Moines 8.

KANSAS *Laws & Where-to-Go*—Forestry, Fish & Game Commission, P. O. Box 581, Pratt.

KENTUCKY *Laws & Where-to-Go*—Director of Public Relations, Dept. of Fish & Wildlife Resources, Frankfort.

LOUISIANA *Laws*—Wildlife & Fisheries Commission, 126 Civil Courts Bldg., New Orleans 16.
Where-to-Go—Dept. of Commerce & Industry, Tourist Information, State Capitol Bldg., Baton Rouge.

MAINE *Laws*—Dept. of Inland Fisheries & Game, State House, Augusta.
Where-to-Go—State Publicity Bureau, Gateway Circle, Portland 4.

MARYLAND *Laws*—Director, Game & Inland Fish Commission, 516 Munsey Bldg., Baltimore 2.
Where-to-Go—Division of Information, Dept. of Economic Development, State Office Bldg., Annapolis.

MASSACHUSETTS *Laws*—Division of Fisheries & Game, 73 Tremont St., Boston 8.
Where-to-Go—Dept. of Commerce, 150 Causeway St., Boston 8.

MICHIGAN *Laws*—Dept. of Conservation, Office of

Information & Education, Mason Bldg., Lansing 26.

Where-to-Go—Michigan Tourist Council, Lansing 4.

MINNESOTA *Laws*—Dept. of Conservation, State Office Bldg., St. Paul 1.

Where-to-Go—Minnesota Tourist Information, 212 State Office Bldg., St. Paul 1.

MISSISSIPPI *Laws*—Game & Fish Commission, P. O. Box 451, Jackson.

Where-to-Go—Agricultural & Industrial Board, 1104 Woolfolk State Office Bldg., Jackson.

MISSOURI *Laws*—Conservation Commission, Jefferson City.

Where-to-Go—Division of Resources & Development, Jefferson Bldg., Jefferson City.

MONTANA *Laws & Where-to-Go*—Fish & Game Dept., Information & Education Division, Helena 3.

NEBRASKA *Laws & Where-to-Go*—Information & Education Division, Game, Forestation and Parks Commission, State Capitol, Lincoln 9.

NEVADA *Laws & Where-to-Go*—State Fish & Game Commission, 51 Grove St., P. O. Box 678, Reno.

NEW HAMPSHIRE *Laws*—Fish & Game Dept., 34 Bridge St., Concord.

Where-to-Go—State Planning & Development Commission, State House Annex, Concord.

NEW JERSEY *Laws*—Division of Fish & Game, Dept. of Conservation & Economic Development, 230 West State St., Trenton 25.

Where-to-Go—Division of Planning & Development, Dept. of Conservation & Economic Development, 520 East State St., Trenton 25.

NEW MEXICO *Laws*—Dept. of Game & Fish, P. O. Box 2060, Santa Fe.

Where-to-Go—State Tourist Bureau, State Capitol, Santa Fe.

NEW YORK *Laws*—State Conservation Dept., State Campus Site, Albany 7.

Where-to-Go—State Dept. of Commerce, 112 State St., Albany 7.

NORTH CAROLINA *Laws*—Wildlife Resources Commission, P. O. Box 2919, Raleigh.

Where-to-Go—State Advertising Division, Dept. of Conservation & Development, Raleigh.

NORTH DAKOTA *Laws & Where-to-Go*—Public Relations Director, Game & Fish Dept., Capitol Bldg., Bismarck.

OHIO *Laws & Where-to-Go*—Information and Education Section, Dept. of Natural Resources, 1500 Dublin Road, Columbus 12.

OKLAHOMA *Laws*—Dept. of Wildlife Conservation, State Capitol, Oklahoma City 5.

Where-to-Go—Tourist Division, Planning and Resources Board, 533 Capitol Ave., Oklahoma City 5.

OREGON *Laws*—Game Commission, 1634 S. W. Alder, Portland 8.

Where-to-Go—Travel Information Division, State Highway Dept., Salem.

PENNSYLVANIA *Laws*—Game Commission, South Office Bldg., State Capitol, Harrisburg.

Where-to-Go—Travel Development Bureau, Dept. of Commerce, South Office Bldg., State Capitol, Harrisburg.

RHODE ISLAND *Laws*—Division of Fish & Game, Veterans' Memorial Bldg., 83 Park St., Providence 8.

Where-to-Go—Publicity & Recreation Division, Development Council, Roger Williams Bldg., Hayes St., Providence 8.

SOUTH CAROLINA *Laws*—Wildlife Resources Commission, P. O. Box 360, Columbia.

Where-to-Go—State Chamber of Commerce, P. O. Box 70, Columbia.

SOUTH DAKOTA *Laws & Where-to-Go*—Dept. of Game, Fish & Parks, Pierre.

TENNESSEE *Laws & Where-to-Go*—Game & Fish Commission, Information & Educational Section, Cordell Hull Bldg., 6th Ave., N., Nashville 3.

TEXAS *Laws*—Game, Fish & Oyster Commission, Austin 14.

Where-to-Go—Highway Dept., Austin 14.

UTAH *Laws*—Fish & Game Commission, 1596 West North Temple St., Salt Lake City 16.

Where-to-Go—Tourist & Publicity Council, State Capitol Bldg., Salt Lake City 16.

VERMONT *Laws*—Fish & Game Service, State Office Bldg., Montpelier.

Where-to-Go—Development Commission, State Office Bldg., Montpelier.

VIRGINIA *Laws*—Commission of Game & Inland Fisheries, 7 North 2nd St., Richmond 13.

Where-to-Go—State Chamber of Commerce, Richmond 13.

WASHINGTON *Laws*—Dept. of Game, 600 North Capitol Way, Olympia.

Where-to-Go—Dept. of Commerce & Economic Development, General Administration Bldg., Olympia.

WEST VIRGINIA *Laws*—Conservation Commission, Division of Education & Information, State Office Bldg., Charleston 5.

Where-to-Go—Industrial & Publicity Commission, State Office Bldg., Charleston 5.

WISCONSIN *Laws & Where-to-Go*—Conservation Dept., State Office Bldg., Madison 1.

WYOMING *Laws*—Game & Fish Commission, P. O. Box 378, Cheyenne.
Where-to-Go—Travel Commission, 213 Capitol Bldg., Cheyenne.

CANADIAN PROVINCES

ALBERTA *Laws & Where-to-Go*—Travel Bureau, Legislative Bldg., Edmonton.

BRITISH COLUMBIA *Laws*—Office of the Game Commission, 567 Burrard St., Vancouver.
Where-to-Go—Government Travel Bureau, Dept. of Recreation and Conservation, Victoria.

MANITOBA *Laws & Where-to-Go*—Travel & Publicity Branch, 254 Legislative Bldg., Winnipeg.

NEW BRUNSWICK *Laws & Where-to-Go*—Travel Bureau, P. O. Box 1030, Fredericton.

NEWFOUNDLAND *Laws*—Wildlife Division, Dept. of Mines & Resources, St. John's.
Where-to-Go—Tourist Development Board, Fort Townshend, St. John's.

NORTHWEST TERRITORIES *Laws & Where-to-Go*—Dept. of Northern Affairs & National Resources, Ottawa, Ontario.

NOVA SCOTIA *Laws & Where-to-Go*—Bureau of Information, Provincial Bldg., Halifax.

ONTARIO *Laws*—Conservation Information, Dept. of Lands & Forests, Parliament Bldgs., Toronto.
Where-to-Go—Information Branch, Dept. of Travel & Publicity, 67 College St., Toronto.

PRINCE EDWARD ISLAND *Laws*—Dept. of Industry & Natural Resources, Charlottetown.
Where-to-Go—Travel Bureau, P. O. Box 1087, 252 Prince St., Charlottetown.

QUEBEC *Laws & Where-to-Go*—Provincial Publicity Bureau, 106 Grande-Allee, Quebec.

SASKATCHEWAN *Laws & Where-to-Go*—Tourist Branch, Dept. of Travel & Information, Legislative Annex, Regina.

YUKON TERRITORY *Laws & Where-to-Go*—Director, Territorial Game Dept., P. O. Box 2029, Whitehorse.

MEXICO

Laws—Secretaria de Agricultura y Ganaderia, Direccion General y de Caza, Mexico, D. F.
Where-to-Go—Secretaria de Marina, Federal District, Mexico City.